Frommer's

New York City
day BY day®
6th Edition

by Pauline Frommer

FrommerMedia LLC

Contents

15 Favorite Moments 1

1 The Best Full-Day Tours 5
The Best in One Day 6
The Best in Two Days 10
The Best in Three Days 14

2 The Best Special-Interest Tours 19
Romantic New York 20
New York with Kids 24
Literary Gotham 28
New York's Unforgettable Architecture 32
NYC Free & Dirt-Cheap 38

3 The Best Museums 41
The Metropolitan Museum of Art 42
Other Must-See Museums 46
The American Museum of
    Natural History 50
The Museum of Modern Art 52

4 The Best Neighborhood Walks 55
The Financial District 56
Historic Harlem 60
Chelsea, the High Line & Hudson Yards 64
Greenwich Village 68
Prospect Park & Park Slope 72
Williamsburg, Brooklyn 76
Chinatown, Little Italy & the Lower
    East Side 80

5 The Best Shopping 85
Shopping Best Bets 86
Downtown Shopping 87
Midtown & Uptown Shopping 88
Shopping A to Z 90

6 The Great Outdoors 99
Central Park 100
The High Line 104
Green-Wood Cemetery 108
Observation Decks 111

7 The Best Dining 113
Dining Best Bets 114
Downtown Dining 115
Midtown & Uptown Dining 116
Restaurants A to Z 118

8 The Best Nightlife 129
Nightlife Best Bets 130
Downtown Nightlife 131
Midtown & Uptown Nightlife 132
Nightlife A to Z 134

9 The Best Arts & Entertainment 139
Arts & Entertainment Best Bets 140
Downtown A&E 141
Midtown & Uptown A&E 142
Broadway Theaters 144
A&E A to Z 145

10 The Best Hotels 153
Hotel Best Bets 154
Downtown Hotels 155
Midtown & Uptown Hotels 156
Hotels A to Z 158

The Savvy Traveler 165
Before You Go 166
Getting There 167
Getting Around 168
Fast Facts 169
A Brief History of New York 173
New York Architecture 174

Index 178

Published by:

Frommer Media LLC

ISBN: 978-1-628-87503-4 (paper); 978-1-628-87504-1 (ebk)

Editorial Director: Pauline Frommer
Editor: Holly Hughes
Production Editor: Lynn Northrup
Photo Editor: Meghan Lamb
Assistant Photo Editor: Phil Vinke
Cartographer: Roberta Stockwell
Indexer: Cheryl Lenser

Front cover photos, left to right: Central Park, T photography; Statue of Liberty, Katharina M; Times Square, Luciano Mortula -
LGM/Shutterstock.com.

Back cover photo: The Vessel, Francois Roux/Shutterstock.com.

For information on our other products and services, please go to Frommers.com.

Frommer's also publishes its books in a variety of electronic formats. Some content that appears in print may not be available in electronic formats.

Manufactured in China

5   4   3   2

About This Guide

Organizing your time. That's what this guide is all about.

Other guides give you long lists of things to see and do and then expect you to fit the pieces together. The Day by Day guides are different. These guides tell you the best of everything, and then they show you how to see it *in the smartest, most time-efficient way*. Our authors have designed detailed itineraries organized by time, neighborhood, or special interest. And each tour comes with a bulleted map that takes you from stop to stop.

Hoping to explore the treasures at the Metropolitan Museum of Art or find trinkets in Chinatown? Planning a walk through Greenwich Village or Harlem, or just a whirlwind tour of the best that Manhattan has to offer? Whatever your interest or schedule, the Day by Days give you the smartest routes to follow. Not only do we take you to the top attractions, hotels, and restaurants, but we also help you access those special moments that locals get to experience— those "finds" that turn tourists into travelers.

The Day by Days are also your top choice if you're looking for one complete guide for all your travel needs. The best hotels and restaurants for every budget, the greatest shopping values, the wildest nightlife—it's all here.

Why should you trust our judgment? Because our authors personally visit each place they write about. They're an independent lot who say what they think and would never include places they wouldn't recommend to their best friends. They're also open to suggestions from readers. If you'd like to contact them, please send your comments our way at feedback@frommers.com, and we'll pass them on.

Enjoy your Day by Day guide—the most helpful travel companion you can buy. And have the trip of a lifetime.

About the Author

Pauline Frommer started traveling with her guidebook-writing parents at the age of 4 months and hasn't stopped since. Her first job in travel was on the website Frommers.com, and eventually she worked her way up to Editor in Chief. Pauline also served as Travel Editor for MSNBC.com for several years, before working with John Wiley and Sons to create the award-winning *Pauline Frommer Guidebooks*, a 14-book series that won the coveted "Best Guidebook of the Year" title 3 years in a row from the North American Travel Journalists Association and once from the Society of American Travel Writers. She is now the Editorial Director of the Frommer's Guidebooks and Frommers.com.

For 4 years, Pauline created weekly travel segments for CNN's *Headline News* and CNN's *Pipeline*. You may also have seen her talking travel on *The Today Show, Live with Kelly, The O'Reilly Factor, NBC Nightly News, ABC World News, Good Morning America, FOX News,* and every local news station you can name. Her writings have been widely published in everything from *Budget Travel Magazine* to the *Dallas Morning News* to *Nick, Jr.* magazine. Her weekly podcast, The Frommer Travel Show, available wherever podcasts are found, was named one of the 13 best for travel by the New York Times.

She resides in New York City with her husband and two daughters and she dedicates this book to them. Trixie, Veronica, and MKS: Exploring NYC together has been one of the highlights of my life. I thank you, and I love you.

An Additional Note

Please be advised that travel information is subject to change at any time—and this is especially true of prices. We, therefore, suggest that you write or call ahead for confirmation when making your travel plans. The authors, editors, and publisher cannot be held responsible for the experiences of readers while traveling. Your safety is important to us, however, so we encourage you to stay alert and be aware of your surroundings.

Star Ratings, Icons & Abbreviations

Every hotel, restaurant, and attraction listing in this guide has been ranked for quality, value, service, amenities, and special features using a **star-rating system.** Hotels, restaurants, attractions, shopping, and nightlife are rated on a scale of zero stars (recommended) to three stars (exceptional). In addition to the star-rating system, we use a **kids icon** to point out the best bets for families. Within each tour, we recommend cafes, bars, or restaurants where you can take a break. Each of these stops appears in a shaded box marked with a coffee-cup-shaped bullet ☕.

The following **abbreviations** are used for credit cards:

AE	American Express	MC	MasterCard
DC	Diners Club	V	Visa

A Note on Prices

In the "Take a Break" and "Best Bets" sections of this book, we have used a system of dollar signs to show a range of costs for 1 night in a hotel (the price of a double-occupancy room) or the cost of an entree at a restaurant. Use the following table to decipher the dollar signs:

Cost	Hotels	Restaurants
$	under $100	under $10
$$	$100–$200	$10–$20
$$$	$200–$300	$20–$30
$$$	$300–$400	$30–$40
$$$$	over $400	over $40

Frommers.com

Now that you have this guidebook to help you plan a great trip, visit our website at **www.frommers.com** for additional travel information on more than 3,600 destinations. We update features regularly to give you instant access to the most current trip-planning information available. At Frommers.com, you'll find scoops on the best airfares, lodging rates, and car rental bargains. You can even book your travel online through our reliable travel booking partners. Other popular features include:

- Online updates of our most popular guidebooks
- Vacation sweepstakes and contest giveaways
- Newsletters highlighting the hottest travel trends

An Invitation to the Reader

In researching this book, we discovered many wonderful places—hotels, restaurants, shops, and more. We're sure you'll find others. Please tell us about them, so we can share the information with your fellow travelers in upcoming editions. If you were disappointed with a recommendation, we'd love to know that, too. Please write to: Support@FrommerMedia.com.

15 Favorite
Moments

15 Favorite Moments

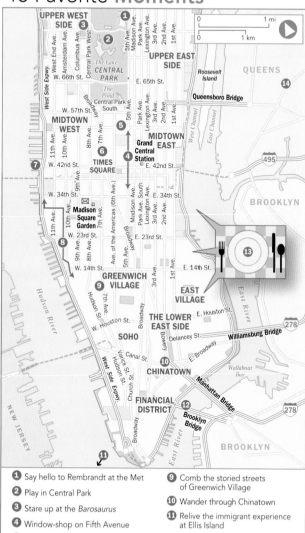

1. Say hello to Rembrandt at the Met
2. Play in Central Park
3. Stare up at the *Barosaurus*
4. Window-shop on Fifth Avenue
5. Chill with the cool kids at MOMA
6. Take in a Broadway show
7. See Manhattan on a sunset cruise
8. Promenade along the High Line
9. Comb the storied streets of Greenwich Village
10. Wander through Chinatown
11. Relive the immigrant experience at Ellis Island
12. Cross the Brooklyn Bridge on foot
13. Dine Outdoors
14. Zip to Queens' Museum of the Moving Image
15. Stay up late

Previous page: Central Park.

New York City is back—and stronger than ever. During the world's "pandemic pause" it added a few tricks to its bag, brushed the dust off some older attractions, and yes, culled a few offerings. But there's still more here for visitors to see and do than in any other place on the planet. What follows are the best of the best.

1 Say hello to Rembrandt at the Met. A vivid self-portrait of the Dutch painter is one of thousands of masterpieces on view at the Metropolitan Museum of Art, the city's premier museum and one of the world's best. It's open until 9pm on Friday and Saturday nights, and evening is a wonderful time to visit—the crowds are smaller then, and you can sip wine in the elegant Great Hall Balcony Bar (or the Roof Garden if it's warm out). See p 42.

2 Play in Central Park. I love the city's backyard not just for its beauty, but for its endless variety: undulating paths and greenswards, formal gardens, boat ponds, a castle, theaters, an ice skating rink, an Egyptian obelisk, a lake, and even a storied carousel. See p 100.

3 Stare up at the *Barosaurus*. The largest freestanding mounted dinosaur in the world is impressive indeed—and the American Museum of Natural History offers even more beyond its giant fossils. The adjacent Rose Center/Hayden Planetarium is

The High Line Park raises a ribbon of green above the streets.

spectacular during the day, and pure magic at night. See p 50.

4 Window-shop on Fifth Avenue. Legendary stores, such as Saks, Bergdorf Goodman, Tiffany & Co., Cartier, and Harry Winston, rub shoulders with va-va-va-voom Gucci, and Versace—with each vying equally hard for attention, it's hard to choose. See p 90.

5 Chill with the cool kids at MoMA. Now that the Museum of Modern Art has added 30% more gallery space, hanging out here is less about the crowds and more about seeing the best contemporary art (and revisiting old faves like Dali's dripping clocks and those trance-inducing Rothkos). See p 52.

6 Take in a Broadway Show. It doesn't have to be *Hamilton*. The Great White Way is home to dozens of shows that will make you laugh, or tap your toes, or even (if you're lucky) help you see your own life in a different light. See p 151 for tips on getting discounted tickets (it can be done).

7 See Manhattan on a sunset cruise. The city that never sleeps begins to glitter at dusk, when millions of lights set it aglow. Take a sunset cruise on the mighty Hudson for wraparound views of the city skyline and its splendid evening sparkle. See p 23.

8 Promenade along the High Line. The High Line redefined what a public park could be. Once an abandoned elevated freight-train track, it was redeveloped into an innovative string of outdoor habitats. Strolling it, you get sweeping

The pedestrian walkway across the Brooklyn Bridge.

river vistas—and eye-level "Peeping Tom" views into the windows of neighboring office and apartment buildings. *See p 64 and 104.*

⑨ Comb the storied streets of Greenwich Village. This historic, human-scale neighborhood has serendipitous charms around every corner—from vintage brownstones to fabled watering holes. Many famous writers, artists, and poets of yesteryear called this former hamlet home. *See p 68.*

⑩ Wander Through Chinatown. Manhattan's Chinatown is a city within the city, with its own pace (rushed), food stores spilling onto the sidewalks, Buddhist temples, souvenir and knock-off stores, and Asian restaurants of every sort, from Fujianese to Cantonese to new-fangled Thai. *See p 80.*

⑪ Relive the immigrant experience at Ellis Island. Some 12 million people passed through this island processing center from 1892 to 1954, the largest migration in human history. Whether or not your family entered America through Ellis Island, a visit here is extremely moving. *See p 16.*

⑫ Cross the Brooklyn Bridge on foot. I recommend many scenic strolls in this guide but few offer the majestic vistas this one does. Don't just look at the cityscapes—the span itself is a graceful engineering marvel, the first steel-wire suspension bridge ever erected. *See p 33.*

⑬ Dine Outdoors. During the pandemic, al fresco meals became the norm, with restaurants across the five boroughs setting up adorable outdoor dining cabins. The effect was so delightful that the "Open Streets" law was passed to make them a permanent part of the cityscape. *See page 114.*

⑭ Zip to Queens to tour the Museum of the Moving Image. Museums don't get more interactive—or fun—than this cutting-edge exploration of film, TV, video games, and digital media. Kids love it and so do their parents. *See p 48.*

⑮ Stay up late. When musicians play Carnegie Hall, Radio City Music Hall, Lincoln Center, Madison Square Garden, and other Gotham venues, it often marks the pinnacle of their careers, whether they're performing jazz, opera, rock and roll, indie, symphonic music, you name it. Cocktail culture is also being shaped here, as are comedy and dance. So ditch your usual bedtime—as the sun goes down, this city is just waking up. *See p 140.* ●

The Best in One Day

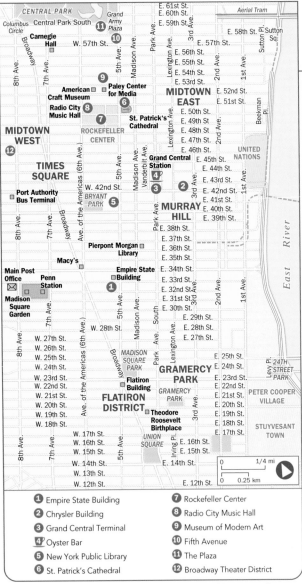

1. Empire State Building
2. Chrysler Building
3. Grand Central Terminal
4. Oyster Bar
5. New York Public Library
6. St. Patrick's Cathedral
7. Rockefeller Center
8. Radio City Music Hall
9. Museum of Modern Art
10. Fifth Avenue
11. The Plaza
12. Broadway Theater District

Previous page: The Top of the Rock observation deck in Rockefeller Center offers prime vistas of Manhattan and beyond.

The most wonderful—and maddening—thing about New York? The endless number of choices. Start your urban exploration in Midtown, the city's business and commercial heart. The shopping opportunities here are legion, and the air space is spiky with corporate skyscrapers—but Midtown is also home to several quintessential New York landmarks. START: **Subway 6 to 33rd Street or B, D, F, M, N, Q, or R to 34th Street.**

Gargoyles perched high on the Chrysler Building.

① ★★ Empire State Building.

King Kong climbed it in 1933. A plane slammed into it in 1945. After September 11, 2001, the Empire State regained its status as New York City's tallest building . . . at least for a few years. Through it all, it has remained one of the city's favorite landmarks. Completed in 1931, the limestone-and-stainless-steel Art Deco dazzler climbs 103 stories (1,454 ft./436m). The best views are from the 86th- and 102nd-floor observatories, but I prefer the former for its windswept deck (upstairs you stay inside). From up here, the citywide panorama is electric. Wait times have diminished in recent years. ⏱ *1.5 hr. 20 W. 34th St. (off Fifth Ave.). www. esbnyc.com.* ☎ *212/736-3100. Basic admission (86th floor) $42 adults, $40 seniors, $36 children 6–12, free for*

children 5 and under. Express passes and 102nd floor observatory tickets more (see website). Observatories open daily 8am–2am; last elevator goes up at 1:15am. Subway: 6 to 33rd St.; B/D/F/M to 34th St.

② ★★★ Chrysler Building.

Built as the Chrysler Corporation headquarters in 1930, this is New York's most romantic Art Deco edifice and, for many New Yorkers, its most endearing visual touchstone. It's especially dramatic at night, when the triangular points in its steely crown are outlined in silvery lights. Go in to see the marble-clad lobby; a mural on the ceiling was actually rediscovered in 1999. A viewing deck will be opening. *See p 35.*

③ ★★ Grand Central Terminal.

An iconic Beaux Arts beauty. The highlight is the vast, imposing main

The Sky Ceiling at Grand Central Terminal.

concourse, where high windows allow sunlight to pour onto the half-acre (.25-hectare) Tennessee-marble floor. Everything gleams, from the brass clock over the central kiosk to the gold- and nickel-plated chandeliers piercing the side archways. The breathtaking *Sky Ceiling* depicts the constellations of the winter sky above New York. *42nd St. and Park Ave. www.grandcentral terminal.com. ☎ 212/340-2210. Subway: 4/5/6/7/S to 42nd St.*

4 **Grand Central Oyster Bar.** Head to the basement to nosh at the iconic Oyster Bar, in biz since 1913. Some 30-plus varieties of oysters are on offer, and they're the top pick, either raw, or in a classic oyster roast. Look up: the arched, tiled ceilings mirror those at Ellis Island (p. 16), both done by the same company.

5 ★ **New York Public Library.** The lions *Patience* and *Fortitude* stand guard outside the grand Fifth Avenue entrance of the **Main Branch (Stephen A. Schwarzman Building)** of the public library, designed by Carrère & Hastings in 1911. It's one of the country's finest examples of Beaux Arts architecture. Sadly, architect John Mervin Carrère never got to enjoy the fruits of his labor; he was killed in a taxi accident 2 months before the library dedication. The majestic white-marble structure is clad with Corinthian columns and allegorical statues. Take the time to watch the excellent 15-minute film on the library's holdings. ⏱ *45 min. Fifth Ave. (btw. 42nd and 40th sts.). www. nypl.org. ☎ 917/275-6975. Free admission. Mon and Thurs–Sat 10am–6pm, Tues–Wed 10am–8pm, Sun 1–5pm. Subway: B/D/F/M to 42nd St.*

6 ★★ **St. Patrick's Cathedral.** This Neo-Gothic white-marble-and-stone wonder is the largest Roman Catholic cathedral in the U.S. Designed by James Renwick, begun in 1859, and consecrated in 1879, St. Patrick's wasn't completed until 1906. You can pop in between services to get a look at the impressive interior. The St. Michael and St. Louis altar came from Tiffany & Co., while the St. Elizabeth altar—honoring Mother Elizabeth Ann Seton, the first American-born saint—was designed by Paolo Medici of Rome. ⏱ *15 min. Fifth Ave. (btw. 50th and 51st sts.). www. saintpatrickscathedral.org. ☎ 212/ 753-2261. Free admission. Daily 6:30am–8:45pm. Subway: B/D/F/M to 47th–50th sts./Rockefeller Center.*

7 ★★★ **Rockefeller Center.** A prime example of civic optimism expressed in soaring architecture, Rock Center was built in the 1930s at the height of the Great Depression. Today it is one of the world's largest privately owned business-and-entertainment centers, with 18 buildings on 21 acres. The **GE Building,** also known as **30 Rock,** at 30 Rockefeller Plaza, is a 70-story showpiece; at its apex is the **Top of the Rock** observation deck. In season the mammoth Rockefeller Center Christmas tree towers over the 30 Rock plaza and its famous skating rink. *Bounded by 48th and 51st sts. and Fifth and Sixth aves. Timed tickets to Top of the Rock from $38 (www.topoftherocknyc.com). Subway: B/D/F/M to 47th–50th sts./ Rockefeller Center.*

8 ★★★ **Radio City Music Hall.** Opened in 1932, this sumptuous Art Deco classic is the world's largest indoor theater, with 6,000 seats. Long known for its Rockettes revues and popular Christmas show, Radio City also has a place in movie history: More than 700 films have opened here since 1933. The Deco "powder rooms" are some of the swankiest in town. *1260 Sixth Ave. (at 50th St.). www.msg.com/ venue-tours/radio-city-music-hall.* ☎ *212/247-4777. 75 min. Stage Door Tour daily 9:30am–5pm. Tickets $31 adults; $27 seniors, students, and children. Subway: B/D/F/M to 47th–50th sts./Rockefeller Center.*

⑨ ★★★ Museum of Modern Art. MoMA houses the world's greatest collection of painting and sculpture from the late 19th century and 20th century—from Monet's Water Lilies and Klimt's The Kiss to 20th-century masterworks by Frida Kahlo and Jasper Johns to contemporary pieces by Richard Serra and Chuck Close. Add to that a vast collection of architectural models, film, video and iconic design objects ranging from tableware to sports cars. ⏱ *3 hr. See p 52.*

⑩ ★★ Fifth Avenue. New York's most famous shopping artery runs up to the southeast corner of Central Park at 59th Street. Some landmarks to note: **Tiffany & Co.,** at no. 727 (btw. 56th and 57th sts.), with its stainless-steel doors and Atlas clock; and the shop that clothes the 1%: **Bergdorf Goodman** at 754 (at 57th St.). *Subway: N/R/W to Fifth Ave./59th St.*

⑪ ★ The Plaza. There's no denying the glamour of the Big Apple's most famous hotel (now divided between hotel rooms and private condos, with restaurants and shops on the lowest floors). This 1907 French Renaissance "palace" has hosted royalty, celebrities, and a legion of honeymooners. Have afternoon tea in the legendary **Palm Court** or sip a flute of bubbly in the **Champagne Bar.** *768 Fifth Ave. (at Central Park South). www.fairmont. com/theplaza.* ☎ *888/850-0909. Subway: N/R/W to Fifth Ave./59th St.*

⑫ ★★★ Broadway Theater District. You can't say you've "done" NYC until you've experienced a big, splashy musical or thought-provoking drama. See p 151 for tips on how to save money on tickets.

Inside St. Patrick's Cathedral on Fifth Avenue.

The Best **in Two Days**

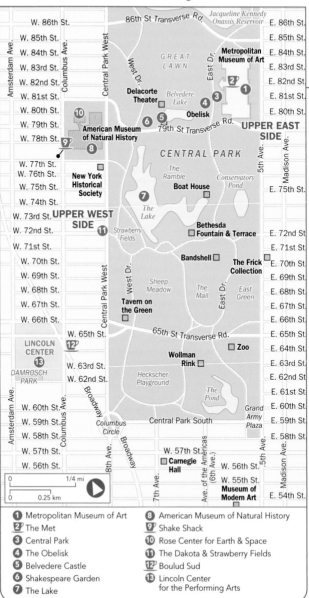

1. Metropolitan Museum of Art
2. The Met
3. Central Park
4. The Obelisk
5. Belvedere Castle
6. Shakespeare Garden
7. The Lake
8. American Museum of Natural History
9. Shake Shack
10. Rose Center for Earth & Space
11. The Dakota & Strawberry Fields
12. Boulud Sud
13. Lincoln Center for the Performing Arts

After the 1-day tour of Midtown, head uptown to Manhattan's artistic soul—the Metropolitan Museum and Lincoln Center. The area is also home to Central Park, an urban oasis that recharges body and mind. This part of town has a wealth of museums—most of them along Fifth Avenue. To avoid burnout, don't try to see them all in 1 day. If you have kids in tow, run, don't walk, to the American Museum of Natural History. START: **Subway 4, 5, or 6 to 86th Street.**

❶ ★★★ Metropolitan Museum of Art. At 1.6 million sq. ft. (148,644 sq. m), this is the largest museum in the Western Hemisphere, attracting five million visitors annually. Nearly all the world's cultures through the ages are on display—from Egyptian mummies to ancient Greek statuary to Islamic carvings to Renaissance paintings to 20th-century decorative arts—and masterpieces are the rule. You could go once a week for a lifetime and still find something new on each visit. Everyone should see the **Temple of Dendur,** the jewel of the Egyptian collection. But let personal preference be your guide to the rest. Touchstones include the exceptional Rembrandts, Vermeers, and other Dutch master painters. Transplanted period rooms—from the elegant 18th-century bedroom from a Venetian castle to the warm and inviting 20th-century Frank Lloyd Wright living room—are equally unmissable. ⏱ *3 hr. See p 42.*

❷ The Met. Eating at the Met gives you options. If you're visiting between May and October, check out the Roof Garden Bar ($) for breathtaking treetop views of Central Park. Year-round you can grab lunch at the American Wing Café ($$), or the elegant Petrie Court Café ($$) with its own park vistas. On Friday and Saturday evenings, cocktails and appetizers are served at the Great Hall Balcony Bar ($) overlooking the Great Hall. *Fifth Ave. (at 82nd St.). www.metmuseum. org.* ☎ *212/535-7710.*

The Metropolitan Museum of Art's American Wing.

3 ★★★ **kids** **Central Park.** Manhattanites may lack yards, but they do have this glorious swath of green. Designed by Frederick Law Olmstead and Calvert Vaux in the 1850s, the park is 2½ miles (4km) long (extending from 59th to 110th sts.) and a half-mile (.8km) wide (from Fifth Ave. to Central Park West). It encompasses a zoo, a carousel, two ice-skating rinks (in season), restaurants, children's playgrounds, and even theaters. *See p 100.*

4 **The Obelisk.** Also called Cleopatra's Needle, this 71-ft. (21m) obelisk is reached by following the path leading west behind the Met. Originally erected in Heliopolis, Egypt, around 1475 B.C., it was given to New York by the Khedive of Egypt in 1880. Continue on the path to Central Park's **Great Lawn** (p 102), site of countless softball games, concerts, and peaceful political protests.

5 ★ **Belvedere Castle.** Built by Calvert Vaux in 1869, this fanciful medieval-style fortress-in-miniature sits at the highest point in Central Park and affords sweeping views. The many birds that call this area home led to the creation of a bird-watching and educational center in the castle's ranger station. To get here, follow the path across East Drive and walk west.

6 **Shakespeare Garden.** Next to the Delacorte Theater, this garden grows flowers and plants mentioned in the Bard's plays.

7 ★★ **The Lake.** South of the garden, you'll reach the Lake, with its iconic photo-op outlooks at **Bow Bridge** and **Bethesda Terrace.** Follow the perimeter pathway lined with weeping willows and Japanese cherry trees east to the neo-Victorian **Loeb Boathouse,** which rents rowboats and bicycles; on summer evenings, you can arrange gondola rides. Returning to the west side, follow paths to exit the park at 77th Street and Central Park West. *See p 102.*

8 ★★★ **kids** **American Museum of Natural History.** The spectacular entrance—featuring a *Barosaurus* skeleton, the world's largest freestanding dinosaur exhibit—is just the tip of the iceberg. Founded in 1869, the AMNH houses the world's greatest

The White Rhinoceros diorama at the American Museum of Natural History.

natural-science collection in a square-block group of buildings made of whimsical towers and turrets, pink granite, and red brick. The diversity of the holdings is astounding: some 36 million specimens, ranging from microscopic organisms to the world's largest cut gem, the **Brazilian Princess Topaz** (21,005 carats). If you only see one exhibit, make it the ★★ **dinosaurs**, which take up the entire fourth floor. *Tip:* The admission lines can be tedious for young kids. If you buy advance tickets online, you can avoid the 20-minute wait. ◯ *2 hr. See p 50.*

9 kids Shake Shack. The food offerings at the AMNH are less impressive than the artifacts. Instead of dining here, duck across the street (west of the museum) to this New York-founded chain for excellent burgers, fries, and creamy shakes. *366 Columbus Ave (at W. 77th St. www.shakeshack.com.* ☎ *646/747-8770. $.*

10 ★★ kids Rose Center for Earth & Space. Part of the American Museum of Natural History, this four-story sphere "floating" in a glass square is astonishing. Even if you're suffering from museum overload, the Rose Center will lift your spirits. The center's **Hayden Planetarium** features spectacular space shows (every half-hour Mon–Fri 10:30am–4:30pm, Wed from 11am; Sat–Sun 10:30am–5pm). *See p 51.*

11 The Dakota and Strawberry Fields. The 1884 apartment house with dark trim and dramatic gables, dormers, and oriel windows is best known as the spot where its most famous resident, John Lennon, was gunned down on December 8, 1980 (Yoko Ono still lives here). Directly across the street from the Dakota in Central Park is

Central Park photo-op: the Imagine mosaic at Strawberry Fields.

Strawberry Fields, a memorial to the songwriter and peace activist. A must for serious Beatles fans. *1 W. 72nd St. (at Central Park West) and Central Park btw. 71st and 74th sts.*

12 ★★ Boulud Sud. Perfect for a pre-Lincoln Center meal, star chef Daniel Boulud's food is downright operatic, a masterful take on Mediterranean fare from the south of France to North Africa. And the room is elegant enough for your concert-going duds, too. *20 W. 64th. St (off Broadway). www.boulud-sud. com.* ☎ *212/595-1313. $$$.*

13 ★★ Lincoln Center for the Performing Arts. New York has countless performing arts venues, but none so multifaceted as Lincoln Center—presenting world-class opera, ballet, theater, jazz, symphonies, and more. After a long day on your feet, relax on the outdoor plaza in front of the fountains or on the tilting roof lawn. At Christmastime, the light displays are lovely, and on summer evenings, the plaza becomes an outdoor dance party. *See p 147.*

The Best in Three Days

Duane St.
Reade St.
Chambers St.
Warren St.   Warren St.
Park Pl. W.
Murray St.
Murray St.   Park Pl.
Barclay St.
Vesey St.

CITY HALL PARK
City Hall ☐ **9**

Woolworth Building

Broadway
Greenwich St.
Church St.
Park Row
Centre St.
Ave. of the Finest

St. James Pl.
Madison St.
Wagner Pl.
Frankfort St.
Spruce St.
Beekman St.
Ann St.

Brooklyn Bridge

WORLD FINANCIAL CENTER

7 WORLD TRADE CENTER SITE **6**

5
8
Dey St.
Cortlandt St.

Nassau St.
William St.
Gold St.
Fulton St.
Pearl St.
Water St.
Front St.
South St.

North End Ave.

BATTERY PARK CITY

Liberty St. **4**

Fed. Reserve Bank
FINANCIAL DISTRICT

John St.
Maiden Ln.
Cedar St.
Pine St.

SOUTH STREET SEAPORT
18
17
15

South End Ave.
West Side Expwy.
Washington St.
Greenwich St.

Thames St.
Albany St.
Rector Pl.
RECTOR PARK
W. Thames St.
3rd Pl.
2nd Pl.
1st Pl.

Wall St. **3**
Rector St.
NY Stock Exchange
Exchange Pl.
Beaver St.
Stone St.
Bridge St.
Whitehall St.

Trinity Pl.
Broadway
New St.
William St.
Pearl St.
Water St.
Front St.
South St.
Old Slip

14
13
11
9

Hudson River

West St.
Battery Pl.
State St.

Coenties Slip
Broad St. **11**

6

East River

Castle Clinton Nat'l. Mon. ☐
BATTERY PARK

Staten Island Ferry Terminal

Ferries to Liberty and Ellis Islands (see map below)

| 0 | | 1/4 mi |
| 0 | 0.25 km | |

Hudson River

FINANCIAL DISTRICT

Manhattan Bridge
Brooklyn Bridge

BROOKLYN

NEW YORK
NEW JERSEY

East River

BATTERY PARK

ELLIS ISLAND
2

GOVERNORS ISLAND

Statue of Liberty
1
LIBERTY ISLAND

1 The Statue of Liberty
2 Ellis Island
3 Trinity Church
4 Eataly
5 St. Paul's Chapel
6 9/11 Memorial & Museum
7 One World Observatory
8 World Trade Center Transportation Hub
9 City Hall Park
10 Foley Square
11 The Dead Rabbit Grocery & Grog

Explore the city's beginnings, its turbulent recent history, and its dynamic present in Lower Manhattan. You'll find colonial influences and cobblestoned streets, a center of city government, and world finance, the Statue of Liberty and Ellis Island, and a neighborhood that still bears the scars of the September 11, 2001, terrorist attacks. (Don't miss the museum and memorial at the World Trade Center site.) We recommend that you start this tour early and book visits to both the 9/11 Museum and Lady Liberty well in advance. For more details on southern Manhattan, see p 56. START: **Subway 4, 5, or 6 to Brooklyn Bridge/City Hall.**

❶ ★★★ kids The Statue of Liberty. For the millions who arrived in New York by ship, Lady Liberty was their first glimpse of America. A gift from France to the U.S., the statue was designed by sculptor Frédéric-Auguste Bartholdi and unveiled on October 28, 1886. Seeing her is as much of a thrill today as it was then. *Note:* Save yourself a long wait by buying and printing tickets ahead of time and getting to the ferry at least half an hour before it starts operating. Standard tickets sell out daily by noon, but you'll need to book as

much as 5 months in advance for tickets to go up to the crown (you'll climb 377 un-air-conditioned steps, but the view, and the sight of Gustave Eiffel's handsome interior scaffolding—yes, THAT Eiffel—is worth it). Only advance tickets include access to the pedestal's observation deck; the new Statue of Liberty museum is open to all and worth a quick look. *Tip:* While only official Statue Cruises dock at Liberty Island, a free 25-minute ride on the Staten Island Ferry (www.siferry.com) also provides spectacular skyline views of Manhattan and is a

The new Statue of Liberty museum.

wonderful way to see the harbor. ⏱ *1 hr. (Statue Cruise ferry also visits Ellis Island, see below.) Liberty Island. www.nps.gov/stli and www. statuecruises.com.* ☎ *212/363-3200 (general info) or 877/523-9849 (tickets). Tickets $23.50 adults, $18 seniors, $12 children 4–12; crown access costs $3 extra. Daily 9am–4pm (last ferry departs around 3pm); extended hours in summer. Subway: 4/5 to Bowling Green; 1/9 to South Ferry.*

❷ ★★★ **Ellis Island Immigration Museum.** For 62 years (1892–1954), this was the main point of entry for newcomers to America. Today it's one of New York's most moving attractions—particularly for the 40% of Americans whose ancestors first set foot in "The New World" here. The self-guided tour follows the path immigrants would have taken (as they underwent health exams, a grilling on their political beliefs, and more) before learning whether or not they'd be admitted into the country. Recently, the un-renovated hospital building has opened for a fascinating extra-cost "hard hat" tour (see website for details). ⏱ *2 hr. Ellis Island. www.nps.gov/elis. For tickets and ferry info see Statue of Liberty, above. Daily 9:30am–5pm; extended hours in summer. Subway: 4/5 to Bowling Green; 1/9 to South Ferry.*

❸ ★★ **Trinity Church.** This neo-Gothic marvel was consecrated in 1846 and is still active today. The main doors, modeled on the doors in Florence's Baptistry, are decorated with biblical scenes; inside are splendid stained-glass windows. Among those buried in the pretty churchyard are Alexander Hamilton and Robert Fulton. ⏱ *25 min. 79 Broadway (at Wall St.). www.trinity wallstreet.org.* ☎ *212/602-0800.*

Trinity Church's cemetery, where founding father Alexander Hamilton is buried.

Mon–Fri 7am–6pm, Sat 8am–4pm, Sun 7am–4pm. Subway: 4/5 to Wall St.

❹ ☕ ★ **Eataly.** The downtown branch of the hugely popular all-Italian food hall. Grab a quick but expertly crafted panini or have a full sit-down meal. *101 Liberty St., just off Broadway (3rd floor). www.eataly. com.* ☎ *212/897-2895. $–$$.*

❺ ★★ **St. Paul's Chapel.** Manhattan's only surviving pre-Revolutionary church was built in 1766 to resemble London's St. Martin-in-the-Fields. George Washington came here to pray right after his inauguration as the first president of the United States. With a light, elegant Georgian interior, the chapel was a refuge for rescue workers after September 11; you'll see exhibits and artifacts from that dark period. ⏱ *15 min. 209 Broadway (at Fulton St.). www.trinitywallstreet.org. ☎ 212/233-4164. Mon–Fri 10am–6pm, Sat 10am–4pm, Sun 7am–3pm. Subway: 2/3 to Park Place; 1/9/4/5/A to Fulton St./Broadway/Nassau.*

⑥ ★★★ 9/11 Memorial and Museum.

The Twin Towers dominated the Manhattan skyline after their construction in 1973, and visitors from around the world have made pilgrimages to this site since their destruction during the September 11, 2001, terrorist attacks. A permanent memorial, *Reflecting Absence*, converts the footprints of the Twin Towers into large reflective pools, incorporating the largest man-made waterfalls in North America. On the same plaza is the 9/11 Museum, a powerful and emotional retelling of the attacks on the towers, the Pentagon, and United Airlines Flight 93 in Pennsylvania. The museum uses artifacts, video and audio recordings, photography, interactive panels and more, to create a sophisticated, multidimensional history lesson, one that may be too intense for children under 12. *Tip:* Guided tours of the museum are available for an additional cost, but we think most visitors will prefer the self-guided tour. ⏱ *2–3 hr. Entrances at intersections of Liberty and Greenwich sts., Liberty and West sts, or West and Fulton sts. www.911memorial.org. ☎ 212/266-5211. Museum admission $26, $20 seniors and students over 13, $15 children 12 and under, $17 veterans, free on Tuesdays 5–8pm. Memorial park open daily 7:30am–9pm; museum open Sun–Thurs 9am–8pm and Fri–Sat 9am–9pm. Subway: A/C/J/Z, 2/3, or 4/5 to Fulton St., 2/3 to Park Place, A/C/E to World Trade Center, R to Rector St., N/R to Cortland St.*

⑦ ★ One World Observatory.

Architect Daniel Libeskind's 1,776-foot-tall (533m) **One World Trade Center** is the tallest building in North America, and near its apex is, you guessed it, an observation deck. You can see for miles through its floor-to-ceiling windows, but because you're kept inside, and because the building is on the tip of Manhattan, rather than in its heart, we don't think it has the visceral thrill of the other decks in town. Still, if you missed going up one of those, this is a worthy second choice. *1 World Trade (entrance on Vesey St. at West St.). http://oneworldobservatory.com. ☎ 844/696-1776. Basic admission $43 adults, $41 seniors, $31 children. Nov–June Fri–Sun, June Thurs–Sun, July–Oct Thurs–Mon. Subway: A, C, J, Z, 2, 3, 4, or 5 to Fulton St., 2, 3 to Park Place, E to World Trade Center, R to Rector St., Subway: A/C to World Trade Center, N/R to Cortland St.*

One World Trade Center.

8 ★ World Trade Center Transportation Hub. The only subway stop in the city that's now an attraction in its own right, this wing-like steel-and-glass canopy, designed by Catalan architect Santiago Calatrava, is an extraordinary work of architecture. *Tip:* If you stand on Broadway, you can get a photo of One World Trade Center rising up between its arms. *At the intersection of Fulton and Church St.*

9 City Hall Park. City Hall has been the seat of NYC government since 1812. You can appreciate the handsome park, highlighted by flickering gaslight lamps, and the 1811 building's French Renaissance exterior. Abraham Lincoln was laid in state in the soaring rotunda. Equally grand is the colossal **Municipal Building** (1 Centre St. at Chambers St.), built on the other side of Centre Street in 1915 by McKim, Mead & White; it was the celebrated firm's first "skyscraper." Across Broadway at no. 233 is that temple of commerce known as the **★★ Woolworth Building.** Built from the proceeds of a nickel-and-dime empire in 1913, this gargoyle-laden masterpiece is the work of Cass Gilbert. Near-daily tours of the lobby are now offered, thanks to the efforts of Gilbert's great-granddaughter. *City Hall Park (btw. Broadway and Park Row). Woolworth building tours $20–$45, depending on length. www.woolworthtours.com.*

10 ★ Foley Square. It's hard to believe that this dignified urban landscape was once a fetid swamp and, in the 19th century, one of the city's most notorious slums, Five Points. Today, with its ring of colonnaded courthouse buildings, Foley Square bustles with judiciary industry. It's also one of the most filmed places in the five boroughs. The exterior of the 1913 **NY State Supreme Court Building** (60 Centre St.) is where Kris Kringle goes on trial in *Miracle on 34th Street* (the original) and also looks very familiar if you are a *Law & Order* fan. The imposing 1932 **Thurgood Marshall U.S. Courthouse** (40 Centre St.) was designed by Cass Gilbert. *Bounded by Centre, Worth and Lafayette sts. Subway: 4/5/6 to Brooklyn Bridge/City Hall.*

11 ★ The Dead Rabbit Grocery and Grog. Grab a punch, a flip, a nog, or some other historically accurate 19th-century cocktail at this charmingly old-timey bar, which was named best bar in the world in 2016, by the mixologists who put together the influential "50 Best Bars" list. A light (but tasty) supper is served. *30 Water St. (near Broad St.). www.deadrabbitnyc.com.* ☎ *212/897-2895. $–$$.*

Plan Ahead

Tis the era of advance reservations, ever since the spiky virus made its first appearance. So be sure to book as soon as you know your plans, as many attractions, eateries, and other sorts of venues may have more limited space than before. ●

Romantic New York

1. Neue Gallery
2. The Lake
3. Picnic in the Sheep Meadow
4. The Plaza
5. Tiffany & Co
6. Summer on the Lincoln Center Plaza
7. Winter on the Rink in Rockefeller Center
8. The Whispering Gallery
9. The Museum of Sex
10. One if By Land, Two if By Sea
11. Harbor Cruise
12. The River Café

ew York is known for its wolves of Wall Street and other all-business movers-and-shakers. But to me, the city harbors a romantic streak as wide as the Hudson River. Here are some places best discovered as a twosome. START: **Subway 4, 5, or 6 to 86th Street.**

Minne sculptures and a Klimt painting in the Neue Galerie.

❶ ★★ Neue Galerie New York.

If you don't think museums can be sexy, you haven't visited the Neue, which does not allow anyone younger than 13 to see its some-times risqué collection of Austrian and German art from 1890 to 1940. Not only does the Galerie house some of Gustave Klimt's most sensual works (including the famed "Woman in Gold"), it's set in an opulent 1912 mansion, designed by the team of Carrere & Hastings, and has a soigné, wood-paneled, Viennese-style cafe perfect for canoodling. The cafe becomes a cabaret on Thursday evenings, attracting some of the top performers in the biz. *1048 Fifth Ave. (at 86th St.). www.neuegalerie.org.* ☎ *212/628-6200. Admission $25 adults, $16 seniors, $12 students. Thurs-Sun 11am-5pm.*

❷ ★★ The Lake.

When you see the shimmering waters edged by weeping willows and Japanese cherry trees, you'll understand why it inspired songwriters Rodgers and Hart ("I love the rowing on Central Park Lake" in "The Lady Is a Tramp"). The green banks along the man-made lake slope gently toward the water and make for an ideal picnic spot. You can rent a rowboat for two at the neo-Victorian Loeb Boathouse at the east end of

Rowing on Central Park Lake.

the lake. The boathouse also has a restaurant and a seasonal outside bar with seating overlooking the lake. It's a thoroughly pleasant place to enjoy a cool summer cocktail. *Midpark from 71st to 78th sts.*

3 Sheep Meadow. Skip the horse-drawn carriage rides, which are pretty pricey (roughly $50 for 20 min.). Head to the Sheep Meadow instead, a large green swath in lower Central Park that, yes, was once a grazing ground. It's got stupendous views of the Central Park South skyline pillowed in trees, perfect for a picnic. *Midpark btw. 66th and 69th sts.*

4 ★★ The Plaza. This historic confection of a hotel has fueled countless romances. Newlyweds Scott and Zelda Fitzgerald famously frolicked in the fountain out front. And who can forget the poignant final scene in *The Way We Were,* when Barbra Streisand and Robert Redford say good-bye in front of the Plaza? The scene was lovingly re-created on TV's *Sex and the City.* Toast to bittersweet romance in the swank Champagne Bar. *768 Fifth Ave. (at 59th St.). www.theplazany. com.* ☎ *212/759-3000. Subway: N/R/W to Fifth Ave. and 59th St.*

5 ★★ Tiffany & Co. Grab a croissant and a coffee and make like Audrey Hepburn in *Breakfast at Tiffany's.* Or just wander through, admiring all the sparkly stuff at this classic jewelry shop. You don't need to buy to enjoy Tiffany's. *727 Fifth Ave. (btw. 56th and 57th sts.).* ☎ *212/755-8000. Subway: E/M to Fifth Ave./53rd St.*

6 Lincoln Center Plaza. On a warm summer night, grab your partner and dance with abandon during "Midsummer Night Swing," the sexy dance party on Josie Robertson Plaza. Every night is a different dance theme, from salsa to swing to ballroom. The fountains and floodlights of the plaza are particularly seductive at dusk. *Columbus Ave. at 64th St. www. lincolncenter.org. See p 145.*

7 ★★ The Rink in Rockefeller Center. A romantic winter rendezvous on the ice-skating rink in the center's Lower Plaza is clichéd, but just try to resist a swirl around the ice during the holidays, with the spectacular Rock Center Christmas tree glittering from above. Avoid crowds by going early or late. *Lower Plaza, Rockefeller Center (btw. 49th and 50th sts).* ☎ *212/332-7654. Admission $25 adults, $15 seniors and children 11 and under; skate rental $12. Mid-Oct to mid-Apr; daily 8:30am–midnight. See p 8.*

8 The Whispering Gallery. Not only is the tiled Gustavino ceiling outside the Grand Central Oyster Bar a beauty, but it creates an acoustical phenomenon. Stand facing one of the pillars with your loved one facing the one directly opposite and whisper sweet nothings. You'll be able to hear one another—and no one else can listen

Skaters on the Rockefeller Center skating rink.

in. *Grand Central Station, 42nd St. and Park Ave. www.grandcentral terminal.com.* ☎ *212/340-2210. Subway: 4/5/6 to 42nd St./Grand Central.*

⑨ ★ Museum of Sex. Okay, so we're stretching the definition of romance with this one. But heck, a visit to this repository of early sex films, S&M displays, painted nudes, blow-up dolls, and other paraphernalia could make your time back at the hotel a bit more interesting. ⏱ *1 hr. 233 Fifth Ave. (at 27th St.). www.museumofsex.com.* ☎ *212/689-6337. Admission $39 adults, but online discounts halve costs. No one under 18 admitted. Sun–Thurs 10:30am–11pm, Fri–Sat 10am–midnight. Subway: N/R to 28th St.*

Please Check

Hours were still shifting, and protocols changing, as we went to press. Please contact the venues in this chapter before showing up, and get advance reservations when you can. It's just smart nowadays.

⑩ ★ One If By Land, Two If By Sea. The former carriage house of Vice President Aaron Burr (Alexander Hamilton's killer) makes the perfect setting for popping the question. Lit by crystal chandeliers and suffused with historic charm, it has a menu as classy as the setting. *17 Barrow St. (btw. Seventh Ave. and West 4th St.). www.oneifbyland.com. $$$$.*

⑪ ★★ Harbor Cruise. Whether you're on a simple spin around the island or an elegant dinner cruise, seeing Manhattan from the water is a thrill. That old reliable, **Circle Line** (www.circleline.com), has the most options, from 2-hour harbor cruises to sunset harbor lights cruises, from $29 to $44. Circle Line leaves from 89 South St. in the Seaport District. **Bateaux New York** (www.bateaux newyork.com) runs dinner cruises in sleek glass boats to the accompaniment of live jazz, from $70 to $140 It leaves from Pier 61 at Chelsea Piers (W. 23rd St.).

⑫ ★ The River Café. The River Café sits on the Brooklyn waterfront practically underneath the Brooklyn Bridge, with magnificent views of downtown Manhattan. Even if you don't come for dinner, you can sit on the terrace, sip a cocktail, and drink in the views. *1 Water St., Brooklyn. www.rivercafe.com.* ☎ *718/522-5200. $$$–$$$$.*

An Art Adventure

Anyone can go to a museum or gallery, but going to an artist's studio is a sophisticated, fascinating excursion, perfect for cosmopolitan couples. To do so, simply download the app **ArtMuse Selects,** and then make a booking on it for a visit. The app, booking process, and visit are all free. The app is also a top resource for info on NYC galleries, pop-up art events, and art fairs. And though there's no pressure to buy, prices are at their lowest when you buy directly from an artist, so you might find a special work for the home you share . . . or will share someday.

New York with Kids

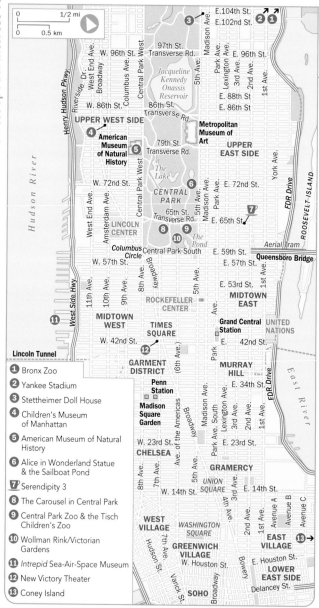

0 | 1/2 mi
0 | 0.5 km

E.104th St.
E.102nd St.
W. 96th St.
97th St. Transverse Rd.
E. 96th St.
Jacqueline Kennedy Onassis Reservoir
E. 88th St
E. 86th St
86th St. Transverse Rd.
UPPER WEST SIDE
American Museum of Natural History
Metropolitan Museum of Art
79th St. Transverse Rd.
UPPER EAST SIDE
The Lake
W. 72nd St.
E. 72nd St.
CENTRAL PARK
65th St. Transverse Rd.
E. 65th St.
LINCOLN CENTER
The Pond
E. 59th St.
Columbus Circle
Central Park South
Aerial Tram
Queensboro Bridge
W. 57th St.
E. 57th St.
E. 53rd St.
ROCKEFELLER CENTER
MIDTOWN EAST
MIDTOWN WEST
Grand Central Station
UNITED NATIONS
TIMES SQUARE
W. 42nd St.
E. 42nd St.
Lincoln Tunnel
GARMENT DISTRICT
MURRAY HILL
Penn Station
E. 34th St.
Madison Square Garden
W. 23rd St.
E. 23rd St.
CHELSEA
GRAMERCY
UNION SQUARE
W. 14th St.
E. 14th St.
WEST VILLAGE
WASHINGTON SQUARE
EAST VILLAGE
GREENWICH VILLAGE
W. Houston St.
E. Houston St.
SOHO
LOWER EAST SIDE
Delancey St.

Hudson River
East River
Henry Hudson Pkwy.
Riverside Dr.
West End Ave.
Broadway
Columbus Ave.
Central Park West
5th Ave.
Madison Ave.
Park Ave.
Lexington Ave.
3rd Ave.
2nd Ave.
1st Ave.
York Ave.
FDR Drive
ROOSEVELT ISLAND
West End Ave.
Amsterdam Ave.
Central Park West
West Side Hwy.
11th Ave.
10th Ave.
9th Ave.
8th Ave.
Broadway
7th Ave.
(6th Ave.)
Ave. of the Americas
5th Ave.
Park Ave. South
Lexington Ave.
3rd Ave.
2nd Ave.
1st Ave.
Madison Ave.
Broadway
8th Ave.
7th Ave.
Park
Hudson St.
Varick St.
Bowery
Avenue A
Avenue B
Avenue C

1 Bronx Zoo
2 Yankee Stadium
3 Stettheimer Doll House
4 Children's Museum of Manhattan
5 American Museum of Natural History
6 Alice in Wonderland Statue & the Sailboat Pond
7 Serendipity 3
8 The Carousel in Central Park
9 Central Park Zoo & the Tisch Children's Zoo
10 Wollman Rink/Victorian Gardens
11 Intrepid Sea-Air-Space Museum
12 New Victory Theater
13 Coney Island

eneath its noise, grit, and air of jaded cynicism, New York City is extremely kid-friendly. It opens its arms to kids of all ages, with some of the top children's attractions in the country, magical kid-centric holidays, and tons of treats for the eyes, ears, and tummy. What kid can resist? Just be sure to budget 3 to 4 days if you want to fit in everything on this tour. START: **Subway 2 or 5 to East Tremont Avenue/West Farms Square.**

Sea lions at the Bronx Zoo.

❶ ★★★ **kids Bronx Zoo.** The largest urban wildlife conservation facility in America, the Bronx Zoo has some 4,000 animals roaming 265 acres (106 hectares). It's hard to believe that you're actually in the Bronx as you watch lions, zebras, and gazelles roam the African Plains, a re-created savanna. Other highlights: Tiger Mountain (Siberian tigers), and the Congo Gorilla Forest, where 23 lowland gorillas, assorted monkeys, and other species live in a 6½-acre (2.6-hectare) African rainforest environment. ⏱ 4–5 hr. Fordham Rd. and Bronx River Pkwy. www.bronxzoo.com. ☎ 718/652-8400. Mon–Fri 10am–5pm, Sat–Sun 10am–5:30pm (extended summer and holiday hours). Admission $24 adults, $23 seniors, $17 children 3-12, free for kids 2 and under. Subway: 2/5 to E. Tremont Ave./W. Farms Sq.

❷ ★★ **kids Yankee Stadium.** Is there a better way to spend a sun-dappled afternoon or warm summer evening than at a baseball game at Yankee Stadium? And the quickest and most convenient way to get to the stadium is the subway. ⏱ 4 hr. 1 E. 161st St. (Jerome Ave.), the Bronx. www.yankees.com. ☎ 718/293-6000. Tickets $15–$85. Subway: B/D/4 to 161st St.

❸ ★ **kids Stettheimer Doll House.** This remarkable dollhouse in the **Museum of the City of New York** was the creation of Carrie Walter Stettheimer, a theater set designer who, with her two equally talented sisters, entertained the city's avant-garde artist community in the 1920s. Among the exquisite furnishings are period wallpaper, paper lampshades, and an art gallery featuring miniatures of such famous works as Marcel Duchamp's *Nude Descending a Staircase*. The museum has other toys on display as well as fascinating, interactive exhibits on the city's history. ⏱ 1½ hr. Museum of the City of New York, 1220 Fifth Ave. (103rd St.). www.mcny.org. ☎ 212/534-1672. Tues–Sun 10am–5pm. Admission $20 adults, $14 seniors, free for children 19 and under. Subway: 6 to 103rd St.

❹ ★★ **kids Children's Museum of Manhattan.** A rambling, indoor/outdoor fun house (shhh . . . it's also educational), CMOM entertains everyone from toddlers to 10-year-olds with interactive science experiments, daily shows, water features, playrooms, and changing exhibits on everything from ancient Greece to the art of Andy Warhol. ⏱ 2 hr. 212

W. 83rd St. (btw. Broadway and Amsterdam). www.cmom.org. ☎ 212/721-1223. Sun–Fri 10am–5pm, Sat 10am–7pm. Admission $15 adults and children, $12 seniors. Subway: 1 to 86th St.

5 ★★★ kids American Museum of Natural History. One word: ★★ **dinosaurs,** which devour the entrance hall and take up the entire fourth floor. Not to mention diamonds as big as the Ritz, and much more. *See p 50.*

6 ★★ kids Central Park's Alice in Wonderland Statue & Sailboat Pond. The 1959 bronze statue of Alice sitting on a giant mushroom becomes one big jungle gym in warm weather. Next to it is Conservatory Water, an ornamental pond where kids sail miniature boats (rented on-site). *Central Park, east side from 72nd to 75th sts.*

7 kids Serendipity 3. The Frrrozen Hot Chocolate is legendary at this whimsical Upper East Side dessert parlor, which also serves kid-friendly burgers, pastas, and chicken potpie. 225 E. 60th St. (btw. Second and Third aves.). www.serendipity3. com. ☎ 212/838-3531. $$.

8 ★★ kids The Carousel in Central Park. A quarter of a million children ride these vintage hand-carved horses every year. *See p 100.*

9 ★★ kids Central Park Zoo. Built in 1988 to replace a 1934 WPA-built structure, the zoo's 5½ acres (2.2 hectare) house more than 400 animals, among them sea lions, polar bears, and penguins. In the small **Tisch Children's Zoo,** kids can feed and pet tame farm animals. Check out the **Delacorte Clock,** with six dancing animals designed by the Italian sculptor Andrea Spadini. *See p 103.*

10 ★★ kids Wollman Rink/Victorian Gardens. Central Park's spacious rink is built for stretching out and perfecting your moves. Plus, it has views of skyscrapers along Central Park South. *See p 103.*

Holiday Magic

New York celebrates the holidays with glitter and gusto. On Thanksgiving, the **Macy's Day Parade** rolls through town; wake up early to find a perch along the parade route. Join the locals the night before for a street party around the Museum of Natural History to watch the giant parade balloons being inflated. From November through early January, the ever-popular **Christmas Spectacular** (www.radiocity.com; ☎ 212/307-1000; tickets $49–$250) plays at Radio City Music Hall, while in the Bronx, the New York Botanical Gardens mounts the wonderful **Holiday Train Show,** where vintage model trains zip around miniature reproductions of New York landmarks—all made *entirely out of plant materials* (www.nybg.org; ☎ 718/817-8700; $25 adults, $22 seniors and students, $12 children 2-12; take Metro-North Railroad from Grand Central to the Botanical Gardens stop).

The New Victory Theater presents kid-friendly shows like Mother Africa; My Home.

⑪ ★★★ kids **Intrepid Sea, Air & Space Museum.** The aircraft carrier known as the "Fighting I" served the U.S. Navy for 31 years, suffering bomb attacks, kamikaze strikes, and a torpedo shot. It's now a very cool sea, air, and space museum on the waterfront. You can crawl inside a wooden sub from the American Revolution, inspect a missile submarine, manipulate the controls in the cockpit of an A-6 Intruder and view an actual space shuttle. ◷ 1½ hr. Pier 86, 12th Ave. and 46th St. http://intrepidmuseum.org. ☎ 212/245-0072. Admission $33 adults, $31 seniors, $24 children 5–12, free for children 4 and under. Apr–Sept Mon–Fri 10am–5pm, Sat–Sun 10am–6pm; Oct–Mar Tues–Sun 10am–5pm. Bus: M42 to 12th St. and Hudson Ave. Subway: 1/2/3/7/9/A/C/E/S to 42th St./Times Sq.

⑫ ★★ kids **New Victory Theater.** Imaginative, kid-appropriate shows from around the globe play here—musicals, circuses, puppet shows, dance, you name it. Many of its offerings over the years have been wondrous. ◷ 2 hr. 209 W. 42nd St. (off Broadway). ☎ 646-223-3010.Tickets start at $16. Subway: 1/2/3/7/9/A/C/E/S to 42th St./Times Sq.

⑬ ★ kids **Coney Island.** This classic summer playground has carny rides, wooden boardwalks, and breezy salt air. It's a long subway ride out, but once you're here you can ride the 1927 **Cyclone** roller coaster or the 1920 **Wonder Wheel,** visit the **NY Aquarium,** or splash in the sea. 1208 Surf Ave., Brooklyn. www.coneyisland.com; https://nyaquarium.com; www.lunaparknyc.com. ☎ 718/372-5159. Ride prices vary. Memorial Day to Labor Day daily noon to late evening; Easter to Memorial Day and Labor Day to end of Oct weekends noon to late evening. Subway: D/N to Coney Island/Stillwell Ave.; F/Q to W. 8th St.

Literary Gotham

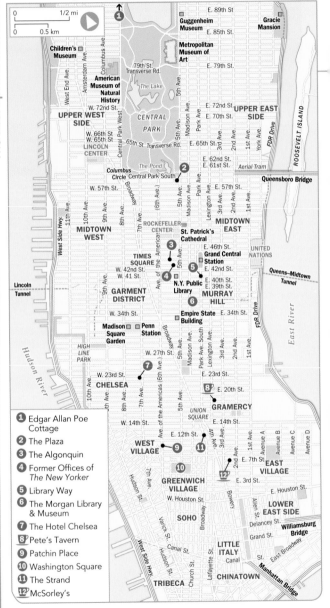

1. Edgar Allan Poe Cottage
2. The Plaza
3. The Algonquin
4. Former Offices of *The New Yorker*
5. Library Way
6. The Morgan Library & Museum
7. The Hotel Chelsea
8. Pete's Tavern
9. Patchin Place
10. Washington Square
11. The Strand
12. McSorley's

There is something about New York life that has long inspired writers. The home of the publishing industry, New York is a town that embraces the written word. Readings by big-name as well as undiscovered authors are a daily occurrence at venues throughout the city. What follows is a tour of some of the city's past and present literary landmarks (we have more in our tour of Greenwich Village, p 68). START: **N, R, or W to Fifth Avenue and 59th Street.**

① ★ Edgar Allan Poe Cottage. In 1846 the great storyteller rented this cabin, built in 1812, in hopes that the clean air of what was then the countryside would cure his beloved wife of tuberculosis. Alas, she died a little over a year after the move, and Poe passed away in 1849. The house is tiny and set today in a park (it was moved in 1913) but looks just as it would have when the Poes were in residence. Raconteur docents help bring their story to life. *2640 Grand Concourse in the Bronx. Thurs–Fri 10am–3pm, Sat 10am–4pm, Sun 1–5pm. $5 entry. Subway: D/4 to Kingsbridge Rd.*

② ★★ The Plaza. Eloise lived here, of course; the celebrated children's book heroine won the hotel "Literary Landmark" status in 1998.

Eloise was written in 1955 by performer Kay Thompson during her stay at the Plaza, and the famous portrait of the mischievous little girl is still displayed in the renovated lobby. *See p 9.*

③ The Algonquin. In the 1920s, this hotel was where such notables as James Thurber and the acid-tongued Dorothy Parker met to drink and trade bons mots at the so-called Round Table. Alas, both the restaurant and lobby have been stripped of their original decor/ambiance. *59 W. 44th St. (btw. Fifth and Sixth aves.). www.algonquin hotel.com. ☎ 212/840-6800. Subway: B/D/F/M to 42nd St.*

④ The former *New Yorker* offices. America's most celebrated literary magazine came into being at the Algonquin Round

The deathbed of Edgar Allan Poe's wife, at the Edgar Allan Poe Cottage.

Table, just a block away from its former office space here. Over the decades, the office has featured such writers as E. B. White, John Cheever, John Updike, and Calvin Trillin; you'll find their names and others on a plaque. *25 W. 43rd St. (btw. Fifth and Sixth aves.). Subway: B/D/ F/M to 42nd St.*

5 ★ Library Way. Along 41st Street between Park and Fifth, 96 bronze plaques embedded in the sidewalk all feature quotations from literature or poetry. Walking west along this street leads you to the legendary New York Public Library. *41st St. (btw. Park and Fifth aves.). Subway: B/D/F/M to 42nd St.*

6 ★★ The Morgan Library & Museum. The former private library of financier John Pierpont Morgan contains one of the world's most important collections of rare books and manuscripts. It was not Morgan himself who bartered with booksellers but his personal librarian, Belle da Costa Greene, a light-skinned African American who passed herself off as white to gain entree into Morgan's world. For more than 40 years, Morgan gave her carte blanche (money was no object) to build the collection. In addition to displaying these treasures (usually a Gutenberg bible is on view), the museum creates special exhibitions on such topics as Emily Dickinson's works or the writings and images of Martin Luther. ⏱ *2 hr. 29 E. 36th St. (btw. Park and Madison aves.). www.themorgan.org. ☎ 212/685-0610. Admission $22 adults, $14 seniors, $13 students, free for children 12 and under. Tues–Thurs 10:30am–5pm, Fri 10:30am–9pm, Sat 10am–6pm, Sun 11am–6pm. Subway: B/D/F/N/Q/R/M to 34th St.*

7 The Hotel Chelsea. Built in 1884, the Chelsea became a hotel in 1905 where artists and writers

were encouraged to stay indefinitely. Among the writers who did: Mark Twain, Thomas Wolfe, Dylan Thomas, O. Henry, Arthur Miller, and Sam Shepard (with his then-lover Patti Smith). If the hotel is still closed (it's been undergoing prolonged renovation) admire it from outside. *222 W. 23rd St. (btw. Seventh and Eighth aves.). www. hotelchelsea.com. ☎ 212/243-3700. Subway: 1/9/A/C to 23rd St.*

8 Pete's Tavern. Literary ghosts abound at this New York City landmark that claims to be the oldest continuing dining establishment in New York (1864). In the second booth from the front writer O. Henry is said to have penned his Christmas fable Gift of the Magi in 1906. In 1939, writer Ludwig Bemelmans used Pete's Tavern as his office to write the first in his Madeline children's book series. These days, instead of thirsty cash-strapped writers, you are more likely to see film crews in and around Pete's trying to re-create that old literary New York look. *129 E. 18th Street (at Irving Plaza). www.petestavern.com. ☎ 212/ 473-7676. $$.*

9 Patchin Place. This sweet little cobblestone mews tucked off Sixth Avenue was at one time a serious literary enclave: The poet e e cummings lived at no. 4 from 1923 to 1962, the reclusive writer Djuna Barnes lived at no. 5 for 40 years, and journalist John Reed and his paramour Louise Bryant lived here while he wrote Ten Days That Shook the World. (The lefty magazine he wrote for, The Masses, had its office a couple of blocks away at 91 Greenwich Ave.) *Patchin Place (off 10th St. and Sixth Ave.). Subway: A/B/C/D/E/F/M to W. 4th St.*

The Strand Bookstore.

10 Washington Square. The literary history of New York is filled with references to this fabled downtown neighborhood—and why not? It's where many great writers grew up or chose to live. Novelist Henry James was born at 21 Washington Place in 1843 and later described the neighborhood in his memorable 1880 novel *Washington Square*. Edith Wharton, whose novels evoked the genteel days when the aristocracy ruled New York society from Washington Square, stayed briefly with her mother at 7 Washington Sq. N. Willa Cather lived at both 60 Washington Sq. S. and 82 Washington Place. *See p 69.*

11 ★ The Strand. You can spend hours browsing the "18 miles" of new and used books crammed into the high, narrow shelves of this 1927 institution/bookstore. *See p 91.*

12 McSorley's. This working 1854 saloon was immortalized by New Yorker writer Joseph Mitchell in "McSorley's Wonderful Saloon,"

found in his classic collection of true New York tales, Up in the Old Hotel and Other Stories. *15 E. 7th St. (btw. Second and Third aves.). www.mcsorleysnewyork.nyc.* ☎ *212/474-9148. $.*

McSorley's Old Ale House.

New York's Unforgettable Architecture

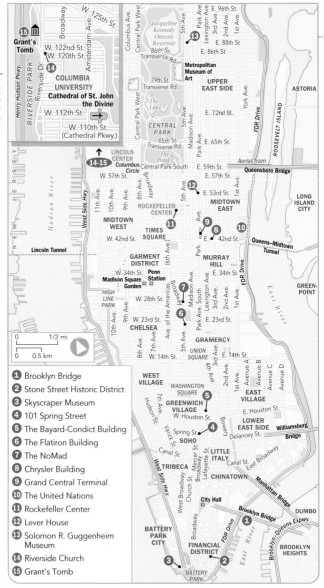

1. Brooklyn Bridge
2. Stone Street Historic District
3. Skyscraper Museum
4. 101 Spring Street
5. The Bayard-Condict Building
6. The Flatiron Building
7. The NoMad
8. Chrysler Building
9. Grand Central Terminal
10. The United Nations
11. Rockefeller Center
12. Lever House
13. Solomon R. Guggenheim Museum
14. Riverside Church
15. Grant's Tomb

Manhattan's muscular skyline is many things: an eclectic architectural landscape; a visual metaphor for the dynamism of America's largest city, perpetually in flux; and a stunning, three-dimensional historical record of how the Big Apple has grown—and grown up—over the years. This tour takes in a bit of all that, in 2 days. START: **Subway 4, 5, or 6 to Brooklyn Bridge/City Hall.**

❶ ★★★ Brooklyn Bridge. It took 16 very difficult years to build, but in 1883 this architectural and engineering marvel was finally finished. The 20- to 40-minute stroll on the bridge's wood-planked walkway is one of New York's must-do activities. Not only is the bridge a wonder to behold, but the views of Manhattan from it are equally stunning. *Subway: 4/5/6 to Brooklyn Bridge–City Hall.*

❷ ★ Stone Street Historic District. This narrow cobblestone street was staked out by the Dutch West India Company in the 1640s. The 15 brick structures that line it were all built in the year after the Great Fire of 1835 leveled the heavily commercial neighborhood, making this one of the most historically cohesive streets in the city. The street is closed to vehicular traffic and filled with the outdoor tables of the taverns and cafes that now inhabit these former warehouses (it's a real party scene in the warmer weather months). *Bounded by Pearl St., Hanover Sq., S. William St. and Coenties Alley. Subway: 2/3 to Wall St.*

❸ ★ Skyscraper Museum. Wowed by New York's sheer verticality? Learn more about the technology, culture, and muscle behind it all at this tiny museum. It contains two galleries: one dedicated to the evolution of Manhattan's skyline, and the other to changing shows. ⏱ *1 hr. 2 West St. (museum entrance faces Battery Place). www.skyscraper.org. ☎ 212/968-1961. Admission $5 adults, $2.50 seniors and students, free for children 11 and under. Wed–Sun noon–6pm. Subway: 1 to Rector St; 4/5 to Bowling Green.*

❹ ★ 101 Spring Street. This 5-story cast-iron building, built by architect Nicholas Whyte in 1870, remains the only intact single-use cast-iron building in SoHo. In 1968, minimalist Donald Judd (1928–1994) bought the former sewing factory and transformed it into a home and studio, now open to the public; the works on view in the building were set in place by the artist himself. Guided visits are $25 and must be reserved well in advance. Check www.juddfoundation.org for times and reservations. *101 Spring St. (btw. Broadway & Mercer St.). Subway: N/R to Prince St.*

Historic Stone Street.

The Flatiron Building.

⑤ ★ **The Bayard-Condict Building.** Renowned Chicago architect Louis Sullivan was Frank Lloyd Wright's boss and, some say, his mentor. The only building Sullivan designed in New York is hidden down a nondescript NoHo

street. It's a beaut, nonetheless: Constructed in 1899, the 13-story building is a creamy confection, with fanciful terra-cotta decoration and ornamental friezes. *65 Bleecker St. (btw. Broadway and Lafayette St.). Subway: 6 to Bleecker St.*

⑥ ★★★ **The Flatiron Building.** This triangular masterpiece is one of the city's most distinctive silhouettes. Its pie-slice form was the solution to a problem—filling the wedge of land created by the intersection of Fifth Avenue and Broadway. Built in 1902, the Flatiron measures only 6 feet (1.8m) across at its narrow end. So called for its resemblance to the laundry appliance, it was originally named the Fuller Building, then later "Burnham's Folly" because people were certain that architect Daniel Burnham's 21-story structure would fall down. The building mainly houses publishing offices, but it has a few shops on the ground floor. The surrounding neighborhood has taken its name—the Flatiron District,

The NoMad's massive fireplace came from a French chateau.

home to smart restaurants and shops. *175 Fifth Ave. (at 23rd St.). Subway: R to 23rd St.*

7 **The NoMad.** *Architectural Digest* named this one of the most "beautifully designed" restaurants in the world, and you'll understand why once you're seated under its pyramidal glass-roofed atrium or next to the ornate and massive fireplace (imported from a French chateau). The gourmet American fare is as sumptuous as the decor. *1170 Broadway (at 28th St.). www.thenomadhotel. com/dining.* ☎ *212/796-1500. $$$$.*

8 ★★★ **Chrysler Building.** This 1930 Art Deco masterpiece was designed to be the world's tallest building—and it was, if only for a year. In the race against other New York architects to build the tallest skyscraper of the era, William Van Alen secretly added a stainless-steel spire inside the fire shaft, hoisting it into place only after his competitors thought his building was completed. *405 Lexington Ave. (at 42nd St.). Subway: 4/5/6 to Grand Central.*

9 ★★★ **Grand Central Terminal.** This magnificent public space is also an engineering wonder. The "elevated circumferential plaza," as it was called in 1913, splits Park Avenue, which is diverted around the building. The network of trains— subway and commuter—that pass through here is vast, but even more impressive is the "bridge" over the tracks, designed to support a cluster of skyscrapers. The main concourse was restored to its original glory in 1998; the *Sky Ceiling* inside depicts the constellations of the winter sky above New York. They're lit with 59 stars surrounded by dazzling 24-karat gold. Emitting light

The United Nations headquarters.

fed through fiber-optic cables, the stars in their intensities roughly replicate the magnitude of the actual stars as seen from Earth. Look carefully and you'll see a patch near one corner left unrestored—a reminder of the neglect this splendid masterpiece once endured. *42nd St. and Park Ave. www.grand centralterminal.com.* ☎ *212/340-2210. Subway: 4/5/6/7/S to 42nd St.*

10 ★★ **The United Nations.** In keeping with the mission of this body, the United Nations complex was designed by an international team, spearheaded by Le Corbusier of France and Oscar Niermeyer of Brazil. Ironically, the institution created to advance the cause of world peace was built upon the grounds of slaughterhouses (the area was known as "Blood Alley"). All of the buildings (erected between 1948 and 1952) were done in the sleek "International" style, appropriately enough. Fascinating tours lead visitors through the lobby, the domed General Assembly chamber, and several other areas. Every member

The Atlas statue at Rockefeller Center.

nation has donated a work of art to the complex. *Entrance First Ave. and 47th St. http://visit.un.org.* ☎ *212/ 963-8687. Tours $22 adults, $15 seniors and students, $13 children 5–12. Children 4 and under not permitted. See website for current schedule. Subway: S, 4, 5, 6, 7 to 42nd St./Grand Central.*

⓫ ★★★ **Rockefeller Center.** Rock Center was erected at the

height of the Great Depression and, by many estimates, kept the city afloat—the nine-year construction employed 75,000 New Yorkers. The focal point is the soaring 70-story **GE Building** at 30 Rockefeller Plaza, which John D. Rockefeller said represented humanity's ability to break new frontiers. Its entrance sculpture, *Wisdom*, by Lee Lawrie, is an Art Deco masterpiece, as is the artist's *Atlas*, at the entrance court of the International Building. The sunken plaza in front of 30 Rock is overseen by the gilded statue *Prometheus* by Paul Manship. *See p 8.*

⓬ ★ **Lever House.** Built in 1952, this High Modern hymn to glass has undergone a spiffy renovation to restore its original sparkle. The clean-lined, relatively small skyscraper was the first in New York to employ the "curtain wall" design philosophy, with a brilliant blue-green glass facade. *400 Park Ave. (btw. 53rd and 54th sts.). Subway: 6 to Lexington Ave.*

⓭ ★★★ **Solomon R. Guggenheim Museum.** Frank Lloyd Wright's only New York edifice— built in 1959—is a brilliant feat of

Contemporary Masterpieces

If you are a fan of today's architecture, New York has more than its share. Check out Frank Gehry's curvaceous 76-story skyscraper at 1 Spruce Street in the Financial District, or his fractured white cube, the **IAC Building** at 555 W. 18th St. Just across the street from the latter is Jean Nouvelle's glass patchwork tower (at **100 Eleventh Ave.**). Look closely: Every single window is a different size. There's also Calatrava's extraordinary **WTC Transportation Hub** (p 18); and in the East Village the game-changing **40 Bond Street,** which looks like a thorn forest topped by a tower.

architecture. The Babylonian-style "inverted ziggurat" has been compared to a wedding cake or a nautilus shell, but it is full of life and movement. Just forget your fantasies about roller-skating down the ramp of the rotunda. ⊘ *1 hr. 1071 Fifth Ave. (at 89th St.). www.guggenheim. org.* ☎ *212/423-3500. Admission $25 adults, $18 seniors and students, free for children 12 and under. Sun–Wed and Fri 10am–5:45pm, Sat 10am–7:45pm. Subway: 4/5/6 to 86th St. Bus: M1/2/3/4.*

⓮ ★ **Riverside Church.** This majestic 2-block-long Gothic church, opened in 1930, has a long history of activism and has hosted such speakers as Martin Luther King, Jr.; Nelson Mandela; and Kofi Annan. The church's soaring bell tower is the tallest in the U.S. Tours of the church's breathtaking interiors—featuring artworks by Heinrich Hofmann—are usually offered several times a week. ⊘ *1 hr. 490 Riverside Dr. (btw. 120th and 121st sts.). www.theriversidechurchny.org. Subway: 1 to 116th St.*

⓯ ★ **Grant's Tomb.** This colossal mausoleum is the crown jewel of a gorgeous stretch of Riverside Park. Ulysses S. Grant, the 18th president and the commander of the Union Army, spent the last 4 years of his life in New York; he's entombed here with his wife, Julia. The deep-red twin granite sarcophagi, viewed from a circular marble mezzanine above, are a moving, almost eerie tribute to the Civil War hero. On the monument's other side is the peaceful Sakura Park, an underrated green space with a delightful Japanese feel. ⊘ *20 min. Riverside Dr. and 122nd St. www. grantstomb.org. Free admission. Summer daily 9am–5pm; spring, fall, and winter Thurs–Mon 9am–5pm. Subway: 1 to 125th St.*

Frank Lloyd Wright's Guggenheim Museum.

NYC Free & Dirt-Cheap

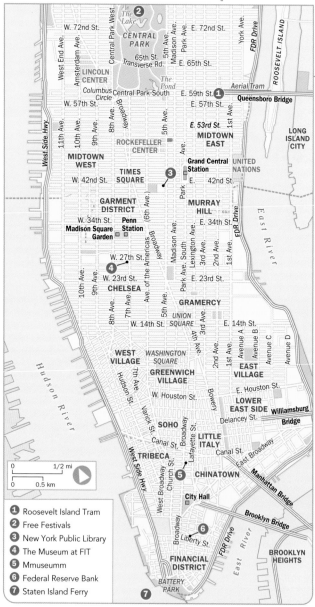

- ❶ Roosevelt Island Tram
- ❷ Free Festivals
- ❸ New York Public Library
- ❹ The Museum at FIT
- ❺ Mmuseumm
- ❻ Federal Reserve Bank
- ❼ Staten Island Ferry

Seeing the sights in New York is often just a matter of turning the corner. Brass bands wailing at Chinatown street funerals, the latest fashions parading down the catwalk that's West Bleecker Street (p 71), the animated holiday window displays at all the department stores—you won't pay a penny for any of it. Nor will you for many museums (see p 41). Here are some other free (or dirt-cheap) ways to savor the Big Apple. START: **Subway 6 to 77th or 86th Street.**

The Roosevelt Island tram.

❶ ★★ Roosevelt Island Tram and FDR Four Freedoms Park. Roosevelt Island residents who ride the tram to and from Manhattan every day are privy to one of NYC's best-kept secrets: The view from it is awe-inspiring. Look down the East River during the 4-minute ride, and you'll see four bridges. On Roosevelt Island, explore serene Franklin D. Roosevelt Four Freedoms Park. Designed by acclaimed architect Louis Kahn, the park was commissioned in 1973. Soon after the announcement, however, Kahn died unexpectedly, New York went bankrupt, and the park plan was shelved for 39 years. The memorial finally opened in 2012, featuring a 1,050-pound bronze bust of Roosevelt by sculptor Jo Davidson. *Closed Tues. Tram at Second Ave. and 59th St. Fare $2.75. Subway: 4/5/6/N/R/W to 59th St.*

❷ ★★★ Free Festivals. We could write an entire book on those! The city is blessed with hundreds each year, the most iconic summer ones being **Shakespeare in the Park** (Central Park; www.publictheater.org) and **New York Philharmonic** evening concerts in parks around the city (https://nyphil.org). For a listing of current fests, try NYMag.com.

❸ ★★★ New York Public Library. This magnificent Beaux Arts building has permanent and temporary exhibitions plus a film about its history and a nice gift shop in the lobby. Oh, and it's all free. *See p 8.*

The New York Public Library's main reading room.

The Staten Island Ferry.

❹ ★★ The Museum at FIT.

That would be the Fashion Institute of Technology (you've seen it on *Project Runway*). This surprisingly erudite museum never charges an entrance fee and covers topics that merge sociology and fashion (like uniforms through the ages, or how denim went from workmen's wear to high fashion). *Seventh Ave. at 27th St. www.fitnyc.edu/museum.* ☎ *212/247-4558. Tues–Fri noon–8pm, Sat 10am–5pm.*

❺ ★★ Mmuseumm.

Take one abandoned elevator shaft, four documentary filmmakers/curators, and lots of dinner-plate-sized (or smaller) contemporary artifacts from around the world, and you get a fascinating, if quirky, mini-museum that explores what it means to be human today. *4 Cortlandt Alley (near White St.). www.* *mmuseumm.com. Free. Warm weather months only, Fri–Sun 11am–6pm.*

❻ ★★ Federal Reserve Bank of New York.

With more gold than Fort Knox—$90 billion of it— you would think this urban fortress would be closed to the public. But no, it offers compelling free tours, covering the history of the Fed, its security measures, and a visit to the gold vault, 50 feet below ground. Advance reservations required. 🕐 *1 hr. 33 Liberty St. (btw. William and Nassau sts.). www.newyorkfed. org.* ☎ *212/720-6130. Subway: 4/5 to Wall St.*

❼ ★★ Staten Island Ferry.

This free 25-minute ride takes you up close and past the Statue of Liberty and Ellis Island. *Whitehall Ferry Terminal. www.siferry.com.* ☎ *718/727-2508.* ●

TV Tapings

It's free—but not easy—to view tapings of such New York–based shows as *The Late Show with Stephen Colbert*, *The Tonight Show Starring Jimmy Fallon*, *Saturday Night Live*, and *The View*. The catch is ordering tickets well in advance. Check the "ticket request" section on each show's website. For a full list of all shows taping in the city, go to **NYC & Company,** the city's official tourism agency (www.nycgo.com/articles/tv-show-tapings).

The Metropolitan **Museum of Art**

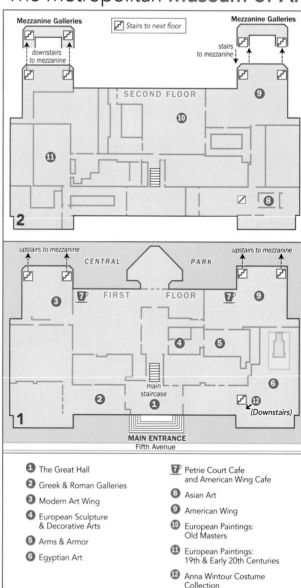

Mezzanine Galleries

📑 Stairs to next floor

Mezzanine Galleries

downstairs to mezzanine

stairs to mezzanine

SECOND FLOOR

❾

❿

⓫

2

❽

upstairs to mezzanine

CENTRAL   PARK

upstairs to mezzanine

❸   ☕ FIRST   FLOOR ☕   ❾

❹   ❺

❻

main staircase

❷   ⓬
(Downstairs)

1

MAIN ENTRANCE
Fifth Avenue

❶ The Great Hall

❷ Greek & Roman Galleries

❸ Modern Art Wing

❹ European Sculpture
& Decorative Arts

❺ Arms & Armor

❻ Egyptian Art

☕ Petrie Court Cafe
and American Wing Cafe

❽ Asian Art

❾ American Wing

❿ European Paintings:
Old Masters

⓫ European Paintings:
19th & Early 20th Centuries

⓬ Anna Wintour Costume
Collection

Previous page: The Great Hall of the Metropolitan Museum of Art.

In 1866, a group of New Yorkers decided their hometown needed a museum that would function as a living encyclopedia of world art. Today, the Metropolitan Museum of Art and the Cloisters fulfill that promise with a collection of more than two million objects dating from the Paleolithic period—that is, the Stone Age—through today.

Thomas Hart Benton's "America Today" in the Modern Art Wing.

❶ **The Great Hall.** The main entrance to the Met makes all who enter feel like royalty. With its soaring ceilings, elegant balconies, and restrained use of Greco-Roman motifs, it's a fine example of neoclassical architecture. The massive sprays of fresh flowers have been a tradition since 1969.

❷ ★★★ **Greek & Roman Galleries.** Some 3,700 people per day visit these spectacular Greek and Roman galleries. The centerpiece is the **Leon Levy and Shelby White Court,** a dramatic peristyle area rich with Hellenistic and Roman art. Among its treasures is a massive statue of **Hercules** with a lion skin draped heroically over his arm. In the galleries, visitors can see **Roman frescoes** long buried under ash after a volcanic eruption; exquisite **gold serpentine armbands;** and the **"Black Bedroom,"** reputedly

made for a villa built by a close friend of the Emperor Augustus.

❸ ★★★ **Modern Art Wing.** Head through the galleries of the Arts of Africa, Oceania, and the Americas to get to the Modern Art Wing, which is full of blockbusters. Must-sees include **Pablo Picasso's** *Gertrude Stein,* **Thomas Hart Benton's** *America Today,* and **Balthus'** *The Mountain.*

❹ ★★ **European Sculpture & Decorative Arts.** In these galleries, a series of period rooms include a handsome bedroom from an 18th-century **Venetian palace** and a mid-18th-century **Tapestry Room** from an English country estate. Especially astonishing is the *Studiolo* from the Ducal Palace in Gubbio, a small Renaissance study paneled in elaborate marquetry—thousands of pieces of different colored wood, giving the illusion of

Practical Matters

The Met (www.metmuseum.org; ☎ 212/535-7710; Sun–Thurs 10am–5:30pm; Fri–Sat 10am–9pm) is located at 1000 Fifth Ave. (at 82nd St.). Admission (for up to 3 consecutive days) is $25 adults, $17 seniors, $12 students, and free for children under 12 and New York State residents. If you're in a rush, skip the main entrance on 82nd and enter at 81st Street. Least crowded times: Friday and Saturday nights or right at opening.

cabinets containing books, musical instruments, and scientific tools.

5 ★ kids Arms & Armor. The full sets of European armor in the courtyard are dazzling, but make sure to pop into the smaller galleries that surround the court. Here you'll find such curiosities as ceremonial saddles carved from bone and pistols inlaid with semiprecious stones. A Turkish saber created in 1876 for the investiture of an Ottoman sultan (who had a nervous breakdown before the ceremony and was deposed) is a miracle of sparkling diamonds, smooth-as-ice jade, and rich gold.

6 ★★★ kids Egyptian Art. The **Temple of Dendur,** built in 15 B.C. and relocated from Egypt, is arguably the most famous object at the Met. Inside, you'll find graffiti from Victorian-era travelers. For a glimpse of daily life in ancient Egypt, check out the 13 wooden models from the **tomb of Meketre,** representations of the nobleman's earthly wealth—a bakery, a dairy, a brewery, and boats—to be taken with him into the afterlife.

7 Cafes. Year-round you can grab a good, filling lunch at one of the Met's onsite cafes—they even have kids' meals. Or, if it's a nice day, head outside the main

entrance and get a snack from one of the carts ($) on the plaza. Eating a pretzel or hot dog while people-watching from the steps of the museum is a quintessential New York experience. For other dining options, *see p 111.*

8 ★ Asian Art. The **Astor Court,** a Chinese scholar's garden based on a Ming Dynasty design, is a wonderfully serene space. The principle of yin and yang, or opposites, gives this space its sense of harmony and tranquility—that, and it's often inexplicably deserted. Also in this section: the Japanese galleries, filled with delicate scrolls, screens, kimonos, and tapestries. Our fave: the elegant **Japanese tearoom/study room.**

9 ★★ American Wing. This airy, light-filled section of the Met is a museum inside a museum containing Hudson River School paintings that are extraordinary in their scope, from the grandeur of **Frederick Church's** *The Heart of the Andes* to the delicate and refined *Lake George* by **John Kensett.** Plenty more is recognizable here, from the iconic *Washington Crossing the Delaware* by **Emanuel Leutze** to **John Singer Sargent's** *Madame X.* The American Wing includes 25 furnished period rooms from the late 17th to the early 20th

Botticelli portrait of a young man, in the European Paintings galleries.

centuries, including **Frank Lloyd Wright**'s suave *Living Room from the Little House.*

⑩ ★★★ European Paintings: Old Masters. Where to start? These galleries hold important works from all the geniuses you studied in Art History 101 (except daVinci). Among the many wonders: **Rembrandt**'s *Aristotle with a Bust of Homer*, **Vermeer**'s *Young Woman with a Water Jug*, **El Greco**'s *Portrait of a Cardinal*, **Velázquez**'s *Juan de Pareja*, **Goya**'s *Don Manuel*, and **Duccio**'s *Madonna and Child.*

⑪ ★★ European Paintings: 19th & Early 20th Centuries. One of the museum's most popular sections, these galleries include a good sampling of Impressionist art. Here you can compare **Gustave Courbet**'s controversial and explicitly sexual *Woman with a Parrot* with a more discreet version by **Edouard Manet.** Or take in **Paul Cézanne**'s *Still Life with Apples and Pears,* with its funky perspectives and innovative use of color, to get a feel for the radical changes in painting that developed in the 20th century.

⑫ ★★ Anna Wintour Costume Collection. A favorite of fashionistas, the Collection puts together blockbuster retrospectives that have, in the past, had museum-goers lining up around the block for entry.

The Cloisters

That big white building on Fifth Avenue? That's just the beginning of what the Met has up its sleeve. Eight miles uptown in Fort Tryon Park, the Met offshoot **The Cloisters** is the only museum in the U.S. wholly devoted to medieval art. It not only displays masterpieces of that era (including the ecstatically beautiful **Unicorn Tapestries**) but does so in a setting that appears airlifted, utterly intact, from a remote corner of the Pyrenees, or a castle-bound town in Bavaria. That's an illusion. The building incorporates elements from five medieval monasteries in France, Spain, and Italy. *Note:* The last stop on the M4 bus is directly in front of The Cloisters. The ride takes 1 hour. Admission is free with same-day Met sticker.

Other **Must-See Museums**

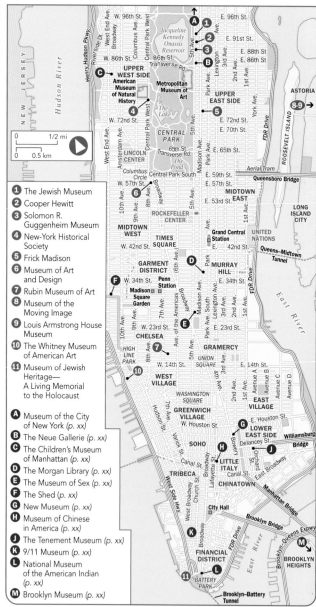

1 The Jewish Museum
2 Cooper Hewitt
3 Solomon R. Guggenheim Museum
4 New-York Historical Society
5 Frick Madison
6 Museum of Art and Design
7 Rubin Museum of Art
8 Museum of the Moving Image
9 Louis Armstrong House Museum
10 The Whitney Museum of American Art
11 Museum of Jewish Heritage— A Living Memorial to the Holocaust

A Museum of the City of New York (p. xx)
B The Neue Gallerie (p. xx)
C The Children's Museum of Manhattan (p. xx)
D The Morgan Library (p. xx)
E The Museum of Sex (p. xx)
F The Shed (p. xx)
G New Museum (p. xx)
H Museum of Chinese in America (p. xx)
J The Tenement Museum (p. xx)
K 9/11 Museum (p. xx)
L National Museum of the American Indian (p. xx)
M Brooklyn Museum (p. xx)

Few cities can match New York in the breadth and depth of its museum collections. Besides the museums you'll find on various other tours in this guide, the following sites would be star attractions in any other city—but all too often fall into second place on New York City visitors' lists (and undeservedly so). *Tip:* Most museums offer free admission on the evenings they stay open late; check websites for details. Also, note that the pandemic did impact hours and prices, so please double check the info in this guide, as much was in transition as we went to press.

① ★★ **The Jewish Museum.** The "humble" goal of this institution is to cover 4,000 years of Jewish history. It does so in dazzling style, with interactive panels, exquisite ceremonial objects (like menorahs and prayer shawls), other Judaica, and folk art. The only topic that doesn't get much coverage is the Holocaust—for that, go to the **Museum of Jewish Heritage** (p 49). ⏱ *2 hr. 1109 Fifth Ave (at 92nd St). www. thejewishmuseum.org.* ☎ *212/423-3200. Admission $18 adults, $12 seniors, $8 students, free to those under 18 and on Saturdays. Sat–Tues 11am–5:45 pm, Thurs 11am–8pm, Fri 11am–4pm. Subway: 6 to 96th St.*

② ★★★ **kids** **Cooper Hewitt.** An offshoot of the Smithsonian, this design museum may be one of the most cutting-edge in the country. Presenting expertly curated exhibits on everything from how Pixar designs films, to the work of Louis Comfort Tiffany, it encourages visitors to use a specially created "pen" to enhance appreciation of the design works on display. You can create your own website filled with whichever objects in the museum interest you (just press the pen to the barcode next to the item), or use the pen to activate responsive tables throughout the museum, to learn more info and interact with the exhibits. ⏱ *2 hr. 2 E. 91st St. (off Fifth Ave.). www. cooperhewitt.org.* ☎ *212/849-2950. Admission $18 adults, $12 seniors, $9*

The Cooper-Hewitt Museum, housed in what was once Andrew Carnegie's mansion.

students, free to those under 18 and on Saturdays 6–9pm. Save $2 by booking online. Thurs-Mon 10am-6pm. Subway: 6 to 96th St.

❸ ★★★ Solomon R. Guggenheim Museum. The building alone is a masterpiece, but what's inside is often as wondrous. Along with of-the-moment themed exhibitions and installations, it offers a stroll through the canon of modern art—everything from an 1867 landscape by Camille Pissaro to important works by Picasso, Kandinsky, and Modigliani. *See p 36.*

❹ ★★ New-York Historical Society. The New-York Historical Society is a major repository of American history, culture, and art, with a special focus on New York. Where else can you find a collection that includes Tiffany lamps, vintage dollhouses, Audubon watercolors, life and death masks of prominent Americans, and even George Washington's camp bed? ⏱ 1½ hr. 2 W. 77th St. (at Central Park West). www.nyhistory.org. ☎ 212/873-3400. Admission $22 adults, $17 seniors, $13 students, $6 children 5–12, free under 5. Thus, Sat-Sun 11am-5pm, Fri 'til 8pm (pay what you wish from 6-8pm). Bus: M79. Subway: 1 to 79th St.

❺ ★★★ Frick Madison. Industrialist Henry Clay Frick, who controlled Pittsburgh's steel industry in the late 19th century, began collecting art after he made his first million. In years past, these works were displayed in his palatial mansion, but that's being renovated, so the works have been moved to this iconic, brutalist building by Marcel Breuer (former home of the Whitney Museum). Paintings by Titian, Gainsborough, Rembrandt, Vermeer, El Greco, Goya are still on view, as always, but because this building has more room than the mansion, many rarely-seen artworks

are also on display. ⏱ 2 hr. 945 Madison Ave (at 75th St.). www.frick.org. ☎ 212/288-0700. Admission $22 adults, $17 seniors, $12 students. Children under 10 not admitted. Thurs–Sun 10am–6pm. Subway: 6 to 77th St.

❻ ★ Museum of Art and Design. Not as spellbinding as the Cooper-Hewitt, this towering museum (with a terrific gift shop) nonetheless has put on some intriguing shows over the years, such as one on designing perfumes (with sniff stations) and another on the brooches Madeline Albright wore as Secretary of State. ⏱ 1 hr. 2 Columbus Circle (at 59th St.). www.madmuseum.org. ☎ 212/299-7777. Admission $18 adults, $14 seniors, $12 students, free for those under 18. Wed–Sun 11am–7pm, half price Thurs 4–7. Subway: A, B, C, D, 1 to 59th St./Columbus Circle.

❼ ★★ Rubin Museum of Art. New York must have good karma: In October 2004, it scored this stunning collection of Himalayan art. In the former Chelsea outpost of Barneys, the Rubin Museum features sculptures, paintings, and textiles. ⏱ 1½ hr. 150 W. 17th St. (btw. Sixth and Seventh aves.). www.rmanyc.org. ☎ 212/620-5000. Admission $19 adults; $14 seniors, students, and artists; free for children 12 and under. Mon and Thurs 11am–5pm, Wed 11am–9pm, Fri 11am–10pm, Sat–Sun 11am–6pm. Subway: 1/9 to 18th St.

❽ ★★★ 🅺🆒 Museum of the Moving Image. For sheer unadulterated fun, no museum in town can beat this one. The first museum anywhere to look at TV, film, and video games together, it explores the craft and technology behind these arts (more recently adding web design and other tech) with imaginative interactive exhibits, art works, video sequences, and artifacts. The museum is just two subway stops

A Simone Leigh sculpture at the Whitney Museum of American Art.

from midtown Manhattan. ◷ *2 hr. 36–01 35th Ave (at 37th St.), Astoria, Queens. www.movingimage.us.* ☎ *718/777-6888. Admission $15 adults, $11 seniors and students, $9 children 3–17. Wed–Thurs 10:30am–5pm, Fri 10:30am–8pm, Sat–Sun 11:30am–6pm. Subway: R to Steinway St. or Q, N to 36 Ave.*

⑨ ★★ Louis Armstrong House Museum. A visit to the only home Satchmo ever owned offers a tuneful trip back in time, accompanied by witty, knowledgeable tour guides (guided tours only). You'll see his prized solid-gold sink, learn what it was like to tour with him, and get a better appreciation for the genial, incredibly brave man who changed music history. ◷ *40 min. 34–56 107th St., Corona, Queens. www.louisarmstronghouse.org.* ☎ *718/478-8274. Admission: $12 adults; $8 seniors, students, and children. Tues–Fri 10am–5pm, Sat–Sun noon–5pm. Subway: 7 to 103 St.-Corona Pl.*

⑩ ★★★ The Whitney Museum of American Art. Reborn in 2016, this mecca of American art is now located in Manhattan's hippest neighborhood, right at the foot of the High Line (p 104). Which is appropriate, as the museum—originally built in 1931 around Gertrude Vanderbilt Whitney's collection of 20th-century art (including works by Edward Hopper, Jasper Johns, and Georgia O'Keefe)—has become a major player in the contemporary art scene, much of which is centered in nearby Chelsea galleries (see p 64). ◷ *2 hr. 99 Gansevoort St. (btw. Washington St. and Tenth Ave.). http://whitney.org.* ☎ *800/ WHITNEY (944-8639). Admission $25 adults, $18 seniors and students, free Thurs 1:30-6pm. Thurs–Fri 10:30am–6pm, Sat–Sun 11:30am–6pm, Mon 1:30pm–5pm. Subway: 6 to 77th St.*

⑪ ★ Museum of Jewish Heritage—A Living Memorial to the Holocaust. Dedicated to teaching people of all backgrounds about 20th-century Jewish life, this award-winning museum was designed in a six-sided shape to symbolize the Star of David and to honor the six million Jews who died in the Holocaust. Inside are photos, artifacts, and moving accounts from survivors. ◷ *2 hr. 36 Battery Place. www.mjhnyc.org.* ☎ *646/437-4200. Admission $16 adults, $12 seniors, $10 students, free for children 12 and under. 11am–7pm Wed-Thurs and Sun. Subway: 4/5 to Bowling Green; 1 to South Ferry.*

The American Museum of Natural History

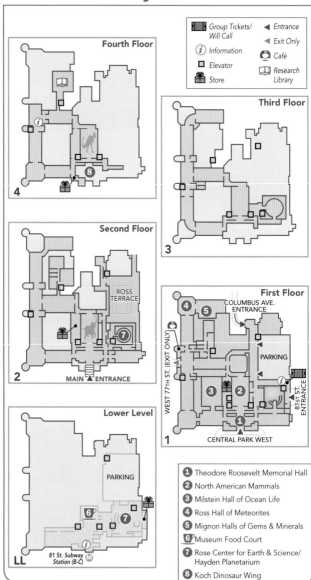

Fourth Floor

4

Third Floor

3

Second Floor

ROSS TERRACE

2

MAIN ENTRANCE

First Floor

COLUMBUS AVE. ENTRANCE

WEST 77TH ST. (EXIT ONLY)

PARKING

81ST ST ENTRANCE

CENTRAL PARK WEST

1

Lower Level

PARKING

LL

81 St. Subway Station (B-C)

Group Tickets/ Will Call
ⓘ Information
Elevator
Store
◀ Entrance
◀ Exit Only
Café
Research Library

1 Theodore Roosevelt Memorial Hall
2 North American Mammals
3 Milstein Hall of Ocean Life
4 Ross Hall of Meteorites
5 Mignon Halls of Gems & Minerals
6 Museum Food Court
7 Rose Center for Earth & Science/ Hayden Planetarium
8 Koch Dinosaur Wing

It's got dinosaurs, giant sapphires, and towering totem poles—and that's just for starters. The American Museum of Natural History has one of the most diverse and thrilling collections in the world—four floors of natural wonders and cultural artifacts for the intrepid explorer in all of us. It's delicious fun for every age.

❶ ★★ Theodore Roosevelt Memorial Hall. The sight of a giant *Barosaurus* fossil in this soaring entrance rotunda provides a smashing opening to the rest of your visit.

❷ ★★ North American Mammals. One of the museum's popular "Habitat Group Dioramas," where skillfully mounted animals are shown in lifelike reproductions of their natural habitats. In one diorama, an Alaskan brown bear, the world's largest living land carnivore, rears up on its hind legs.

❸ ★★ Milstein Hall of Ocean Life. This vast first-floor room explores life in the deep blue sea, with lighted fish dioramas and a spectacular replica of a giant blue whale overhead.

❹ ★★ Ross Hall of Meteorites. On display is a 34-ton meteorite, said to be merely a fragment of a massive meteorite that scientists estimate weighed around 200 tons.

❺ ★★★ Alison and Roberto Mignone Halls of Gems and Minerals. This collection of precious gems includes the biggest sapphire ever found, the 563-carat Star of India.

❻ Museum Food Court. Sustenance for the whole family, including barbecue, paninis, and sandwiches. *Lower level. $–$$.*

❼ ★★★ Rose Center for Earth & Space/Hayden Planetarium. A sphere inside a seven-story glass cube holds the Hayden Planetarium, where you can take a virtual ride through the Milky Way. Prepare to be blown away by the planetarium **Space Show**, narrated by Neil deGrasse Tyson. Buy tickets in advance for the Space Show to guarantee admission (they're available online).

❽ ★★★ Koch Dinosaur Wing. The fourth floor contains the largest collection of real dinosaur fossils in the world. Among the treasures is the *Tyrannosaurus rex*, with 6-inch-long teeth, and the first *Velociraptor* skull ever found.

Practical Matters

The AMNH (www.amnh.org; ☎ 212/769-5100; daily 10am–5:45pm) is on Central Park West (btw. 77th and 81st sts.). Admission (includes entrance to Rose Center) is $23 adults, $18 seniors and students, $13 children 2-12; museum admission plus special exhibits $28 adults, $23 seniors, $16.50 children 2 to 12. You'll need about 4 hours to see the whole thing. Buy tickets in advance for specific IMAX shows or special exhibitions. Subway: B, C to 81st St.

The Museum of **Modern Art**

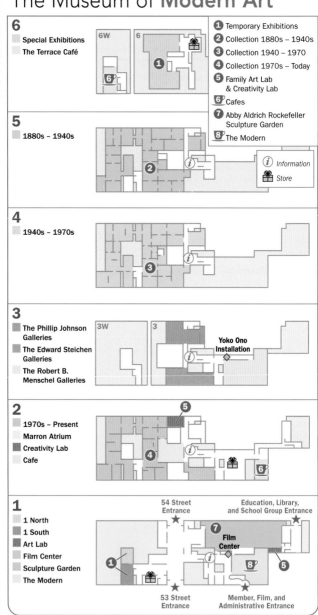

6
- Special Exhibitions
- The Terrace Café

6W 6

1. Temporary Exhibitions
2. Collection 1880s – 1940s
3. Collection 1940 – 1970
4. Collection 1970s – Today
5. Family Art Lab & Creativity Lab
6. Cafes
7. Abby Aldrich Rockefeller Sculpture Garden
8. The Modern

i Information
🎁 Store

5
- 1880s – 1940s

4
- 1940s – 1970s

3
- The Phillip Johnson Galleries
- The Edward Steichen Galleries
- The Robert B. Menschel Galleries

3W 3

Yoko Ono Installation

2
- 1970s – Present
- Marron Atrium
- Creativity Lab
- Cafe

1
- 1 North
- 1 South
- Art Lab
- Film Center
- Sculpture Garden
- The Modern

54 Street Entrance

Education, Library, and School Group Entrance

Film Center

53 Street Entrance

Member, Film, and Administrative Entrance

For art that's termed "modern"—the stuff that was created from the 1880s to the 1970s—this museum is without peer. For contemporary art, it now has important rivals (we're looking at you, Whitney). Still, the strength of its collection makes it an essential stop on any New York jaunt. A 2019 remodeling expanded the gallery space by a full third, which should help alleviate overcrowding. To keep things fresh, a third of the galleries will be rehung every 6 months, creating exhibitions that are "conversations" between artists, sometimes juxtaposing artists of different eras and mediums (film, photography, decorative arts). The plan should allow MoMA to feature more diverse voices, although it may mean that some famous works may not be on display when you visit.

❶ Temporary Exhibitions. Retrospectives, of movements in art or particular artists (like Donald Judd), are the focus of these two floors. If this is your first visit, head first to the 2nd, 4th, and 5th floors, which hold MoMA's canonical works.

❷ ★★★ Collection 1880s–1940s. Go to the eastern side of the building (look for the hanging helicopter) and up the elevator to see the museum's treasures in roughly chronological order; gallery numbers with the floor and then the room number can help you stay on track. Most popular are **Vincent van Gogh**'s *The Starry Night* (always in room 501), **Picasso**'s *Les Demoiselles d'Avignon*, **Monet's** *Water Lilies*, and **Henri Rousseau**'s *The Sleeping Gypsy*. Look also for celebrated works by Frida Kahlo, Paul Gauguin, Marc Chagall, Paul Cézanne, Edward Hopper, Salvador Dali, René Magritte, and Constantine Brancusi. Mixed in will be important works of photography (Man Ray, Berenice Abbott), furnishings (an Eames chair, Frank Lloyd Wright windows), and film.

❸ ★★★ Collection 1940–1970. Andy Warhol and Jackson Pollock are, arguably, the big stars of this floor, although they get major competition from Mark Rothko, Louise Bourgeois, Alexander Calder, Lee Krasner, and Henri Matisse (his later works). "The Studio" is for screenings, performances, and the works of artists in residence.

❹ ★★ Collection 1970s–Today. I expect this floor to have the most turnover, in terms of which works are deemed iconic enough to remain on view, but I think it's fairly risk-free to say you'll likely get some works by Cindy Sherman, Jean-Michel Basquiat, Kara Walker, and Jeff Koons (but really, who knows?). Richard Serra's *Equal*—monolithic metal cubes—will definitely be in gallery 210, as the work is too big to move often.

Practical Matters

The MoMA (www.moma.org; ☎ 212/708-9400; daily 10:30am–5pm, til 7pm Sat) is at 11 W. 53rd St. (btw. Fifth and Sixth aves.). Admission is $25 adults, $18 seniors, $14 students, and free for kids 16 and under. You'll need 3 hours to do it justice. Subway: E,M to Fifth Ave/53rd St.

Paintings by Picasso and Ringgold at the Museum of Modern Art.

Travel Tip

MoMA's museum-wide Wi-Fi allows visitors to access to excellent audio tours. Content is available in specialized versions for children, teenagers, and the visually impaired.

5 ★ **Family Art Lab & Creativity Lab.** Drop-in spaces for those who are feeling inspired and would like to make their own art. The first is for children, the second for anyone, but the programs at both—arts and crafts classes, lectures, gallery walks—are fun and informative.

6 ★ **Cafes.** The museum now has two lovely cafes (the sixth floor one has an outdoor terrace), serving bougie fare like artisanal cheeses, paninis, and decent wines. *2nd and 6th floors. $–$$.*

7 ★★ **Abby Aldrich Rockefeller Sculpture Garden.** This landscaped outdoor space holds such gems as **Picasso**'s whimsical *She-Goat* (1950) and **Alberto Giacometti**'s long, lean *Tall Figure III* (1960), as well as installations by contemporary artists such as **Richard Serra**.

8 ★★ **The Modern.** Whether you're here for lunch, dinner, or a cocktail, this is a destination in itself. It's sleek and fabulous, with big glass windows overlooking the sculpture garden and superb food. *1st floor. www.themodernnyc.com.* ☎ *212/333-1220. $$$.* ●

P.S. 1 Contemporary Art Center

If you're interested in new work that's thrillingly cutting-edge, this MoMA affiliate is worth the trip—one stop outside Manhattan in Queens. Originally a public school, **P.S. 1** (22–25 Jackson Ave. at 46th Ave., Long Island City; www.ps1.org; ☎ 718/784-2084; Thurs–Mon noon–6pm) is one of the country's largest nonprofit art institutions, exhibiting contemporary art from America and abroad. The array of works includes large-scale exhibitions by such artists as Niki de Saint Phalle and virtual reality pieces by Bjork. Museum admission is $10 adults, $5 seniors and students, free for children under 16. Subway: E or M to 23rd Street/Ely Avenue, 7 train to 45th Rd./Court House Square.

The Financial District

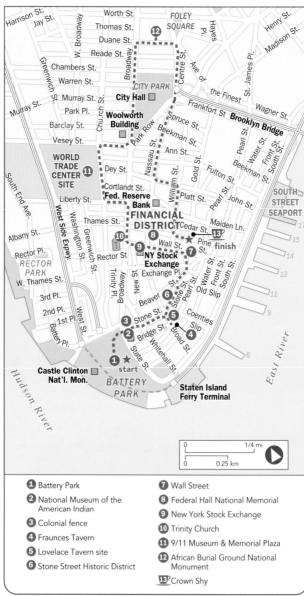

1 Battery Park

2 National Museum of the American Indian

3 Colonial fence

4 Fraunces Tavern

5 Lovelace Tavern site

6 Stone Street Historic District

7 Wall Street

8 Federal Hall National Memorial

9 New York Stock Exchange

10 Trinity Church

11 9/11 Museum & Memorial Plaza

12 African Burial Ground National Monument

13 Crown Shy

Previous page: The City Reliquary in Williamsburg, Brooklyn, displays NYC-themed nostalgia.

The southern tip of Manhattan is where the city as we know it began. You'll explore 17th-century cobblestone alleyways, the seaport where 18th-century commerce helped build the city, historic landmarks of the American Revolution, and the canyons of Wall Street, constructed in outsize Deco style in the early 20th century. START: **Subway 4/5 to Bowling Green or 1 to South Ferry.**

① ★★ Battery Park. Look out at the river: It's the reason this great city was built. When Henry Hudson sailed up it in 1609, mistakenly thinking he'd find Asia at its mouth, little did he know he was setting into motion a chain of events that would still be shaping lives over 400 years later. Hudson's reports about the trading possibilities of the area (particularly for valuable animal pelts), plus his amazement at the great natural harbor, spurred the Dutch to create settlements. They guessed—rightly, it turned out—that the harbor of New York would be the linchpin connecting Europe (via the Atlantic Ocean) with the interior of this vast and wealthy continent (via the Hudson River). Gaze across the harbor to see the **Statue of Liberty.** (See p 15 for more.)

② ★★★ National Museum of the American Indian. Once you leave the park, head to this landmark, though you don't have to go inside (an offshoot of the Smithsonian, with only touring shows, the exhibits can be hit-or-miss). Instead study the facade: This was once the Alexander Hamilton U.S. Custom House. Before 1913, when personal income tax was instituted, the federal government's revenue came almost entirely from customs on goods imported into the States. And a full 75% of this revenue came from the Port of New York, where it was processed in this appropriately grand Beaux Arts colossus, completed in 1907. Daniel Chester

The National Museum of the American Indian is located within the historic Alexander Hamilton U.S. Custom House.

French (who did the moving sculpture of Lincoln at the Lincoln Memorial in Washington, D.C.) created the sculptures out front; his choice of symbols could be used as a treatise on the prejudices of Victorian America. The four seated women represent the four "great" continents of the world. From left to right as you look at them, they are Asia (seen in meditation); the Americas (South America, barely present, is the Aztec-like structure that North America has her foot on); Europe; and a slumbering Africa. In the footstep of this building stood the Dutch settlers' original fort. *1 Bowling Green. www.nmai. si.edu. ☎ 212/514-3700. Free admission. Daily 10am–5pm.*

Fraunces Tavern.

❸ ★★ **Colonial Fence.** The fence that rings Bowling Green Park is the original, one of the few Colonial structures of any sort left in Manhattan. When it was first erected, its spokes had royal crowns at their tips. These were destroyed by colonists on July 9, 1776, when the Declaration of Independence was first read aloud in this very park.

❹ ★ **Fraunces Tavern Museum.** It was on this site that George Washington bade farewell to his officers at the end of the American Revolution. The museum here (in a 1907 replica of the original 1717 tavern) has period rooms, art, and artifacts including a lock of Washington's hair and one of his false teeth. In 1975, an extremist Puerto Rican nationalist group bombed the tavern, killing four. ⏰ 45 min. 54 Pearl St. (near Broad St.). www.frauncestavernmuseum. org. ☎ 212/425-1778. Admission $7 adults; $4 seniors, students, and children 6–18; free for children 5 and under. Wed-Sun noon-5pm.

❺ ★ **Lovelace Tavern Site.** Little is left of 17th-century New York, but an excavation in 1979 led to the discovery of the foundation of Lovelace Tavern, built in 1670. In an ingenious move, the underground excavation was left in place—as was an early-18th-century cistern— and the sidewalk above it was replaced with Plexiglas, so that anyone walking by can look down and see the old foundation and artifacts. Pearl St. at Coenties Alley.

❻ ★★ **Stone Street Historic District.** This 17th-century cobblestone alley, the oldest street in Manhattan, has become a diningand-drinking enclave, with outdoor restaurants and bars. See p 33.

❼ ★★★ **Wall Street.** The street synonymous with high finance began, literally, in 1653 as a 12-foot-high (3.6m) wooden palisade built by the Dutch to keep out the British. (Whoops! They eventually invaded by sea.) Today, it's home to some of the city's most magnificent architecture, skyscraping Jazz Age marvels made all the more impressive by the narrowness of the streets. Check out the BNY Mellon Building, 1 Wall St., a tiered limestone Art Deco gem built in 1931. In 1920, a bomb exploded in front of 23 Wall St.— then the headquarters of J. P. Morgan—killing 38 people and injuring 400; no one knows who set it, but you can still see the pock marks it caused in the wall of the building. Farther down the block at 40 Wall St. is a building that was for a nanosecond the tallest in the world; the 1930 Deco beauty was soon overtaken in height by the Chrysler Building (p 35). Wall St. (btw. Broadway and FDR Dr.).

❽ ★ **Federal Hall National Memorial.** This majestic 1842

structure is one of Wall Street's most recognizable monuments. On this site, before the Revolutionary War, the Stamp Act Congress met to rail against "taxation without representation." Later, the First Congress wrote the Bill of Rights here, and out in front George Washington was inaugurated, on April 30, 1789 (right where his statue stands today).Head inside to see the magnificent rotunda, one of the loveliest public spaces in the city. The capital moved to Philadelphia in 1790, and the original Federal Hall was torn down in 1812. ⏱ *15 min. 26 Wall St. (btw. Nassau and William sts.). www.nps.gov/feha.* ☎ *212/825-6888. Free admission. Mon–Sat 9am–5pm.*

⑨ ★ New York Stock Exchange. The world's largest securities exchange, the NYSE came into being in 1792, when merchants met daily under a nearby buttonwood tree to trade U.S. bonds that had funded the Revolutionary War. In 1903, traders moved into this Beaux Arts building designed by George Post. Surrounded by heavy security, the NYSE is not open to the public. *At Broad and Wall sts.*

⑩ ★★ Trinity Church. Alexander Hamilton is buried in the church's south cemetery. The original building was erected in 1698, although the present structure dates from 1846. *See p 16.*

⑪ ★★★ 9/11 Museum and Memorial Plaza. One of the nation's greatest history museums and most sobering memorials. A must-see. *See p 17 for more.*

⑫ African Burial Ground National Monument. During construction of an office tower here in 1991, masses of human remains were unearthed. Research revealed that the area was a burial ground for slaves and freedmen. The site was designated a National Historic Landmark, and in 2007 a granite memorial was built to pay tribute to the estimated 15,000 Africans and African Americans who were buried here. *Duane and Elk sts. Visitor center at 290 Broadway. www.nps.gov/afbg.* ☎ *212/637-2019. Daily 9am–5pm (till 4pm in winter); visitor center and indoor exhibitions Tues–Sat 10am–4pm. Free admission.*

⑬ ★★★ Crown Shy. End a long day of sightseeing in the company of Wall Street tycoons. Its pricey but impeccable service, majestic high-ceilinged setting, and Instagram-worthy food make this the meal you'll brag about when you get home. *70 Pine St. www.crownshy.nyc.* ☎ *No phone. $$$$*

Statue of George Washington outside the Federal Hall National Memorial.

Historic **Harlem**

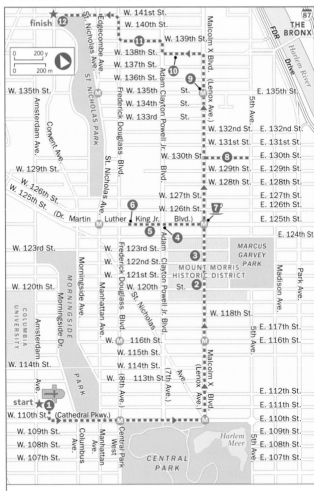

1 The Cathedral of St. John the Divine

2 Mt. Olivet Baptist Church

3 Mount Morris Park Historic District

4 Corner of Adam Clayton Powell, Jr. Blvd. & 125th St.

5 Blumstein's Department Store

6 Apollo Theater

7 Red Rooster Harlem

8 Astor Row

9 Schomburg Center for Research in Black Culture

10 Abyssinian Baptist Church

11 Strivers' Row

12 Hamilton Grange

It wasn't until the mid–19th century that Nieuw Amsterdam and Nieuw Haarlem—the two towns the Dutch founded on the isle of Manhattan—became one. Claimed by a number of different immigrant communities over the years, the neighborhood became renowned in the 1920s (the "Harlem Renaissance") as a mecca of black culture, and still retains that identity today. START: **Subway 1 to 110th St.**

The elaborate front facade of St. John the Divine.

① ★★★ **The Cathedral of St. John the Divine.** The largest cathedral in the world is *not* St. Peter's in Rome (which is technically a basilica). It's this Episcopalian house of worship. Construction on it began in 1892, but the building is not expected to be completed for another 100 years. That's because the 121,000-square-foot structure, a blend of Romanesque and Gothic elements, is being built without steel, in the classic Gothic manner (a fascinating process for visitors to watch). There's still much work to be done, but what's in place—and there's a lot—is quite beautiful, especially the Rose Window in the apse, the largest in North America. ⏱ 45 min. 1047 Amsterdam Ave. (btw. 111th and 112th sts.). www. stjohndivine.org. ☎ 212/316-7490. Self guided tours $5. Mon-Fri

9:30am-6pm, Sat-Sun 9:30am–6pm. Subway: 1/9 to 110th St.

② ★ **Mt. Olivet Baptist Church.** Look closely and you'll notice something one doesn't usually see on the facade of a church: Stars of David. This church epitomizes the neighborhood's demographic transformation from Irish immigrants, to those from Eastern Europe, to blacks escaping the American South. It was built (in 1907) to be the area's first synagogue, by the first Jewish architect licensed in New York State. He based its design on that of the Second Temple in Jerusalem, which had just been excavated, making worldwide headlines. *120th St. and Malcolm X Blvd.*

③ **Mount Morris Park Historic District.** This impressively preserved collection of handsome 19th- and 20th-century brownstones features various styles, from Romanesque Revival to Queen Anne. *Bounded by 119th St., 124th St., Adam Clayton Powell Blvd., and Mount Morris Park West.*

④ ★★ **Corner of Adam Clayton Powell, Jr. Blvd and 125th St.** Look first at the statue of Adam Clayton Powell, Jr., Harlem's first African American congressman. Where it stands is the spot where Malcolm X spent many long hours giving speeches on behalf of the Nation of Islam. Now, look across the street at the tall white building with geometric patterns, the former Hotel Theresa. In 1960, a young

Fidel Castro was asked to speak at the United Nations and stayed here. Repeated clashes between pro- and anti-Castro forces outside the hotel kept the 258-police contingent assigned to Castro busy. On his second day at the Theresa, Nikita Khrushchev came to visit, and his police contingent plus Castro's created the greatest show of force Harlem's ever witnessed. Four years later, when Malcolm X broke with the Nation of Islam to found his own Organization of Afro-American Unity, he took offices in the Teresa. When he was assassinated in 1965, this is where massive crowds gathered to mourn.

⑤ Blumstein's Department Store. Now just a faded facade, this was once the neighborhood's most fashionable store and the site of a paradigm-shifting social crusade. In 1934, the Urban League began a campaign to boycott and picket the store until it changed its hiring practices. Up until that point, although the vast majority of its clientele was African American, Blumstein's refused to hire any black store clerks. The action lasted 2 months, until Blumstein's finally

relented. Dr. Martin Luther King, Jr. often spoke of this strike as an example of the power of non-violent protest. Many years after the boycott, a would-be assassin stabbed King while he was doing a book-signing at the store. He survived, but spent weeks in the hospital recuperating. *230 W. 125th St. (Frederick Douglass Blvd.).*

⑥ ★★★ Apollo Theater. This legendary venue has featured them all—Count Basie, Billie Holiday, Louis Armstrong, Duke Ellington, Marvin Gaye, Aretha Franklin, and more. "Amateur Night at the Apollo" launched the careers of Ella Fitzgerald, James Brown, Lauryn Hill, and the Jackson 5—and it's still going strong. *253 W. 125th St. (Frederick Douglass Blvd.). www. apollotheater.org.* ☎ *212/531-5300.*

⑦ ★★ Red Rooster Harlem. For a taste of modern Harlem, hit up chef Marcus Samuelsson's cheerful comfort-food hot spot. Don't miss the shrimp and grits. *310 Lenox Ave. (btw. 125th and 126th sts.). www.redroosterharlem.com.* ☎ *212/792-9001. $$–$$$.*

Statue of Adam Clayton Powell Jr. on 125th Street.

The Jazz Foundation of America celebrates A Great Night in Harlem at The Apollo Theater.

8 **Astor Row.** Built by the Astor family in the 1880s, this 28-home row of red-brick town houses might remind you of a sleepy block in Savannah, Georgia, thanks to the front yards and porches (a rarity in NYC). ① *20 min. 130th St. (btw. Fifth and Lenox aves.). Subway: 2/3 to 135th St.*

9 ★★★ **Schomburg Center for Research in Black Culture.** This national research library has more than five million items documenting the experiences of African Americans, including manuscripts, rare books, moving images, artifacts, and more. ① *45 min. 515 Malcolm X Blvd. (btw. 135th and 136thsts.).www.nypl.org.* ☎ *212/491-2200. Free admission. Mon–Wed noon–8pm, Thurs–Fri 11am–6pm, Sat 10am–5pm. Subway: 2/3 to 135th St.*

10 **Abyssinian Baptist Church.** This Baptist church's congregation first gathered downtown in 1808, when a group of African Americans and Ethiopians withdrew from the First Baptist Church to protest its segregated seating. The congregation grew here in 1922 under the leadership of activist Adam Clayton Powell, Sr. You can join Sunday services at 9am and 11am. ① *20 min. 132 W. Odell Clark Place (formerly 138th St., btw. Malcolm X and Adam Clayton Powell, Jr., blvds.). www. abyssinian.org.* ☎ *212/862-7474. Subway: 2/3 to 135th St.*

11 ★ **Strivers' Row.** Hardly a brick has changed on these McKim, Mead & White neo–Italian Renaissance town houses since they were built in 1890. Once the original owners had moved out, the brownstones attracted the cream of the new Harlem, including such "strivers" as composers Eubie Blake and W. C. Handy. *W. 139th St. (btw. Adam Clayton Powell, Jr., and Frederick Douglass blvds.).*

12 ★ **Hamilton Grange.** The only house founding father Alexander Hamilton ever owned (built in 1802), it's a poignant visit for fans of the musical, despite the fact that almost none of the original furnishings survive. Ranger-guided tours are informative. ① *1 hr. 414 W. 141st St. (btw. St. Nicholas and Convent aves). www.nps.gov/hagr.* ☎ *212/825-6990. Free admission. Daily 9am–5pm.*

Chelsea, the High Line & Hudson Yards

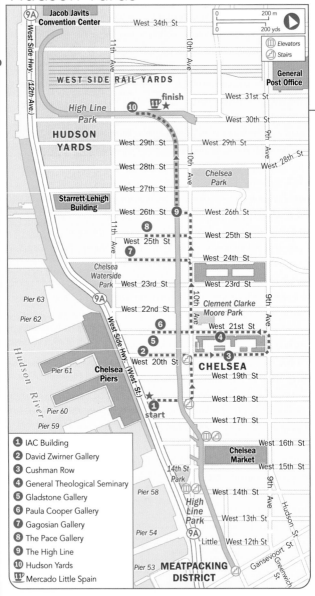

0   200 m
0   200 yds

Elevators
Stairs

9A

Jacob Javits Convention Center

West Side Hwy. (12th Ave.)

West 34th St

11th Ave

10th Ave

9A

General Post Office

West 31st St

finish

10 ★

High Line Park

West 30th St

HUDSON YARDS

West 29th St

West 29th St

9th Ave

West 28th St

West 28th St

Chelsea Park

West 27th St

West 26th St

9

West 26th St

Starrett-Lehigh Building

8

West 25th St

West 25th St

7

West 24th St

10th Ave

11th Ave

Chelsea Waterside Park

West 23rd St

West 23rd St

9A

West 22nd St

Clement Clarke Moore Park

Pier 63

West Side Hwy. (West St.)

West 21st St

4

9th Ave

Pier 62

6

West 20th St

5

2

CHELSEA

West 19th St

Pier 61

Chelsea Piers

1

start

West 18th St

Hudson River

Pier 60

West 17th St

Pier 59

West 16th St

10th Ave

Chelsea Market

West 15th St

1 IAC Building

2 David Zwirner Gallery

3 Cushman Row

4 General Theological Seminary

5 Gladstone Gallery

6 Paula Cooper Gallery

7 Gagosian Gallery

8 The Pace Gallery

9 The High Line

10 Hudson Yards

Mercado Little Spain

14th St Park

Pier 58

West 14th St

High Line Park

West 13th St

Pier 54

9A

Pier 53

Little West 12th St

MEATPACKING DISTRICT

Gansevoort St

Greenwich St

Hudson St

NYC has more galleries than any other city in the world, making it the de facto contemporary art capital. The densest concentration of them is in Chelsea, though rising rents have pushed some to the Lower East Side (p 81) and to Williamsburg, Brooklyn (p 76). Spending an afternoon wandering from one to the next is a good way to get a handle on the cultural zeitgeist of today. We've listed a few of the biggest players in this tour, but if you see a gallery that intrigues you, head in—you'll likely be rewarded. Then it's a quick stroll on the famed High Line Park to Hudson Yards, the largest private real estate development in American history, and home to the newest icons of NYC. START: **Subway C, E to 23rd St.**

❶ ★★★ IAC Building. We'll start with the art of architecture, which took a big leap forward in 2004 when this billowy building (at 555 W. 18th St.) made its debut. It's the first Frank Gehry structure to have an all-glass exterior, and it's a very special glass, warped into curves and covered with a dotted insulation that makes the building energy-efficient. Across the street is French architect Jean Nouvel's equally whiz-bang building (at 100 Eleventh Ave.) with its pixilated curtain wall inspired by the eyes of insects (lots of panes of glass, each of a different diameter and tilt).

❷ ★★★ David Zwirner Gallery. Zwirner's majestic two-floor gallery shows artists as varied as cartoonist R. Crumb and minimalist John McCracken. *537 W. 20th St. (btw. Tenth and Eleventh aves.). www.davidzwirner.com.* ☎ *212/517-8677. Tues–Sat 10am–6pm.*

❸ ★ Cushman Row. In the late 1830s, much of Chelsea's real estate was developed by merchant Don Alonzo Cushman. His little empire included these 1840 Greek Revival houses, considered to be among the best of that style in the nation. *406–418 W. 20th St. (btw. Ninth and Tenth aves.).*

❹ ★★ General Theological Seminary and High Line Hotel.

The campus of the General Theological Seminary.

Filling up an entire city block, this historic property holds both the hip High Line Hotel (p 159) and the General Theological Seminary of the Episcopal Church, the denomination's oldest seminary, founded in 1817. It's a private working seminary, but visitors can tour the grassy grounds (the land was donated by Clement Clarke Moore, author of *'Twas the Night Before Christmas*), the stunning 1888 **Chapel of the Good Shepherd,** and the exquisite vaulted **Refectory** in Hoffman Hall. *440 W. 21st St. (btw. Ninth and Tenth aves.). www.gts.edu.* ☎ *212/243-5150. Mon–Fri 10am–3pm.*

The Gladstone Gallery.

⑤ ★★ Gladstone Gallery.

Gladstone's sizable roster of American and European artists includes such famous names as German artist Rosemarie Trockel and Keith Haring. A second location is at 515 W. 24th St. And pop into Gagosian's (above), a second Chelsea gallery at 522 W. 21st. *530 W. 21st St. (btw. Tenth and Eleventh aves.). www.gladstonegallery.com.* ☎ *212/206-7606. Tues–Sat 10am–6pm.*

⑥ ★ Paula Cooper Gallery.

Works by such major artists as Donald Judd, Sol Lewitt, and Jennifer Bartlett can be found in this loft-like space. *534 W. 21st St. (btw. Tenth and Eleventh aves.). www.paula coopergallery.com.* ☎ *212/255-1105. Tues–Sat 10am–6pm.*

⑦ ★★★ Gagosian Gallery.

Most of Chelsea's galleries aren't large enough to hold more than one major exhibition at a time, but the white high-ceilinged rooms in the Gagosian feel like a mini-museum. The gallery pulls off major feats like 2016's acclaimed show of Richard Serra's monolithic steel slabs. *555 W. 24th St. (btw. Tenth and Eleventh aves.). www.gagosian.com.* ☎ *212/741-1111. Mon–Sat 10am–6pm.*

⑧ ★ The Pace Gallery.

One of the world's best-known galleries, it displays only major artists, both living and dead—from Chuck Close to Mark Rothko. Pace has another Chelsea outpost at 534 W. 25th St. *508–510 W. 25th St. (btw. Tenth and Eleventh aves.). www.thepacegallery.com.* ☎ *212/989-4258. Tues–Sat 10am–6pm.*

⑨ ★★★ The High Line.

Ascend the stairs at 26th street for a short stroll on this elevated park (see

The Paula Cooper Gallery.

The interlacing stairways of Hudson Yards' Vessel.

p. 104), following the signs to Hudson Yards.

🔟 ★★ **Hudson Yards.** This skyscraper-bristling, new 28-acre neighborhood is built atop a technologically advanced platform that covers working train tracks. First stop here should be **The Shed ★★★**, a museum/performing arts space that features exhibits and performances created specifically for this venue by top artists (prices vary, see p 148). Then climb **Vessel ★★**, the rose-gold folly of interlinking stairs that is a hoot to photograph. It requires timed tickets (free for the first hour, $10 after); solo climbers aren't allowed, due to a number of suicides here. Even more expansive views can be had at **Edge ★★**, the tallest observation deck in this hemisphere, set on the 101st floor of 30 Hudson Yards (daily 8am–midnight; $38 adults, $36 senior, $33 child, $2 less if you buy online). Finally, if you have time, stop into the **Shops at Hudson Yards**, a glitzy mall. *30th St. to 25th St., Tenth Ave. to the River. www.hudsonyardsnewyork.com.*

🍵 ★★ **Mercado Little Spain.** Go tapas hopping in the city's most fun food hall, on the ground floor of Hudson Yard's mall. Founded by celeb chef Jose Andres, it has kiosks for all of Spain's greatest hits—big sizzling platters of paella, icy gazpacho soups, plates of cheese and sliced ham, sherry tipples, and more—allowing visitors to graze. A real party. *10 Hudson Yards. $–$$.*

Practical Matters

Most galleries in Chelsea are closed on Sundays and Mondays, have special summer hours, and close temporarily (and randomly) for exhibition changes. Almost all are free to visit.

Greenwich Village

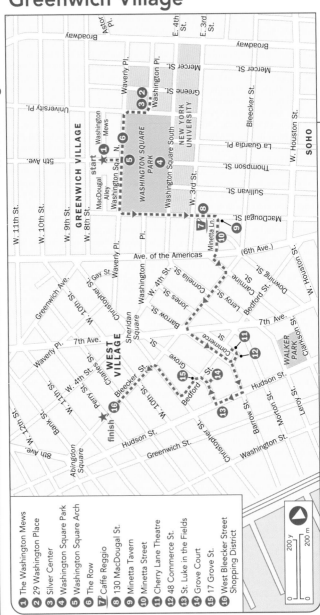

1 The Washington Mews
2 29 Washington Place
3 Silver Center
4 Washington Square Park
5 Washington Square Arch
6 The Row
7 Caffe Reggio
8 130 MacDougal St.
9 Minetta Tavern
10 Minetta Lane
11 Cherry Lane Theatre
12 48 Commerce St.
13 St. Luke in the Fields
14 Grove Court
15 17 Grove St.
16 West Bleecker Street Shopping District

200 y
200 m

Greenwich Village started as its own village, a place where the well-to-do fled on a yearly basis to escape the plagues of Nieuw Amsterdam and New York (yellow fever, primarily). Building began in earnest in the 1820s in this genteel "suburb". When the hoi polloi moved in, the blue bloods did the 19th-century version of urban flight and moved a mile uptown. Swank town houses were subdivided into cheap apartments and boarding houses, and the neighborhood became one of factories and immigrants, and later artists. It's a wealthy area today, but retains its artistic spirit. START: Subway N/R to 8th St.

❶ ★ The Washington Mews. Visitors who stumble upon this cobbled alleyway discover a living slice of old New York. The north side of the mews consists of original 19th-century stables converted into stuccoed houses. *Enter at University Place or Fifth Ave. (btw. 8th St. and Waverly Place).*

❷ ★★ 29 Washington Place. On March 25, 1911, a horrific tragedy here reshaped the history of the American labor movement. Some 600 young women, Jewish and Italian immigrants between the ages of 13 and 23, were laboring inside what was the Triangle Shirtwaist factory when a fire started. Because the owners had locked the women inside (to prevent theft, they later said), many couldn't escape. Girls started jumping to their deaths in front of horrified passersby; in all 146 were killed. As a result, New York's labor code was rewritten to become the most stringent in the nation, and the Ladies Garment Workers Union grew in strength. The building, now part of New York University, is the original one. *At the NW corner of Washington Pl. and Greene St.*

❸ Silver Center. Dash-dot-dot-dash—this is the birthplace of the telegraph. In 1836, New York University painting professor Samuel Morse formulated the rudiments of the telegraphic alphabet (Morse Code). In 1837, using 1,700 feet of copper wire (which he coiled around his room), he sent the first wire dispatches from one end to the other. Witnessing the experiment, student William Vail, scion of a wealthy iron-making family, convinced his father to invest in the new technology—and together they created a revolution in communications. *Corner of Washington Square E. and Washington Square N.*

❹ ★★★ Washington Square Park. Originally drained marshland given to freed slaves to farm in 1641 (they had to hand over much of their harvest each year), in 1797

Skateboarding in Washington Square Park.

this then-remote area became a potters field, where some 20,000 souls were buried (many in 1798, when yellow fever wiped out 5% of the city's population). In 1826 it became a military parade ground, and tales abounded of marching soldiers crunching their boots down on shroud-covered skeletons; there were also public hangings from the massive elm still standing on its northwest corner. In 1850, when Greenwich Village became fashionable, it was re-landscaped as a formal park. By the 1960s it had become a hang-out spot for students, hippies, artists, and musicians performing for pocket change—a tradition that continues today. *Bordered by University and Waverly places and W. 4th and MacDougal sts.*

⑤ ★★★ **Washington Square Arch.** Designed by Stanford White, the first arch here was built of wood in 1889 to commemorate the centennial of George Washington's inauguration; the current 1891 version is white marble. The statues of George Washington were done by Alexander Stirling Calder, father of modern artist and mobile-maker Alexander Calder. *Fifth Ave. and Waverly Place.*

⑥ ★★ **The Row.** Built in the 1830s for society's blue bloods, this is the longest string of Greek Revival town houses in the country. Henry James's heroine in *Washington Square* lived here, as did many memorable characters in Edith Wharton's novels. By the early 20th century, the strip had become run down and many of the Village's best-known "bohemians" moved in, including painters Edward Hopper and Thomas Eakins and writer John Dos Passos (all lived at #3). *1–26 Washington Sq. N. (btw. Fifth Ave. and University Pl).*

⑦ ★ **Caffe Reggio.** The quintessential Village cafe—art-filled and cozy—claims to have brought the first espresso machine to the US. *119 MacDougal St. (at West 3rd. St.)* www.caffereggio.com. ☎ *212/475-9577. $.*

⑧ ★ **130 MacDougal St.** This perfect little brick federal town

Minetta Street.

house is where Louisa May Alcott probably wrote *Little Women*.

⑨ ★★ **Minetta Tavern.** Formerly a speakeasy called the Black Rabbit, this was a major literary hangout, serving up poetry-inspiring booze and spaghetti to such notables as Ezra Pound, e.e.cummings, and Ernest Hemingway in the 1920s, and Allen Ginsberg and Jack Kerouac in the 1950s. *At 113 MacDougal St.*

⑩ ★★★ **Minetta Street.** Listen carefully: A stream runs below this street and sometimes it's possible to hear it gurgling. When the stream was at street level, this was a muddy ghetto called "Little Africa" and inhabited entirely by free blacks from the 1820s to the 1910s. In 1863 when Civil War draft riots sparked the worst violence in the city's history, the residents of this street were able to successfully barricade it for 5 days against the hooligans who killed 105 African Americans in other neighborhoods.

⑪ ★ **Cherry Lane Theatre.** Poet Edna St. Vincent Millay and her artist peers converted an 1817 box factory into the Cherry Lane Playhouse in 1924. It's still a working theater. *38 Commerce St. (at Bedford St.). www.cherrylanetheatre. org.* ☎ *212/989-2020.*

⑫ **48 Commerce St.** Note the working gas lamp in front of this 1844 home. The New York Gas Light Company began laying gas pipes in 1823, and gas lamps—many with ornamental posts—continued to shine into the 20th century. *48 Commerce St. (at Barrow St.).*

⑬ ★ **St. Luke in the Fields.** This charming little church is a reconstruction of the original, which was built in 1822 and badly damaged by fire in 1981. One of the

The private entrance at Grove Court.

church's founding wardens was Clement C. Moore, the author of *'Twas the Night Before Christmas*. *487 Hudson St. (at Grove St.).*

⑭ ★ **Grove Court.** This charming gated mews was once considered a slum; it was built for working men around 1853, when it was known as "Mixed Ale Alley" (because residents could only afford to drink from the dregs at the "bottom of the barrel"). Today this is one of the city's most coveted addresses. *10–12 Grove St. (btw. Hudson and Bedford sts.).*

⑮ ★★ **17 Grove St.** This 1822 house is one of the last remaining wood-framed houses in the Village. The building across the street was used in the TV show *Friends* (Monica and the gang "lived" here). *17 Grove St. (at Bedford St.).*

⑯ ★ **West Bleecker Street Shopping District.** Bleecker Street, from Christopher to Bank streets, is a trendy boutique alley that's a heckuva lot of fun to stroll. *W. Bleecker St. (btw. Christopher and Bank sts.).*

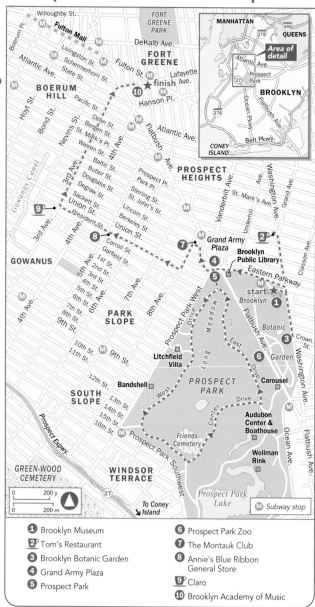

Prospect Park & Park Slope

1. Brooklyn Museum
2. Tom's Restaurant
3. Brooklyn Botanic Garden
4. Grand Army Plaza
5. Prospect Park
6. Prospect Park Zoo
7. The Montauk Club
8. Annie's Blue Ribbon General Store
9. Claro
10. Brooklyn Academy of Music

The attractions in and around Prospect Park are well worth the 25-minute subway ride from midtown Manhattan. Expect gorgeous parkland designed by Frederick Law Olmsted and Calvert Vaux (the masterminds of Central Park), the city's second-largest art museum, plus lovely 19th-century brownstones and hip boutiques. START: Subway 2/3 to Eastern Parkway.

① ★★★ kids **Brooklyn Museum.** In any other city, this spectacular museum would be *the* star attraction, but in New York it's often overlooked because of all the competition. The collection is New York's second-largest. Highlights include the stellar **ancient Egyptian collection**, the **Asian art collection** (which specializes in both classic and contemporary works from Japan), and the **Luce Center for American Art** (an "open storage" annex holding 9,000 works, from Tiffany lamps to 19th-century furniture by local artisans). Designed by architects McKim, Mead, and White in 1897, the museum received a dramatic plaza complete with fountains in 2004. ⏱ 2–3 hr. 200 Eastern Pkwy. (at Washington Ave.). www.brooklyn museum.org. ☎ 718/638-5000.

The Beaux-Arts courtyard of the Brooklyn Museum.

Admission $16 adults, $10 seniors and students, free for ages 19 and under. Sun and Wed–Thurs 11am–6pm, Fri–Sat 11am–8pm. Subway: 2/3 to Eastern Pkwy.

② **Tom's Restaurant.** Really a diner, flag-bedecked Tom's serves the best lemon poppy pancakes on the planet, and (a rarity these days) authentic Noo Yawk egg creams. Service is grandmotherly in its sweetness. Breakfast and lunch only. 782 Washington Ave. (at Sterling Place). ☎ 718/636-9728. $.

③ ★★★ **Brooklyn Botanic Garden.** This tranquil, elegant retreat is one of the most beautiful gardens in the city. It encompasses the **Cranford Rose Garden**, a **Children's Garden**, the **Osborne Garden** (3 acres/1.2 hectares of formal gardens), the **Fragrance Garden** (designed for the visually impaired but appreciated by all), and the **Japanese Hill-and-Pond Garden.** In colder weather, you can investigate one of the world's largest collections of bonsai in the **C. V. Starr Bonsai Museum** and indoor plants (everything from cacti to orchids) in the **Steinhardt Conservatory.** If you come in April or May, seek out the lush carpet of bluebells and check the website for the timing of the **Cherry Blossom Festival.** ⏱ 1–2 hr. 1000 Washington Ave. (at Eastern Pkwy.). www.bbg.org. ☎ 718/623-7200. Admission $18 adults, $12 seniors and students, free for children 12 and under. Mar–Oct

Soldiers' and Sailors' Memorial Arch at Grand Army Plaza.

Tues–Fri 8am–6pm, Sat–Sun 10am–6pm; Nov–Feb until 4:30pm.

④ **Grand Army Plaza.** This multilane traffic circle and the tremendous **Soldiers' and Sailors' Memorial Arch** at its center may remind you of Paris's Place Charles de Gaulle and the Arc de Triomphe. The arch was built in 1892 to honor Union soldiers who died in the Civil War. *At the intersection of Flatbush Ave., Prospect Park W., Eastern Pkwy. and Vanderbilt Ave.*

⑤ ★★★ kids **Prospect Park.** Central Park designers Frederick Law Olmstead and Calvert Vaux considered Prospect Park to be their masterpiece. The park has 562 acres (225 hectares) of woodland—including Brooklyn's last remaining virgin forest—plus meadows, bluffs, and ponds. For the best views, enter at Grand Army Plaza and walk to your right either on the park's ring road (called West Dr. here) or on the parallel pedestrian path to Meadowport Arch, and proceed to **Long Meadow.** Overlooking Long Meadow is **Litchfield Villa,** an 1857 mansion that became the headquarters for the New York parks system. Eventually West Drive turns into Center Drive, which will take you past the **Friends' Cemetery** Quaker burial ground. Center Drive leads to East Drive, which on its way back to Grand Army Plaza passes the 1906 Beaux Arts **boathouse;** the 1912 **carousel;** the **zoo** (see below); and **Lefferts Homestead Children's Historic House**

Prospect Park's Boathouse.

Picnic in Prospect Park.

Museum (☎ 718/789-2822), a 1783 Dutch farmhouse with a museum of period furniture and exhibits. *Bounded by Prospect Park W., Parkside Ave. and Flatbush Ave. www.prospectpark.org.* ☎ *718/965-8951.*

6 ★ kids **Prospect Park Zoo.** Families won't want to miss the zoo at the eastern end of the park. Children in particular take delight in encountering the animals up close, including wallabies and prairie dogs. ⏱ *1 hr. 450 Flatbush Ave. www.prospectparkzoo.com.* ☎ *718/399-7339. Admission $8 adults, $6 seniors, $5 children 3–12. Mon–Fri 10am–5pm, Sat–Sun 10am–5:30pm.*

7 ★ **The Montauk Club.** The northwestern side of Prospect Park is home to the upscale neighborhood of Park Slope, and its tree-lined streets are delightful to explore. Many of the late-19th-century brownstones have been lovingly restored (walk along Montgomery Place between Eighth Ave. and Prospect Park W. to see what we mean). If there were an award

for most stunning building, it would go to the **Montauk Club,** which was designed in 1891 by architect Francis H. Kimball to resemble a Venetian palace. It's a private club. *25 Eighth Ave. (at Lincoln Place).* ☎ *718/638-0800.*

8 ★★ **Annie's Blue Ribbon General Store.** Fashion Institute of Technology prof Ann Cantrell sells handsome and giftable housewares, stationery, toys, and tchotchkes, most of them made in Brooklyn (and many NYC-themed). Souvenir hunters: You're welcome. *232 Fifth Ave (btw. Carroll and President sts.). www.blueribbongeneralstore.com.*

9 ★★★ **Claro.** Hoof it 2 blocks to this Oaxacan bistro, which serves creative and authentic takes on Mexican cuisine. All the dishes are delectable, but don't believe the waitress when she says you need two-to-three per person: A plate of hearty mole (a must-order) is big enough to share, sided by two appetizers, tops. There's also an impressive range of mescals. *284 Third Ave. www.clarobk.com.* ☎ *347/721-3126. $$–$$$.*

10 ★★★ **Brooklyn Academy of Music.** Hop the R or W subway to nearby Fort Greene, home to this always entertaining and intellectually challenging pair of theaters. On the roster might be Peter Brooks' latest directing venture, dance by Anna Teresa De Keersmaeker, an opera, or a conversation with a trendsetter like José Andres or Malala Yousafzai. *Peter Jay Sharp Building, 30 Lafayette Ave. (btw. Ashland Pl. and St. Felix St.). www.bam.org.* ☎ *718/636-4100. Subway: 2/3/4/5/B/D/N/R/Q to Atlantic Ave.*

Williamsburg, Brooklyn

McCarren
Park
7

Bushwick
Inlet Park

Martha P. Johnson
State Park **9**

N. 12th St.
N. 11th St.
N. 10th St.
N. 9th St.
N. 8th St.
N. 7th St.
N. 6th St.
N. 5th St.
N. 4th St.
N. 3rd St.

Driggs Ave.
Lorimer St.
Bayard St.
Richardson St.
Frost St.

8
6
5
4
12
finish ★

Kent Ave.
Wythe Ave.
Berry St.
Bedford Ave.
Driggs Ave.
Roebling St.
Havemeyer St.

10

Brooklyn-Queens Expwy.

Metropolitan Ave.
N. 1st St.
Grand St.
S. 1st St.
S. 2nd St.
S. 3rd St.
S. 4th St.

11

East River

3

Havemeyer St.

Rodney St.

S. 6th St.
Broadway

Williamsburg Bridge

S. 8th St.
S. 9th St.
S. 10th St.

Bedford Ave.

Roebling St.

Marcy Ave.

2

Marcy Ave.
Keap St.
Hooper St.

Division Ave.
Bedford Ave.
Clymer St.
Taylor St.
Wilson St.
Rose St.
Lee Ave.

1 ★
start

0   1/10 mi
0   0.10 km

1 Lee Avenue
2 Shalom Japan
3 City Reliquary
4 Brooklyn Art Library
5 New York Distilling Company
6 Cathedral of the Transfiguration of Our Lord
7 McCarren Park

8 Brooklyn Brewery
9 Martha P. Johnson State Park & Bushwick Inlet Park
10 Artists & Fleas
11 Bedford Avenue
12 Lilia

Hipsters and Hasidim—those are the primary residents of this beguiling neighborhood. While you won't find the elegant architecture that graces other areas of the city—Williamsburg was once mostly factories, warehouses, and hastily built low-rise apartment buildings for workers—you will encounter a neighborhood bursting with artistic energy, *joie de vivre* . . . and stark contrasts. *Tip:* Walking between the Hasidic enclave at the start of the tour and the heart of Williamsburg takes a good 25 minutes. If you're short on time, start this tour at stop #3 (take either the G to Metropolitan Ave. or the L to Bedford to get there). *Important:* Some venues on this tour are only open on weekends, so plan accordingly. START: Subway J, Z or M to Marcy Ave.

Many Hasidic Jewish families live around Lee Avenue.

1 ★ Lee Avenue. This stretch, between Taylor and Heywood, is the commercial center of the largest Hasidic community (70,000-plus ultra-Orthodox Satmar Jews) anywhere. Hebrew lettering adorns storefronts; inside, goods include silver candlesticks and menorahs, wigs (married women must wear them), wide-brimmed black hats, and Eastern European noshes. You'll see many kids; families in this neighborhood average 5 to 7 children. ⏱ *25 min.*

2 ★★ Shalom Japan. An "authentically inauthentic" fusion resto that puts matzoh balls into ramen soup, and slathers sashimi with tahini—all to delicious effect. *310 S. 4th St. (at Rodney St.) www.shalom japannyc.com.* ☎ *718/388-4012. $$.*

3 ★★ City Reliquary. An itsy-bitsy museum, the Reliquary displays the ephemera of Big Apple life—a wooden brick from the last wood sidewalk in the city, branded seltzer bottles from long-gone delis, Statue of Liberty statuettes in every form imaginable, and more. A cabinet of nostalgia. ⏱ *30 min. 370 Metropolitan Ave. (at Havermeyer St.). www.cityreliquary.org.* ☎ *718/782-4842. Admission $7 adults, $5 seniors and students, free to children 12 and under. Sat-Sun noon–6pm.*

4 ★ Brooklyn Art Library. Home to the "Sketchbook Project," which collects handwritten (and hand-drawn) books from artists—including self-taught artists—from around the world (over 160,000 books!). Step in to read one or two of these fascinating, one-of-a-kind tomes. ⏱ *20 min. 28 Frost St. (btw. Union and Lorimer sts.). www.sketch bookproject.org.* ☎ *718/388-7941. Free. Tues–Sun noon–6pm.*

5 ★★ New York Distilling Company. The first legal distilling company in the city since Prohibition leads free tours of its facilities on weekend afternoons at 1pm. Afterwards, belly up to the bar (called **The Shanty**) for an expertly mixed cocktail, featuring the gins and ryes you just witnessed bubbling away. ⏱ *45 min.* 79

Richardson St. (btw. Leonard and Lorimer sts.). www.nydistilling.com. ☎ 718/878-3579. Free. Weekends 2:30–5:30pm.

⑥ ★★★ Cathedral of the Transfiguration of our Lord. It was only after the end of World War II that sermons began to be delivered in English at this exquisite onion-domed Russian Orthodox church. It's still a gathering place for a community that originally emigrated in the 1920s from Europe's Carpathian Mountains (services are in Old Church Slavic, which is similar to Russian). If it's open, step inside to see a host of dazzling gold-painted religious icons; this is the only example of Byzantine Revival architecture on the East Coast. The church was featured in an episode of *Seinfeld*. ⏱ *20 min. At the corner of Driggs and 12th sts. Free admission. Hours vary.*

⑦ McCarren Park. This handsome park was a grungy outdoor bazaar for drug dealers in the 1960s

Bushwick Inlet Park.

and 1970s. While the entire city was in decline then, Williamsburg was particularly hard-hit, with several of its factories closing. Many police officers colluded with the dealers in the dangerous park (nicknamed "The Killing Fields" back then),

A street mural near Bedford Avenue.

Quirky merchandise at Artists & Fleas.

between May and November, the fab food festival **Smorgasburg** will be in session at Martha P. Johnson State Park. The park is named for the trans activist, and is the state's only park named for an LGBTQ person. *Entrance on Kent Ave.*

⓬ ★★ Artists & Fleas. In this hangar-like space, filled with small tables piled high with wares, you'll find all sorts of chic and/or quirky clothing, accessories, and household goods, often sold by the artist who made them. ⏱ *30 min. 70 North 7th St. (btw. Kent and Wythe aves.). www.artistsandfleas.com. Sat–Sun 10am–7pm.*

⓭ ★★ Bedford Avenue. Billy-burg's main drag is a gallery and boutique-lined fun fest, with shops from multinational chains (like Apple and Madewell), along with cute local shops. Don't skip the **Mini-Mall** (at 218 Bedford), which holds a terrific bookstore, a well-curated vintage clothing shop, and accessories shops with real flair. In the streets off Bedford, look for street murals—a number of name artists paint them to help raise the prices on the pieces they're selling in galleries (no guerilla art here!).

until a brave cop named Frank Serpico—you might have seen the film about him or read the book—exposed the corruption in the neighborhood.

⓼ ★ Brooklyn Brewery. Another booze tour! As at the distillery, you'll be both well informed and tipsy by the end. The brewery was founded in 1988 by Steve Hindy, who learned to home brew out of necessity while serving as a correspondent for the Associated Press in the dry Middle East. ⏱ *30 min. 79 North 11th St. (btw. Berry St. and Wythe Ave.). www.brooklyn-brewery.com. Free tours weekends between noon and 6pm, weekday tastings, classes, and tours at 5pm, from $18.*

⓽ ★★ Martha P. Johnson State Park and Bushwick Inlet Park. Wander into these small parks for spectacular views of the Manhattan skyline. If it's a Saturday

⓮ ★★★ Lilia. Put down this book, and get on Resy.com right now to snag a reservation at this sublime palace of pasta. Run by Chef Missy Robbins, it's one of the hardest tables in the city to get, but those who do are rewarded with an Italian meal more memorable than many you'd have in Rome. *567 North 10th St. (at Union St.). www.lilianewyork.com.* ☎ *718/576-3095. $$$*

Chinatown, Little Italy & the Lower East Side

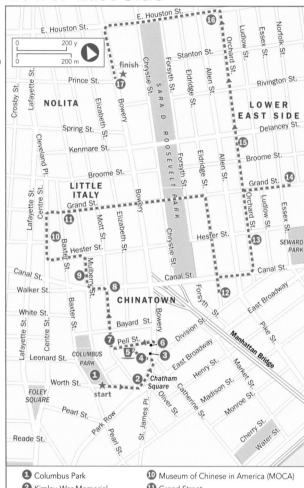

1 Columbus Park
2 Kimlau War Memorial
3 Lin Sister Herb Shop
4 Doyers Street
5 Nom Wah Tea Parlor
6 Edward Mooney House
7 Mott Street
8 Canal Street
9 Mulberry Street
10 Museum of Chinese in America (MOCA)
11 Grand Street
12 Museum at Eldridge
13 Orchard Street
14 Kossar's Bialys
15 The Tenement Museum
16 Russ & Daughters
17 New Museum

Long known for its vibrant street life, the Lower East Side was also home to notorious slums (including the Five Points) where Irish, Italian, Jewish, and Chinese immigrants crowded into tenements. Although much survives from that era—including many of the tenement buildings—today the neighborhood buzzes with the energy of new restaurants, galleries, bars, and live-music clubs. START: **Subway 4/5/6 to Brooklyn Bride or J/Z to Chambers St.**

Chinatown's Columbus Park.

❶ ★ **Columbus Park.** New York's worst slum, known as Mulberry Bend, once stood where this park is, surrounded by tenements with such names as Bone Alley, Kerosene Row, and Bandits' Roost. Most of the houses were torn down in the early 20th century. Today the park is filled with Chinese immigrants practicing tai chi and playing games of chance at the stone tables. It's quite a scene. *Bounded by Mosco, Mulberry, Bayard, and Baxter sts.*

❷ **Kimlau War Memorial.** This memorial arch in Chatham Square was erected in 1962 to honor the Chinese Americans who gave their lives fighting in World War II. The square also contains an imposing statue of Lin Zexu, a 19th-century antidrug hero in China. *Chatham Sq.*

❸ ★★ **Lin Sister Herb Shop.** This three-story apothecary is a marvel. A wall of wooden drawers, each containing medicinal herbs, dominates the first floor. On the upper levels, reflexology massage and acupuncture treatments are offered, and a homeopathic doctor is available for consultations. *4 Bowery (at Division St.). www.linsister. com.* ☎ *212/962-5417.*

❹ ★★ **Doyers Street.** Walk a few feet back to Doyers Street, a narrow, crooked alleyway once notorious for activity by gangs known as tongs. The bend in the street allowed the thugs to jump victims and attack them with hatchets (hence the term "hatchet

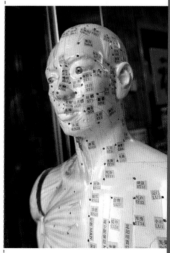

Acupuncture model at a Chinese pharmacy.

Yunhong Chopstick Shop.

man"). You'll see an unusually large number of barbershops on this street and the next. There's a historic reason for that: When the Chinese Exclusion Act of 1882 barred Chinese women from coming to this country, Chinatown businesses popped up to do the work that wives usually did for Chinese men now stranded here, like cooking (hence all the Chinese restaurants) and grooming.

5 ★★ **Nom Wah Tea Parlor.** Nom Wah opened in 1920, making it the oldest dim sum joint in Chinatown. Formica tables, wood booths, red chairs—this oldie is definitely a goodie. Order the egg roll, which it claims is the "original." *13 Doyers St. (btw. Bowery and Pell St.). www. nomwah.com.* ☎ *212/962-6047. $.*

6 **Edward Mooney House.** This Georgian brick structure, painted red, is the oldest row house in the city, dating from George Washington's New York days. Wealthy merchant Edward

Mooney had the house built in 1785 on property abandoned by a Tory during the American Revolution. *18 Bowery (at Pell St.).*

7 ★ **Mott Street.** The heart of old Chinatown, this is the epicenter of the boisterous yearly Chinese New Year celebrations—and a nifty place to wander and shop any time of year. Some addresses to note: no. 17, where, down a set of steps, you will dine in grungy glory on such Chinese-American classics as sweet and sour chicken at legendary **Wop Hop;** and a charming outpost of the famous Taiwanese chain **Ten Ren Tea** (at no. 75), which has a museum-worthy display of teapots. Also do stop by the dazzling **Yunhong Chopstick Shop** (at no. 50). Respectful visitors are welcome at the **Eastern Buddhist Temple** no. 4).

8 **Canal Street.** From West Broadway to the Manhattan Bridge, this is one of the city's liveliest and most congested thoroughfares. Stalls hawk everything from "designer" handbags to electronics.

Kam Man, at no. 200, is our favorite stop: a combo grocery/electronics/home goods superstore, selling wares from across Asia.

⑨ Mulberry Street. A tiny taste of the little that's left of Little Italy. More authentic sites are coming a bit later in this walking tour.

⑩ ★★ kids Museum of Chinese in America (MOCA). It is difficult to comprehend the cruel hardships that the first generations of Chinese suffered in New York. This museum documents the history and culture of the Chinese in America from the early 1800s to the present. ⏲ *45 min. 215 Centre St. (btw. Howard and Grand sts.). www.mocanyc.org.* ☎ *212/619-4785. Admission $12 adults, $8 seniors and students, free for kids 12 and under. Tues–Sun 11am–6pm, Thurs until 9pm. Subway: N/R/Q/J/Z/6 to Canal St.*

⑪ ★ Grand Street. East meets West on this thoroughfare, with genuine Italian grocery stores (stop into De Palo at no. 200 and Piemonte Ravioli at no. 180) and historic red-sauce joints on some blocks, Chinese herb shops and kung fu studios on others. Look up: A lot of the intricate fire escapes you'll see were crafted by Italian immigrants who learned their trade in the old country working on palazzos.

⑫ ★★★ Museum at Eldridge. When this former synagogue was built by Eastern European Jews in 1887, it was the most magnificent on the Lower East Side. Its congregation once included such luminaries as Eddie Cantor, Jonas Salk, and Edward G. Robinson. Over the years, however, membership declined, and the structure fell into disrepair in the 1950s. A recent $20-million renovation restored the building to its former glory—and

Guided tour at the Tenement Museum.

then some. ⏲ *20 min. 12 Eldridge St. (btw. Canal and Division sts.). www.eldridgestreet.org.* ☎ *212/ 219-0302. Admission $14 adults, $10 seniors and students, $8 children 5–18, free for children 4 and under; free for all Mon. Sun–Thurs 10am– 5pm, Fri 10am–3pm. Subway: B/D to Grand St. or 6.*

⑬ ★★ Orchard Street. In the 19th century, this street was a vast outdoor marketplace lined with rows of pushcarts. Today, stores for fabric, lingerie, suits, and dresses have replaced the carts, but in the spirit of tradition, some shop owners are still willing to haggle over prices. Also lining the street: stylish little boutiques, art galleries, and cafes with outdoor seating (in nice weather). It's a brand-new melting pot. On Sundays, Orchard is closed to vehicular traffic between Delancey and Houston streets so that wares can be sold in the open air.

⑭ Kossar's Bialys. A true New York treat, bialys are like bagels but hole-less and less uniform in shape.

Kossar's is the oldest bialy bakery in the U.S. and they're still using their original recipes—why fix what isn't broken? *367 Grand St. (btw. Essex and Norfolk sts.).* ☎ *212/473-4810. $.*

⓯ ★★★ The Tenement Museum. This tremendously moving museum documents the lives of immigrant residents in a six-story tenement built in 1863 at 97 Orchard Street (accessible only via fascinating guided tours). The tenement rooms are eerily authentic, and for good reason: 97 Orchard was essentially boarded up from 1935 to 1987; when it was finally re-opened, everything was exactly as it had been left, a virtual time capsule of 1935 tenement life. Artifacts found a range from the mundane (medicine tins and Russian cigarettes) to the personal (a 1922 Ouija board and an infant's button-up shoe). Visitors choose from among several tours, each of which profiles a different family and/or apartment (there are also neighborhood walking tours). Book well in advance in high season—this is one of New York's most popular museums. ⏲ *1–1½ hr. 103 Orchard St. (at Delancey St.). www.tenement.org.* ☎ *212/982-8420. Tours $27 adults, $22 seniors and students. Tours daily.*

⓰ ★★ Russ & Daughters. This iconic deli was the first business in the United States to have "& Daughters" in its name—added in 1935 when the owner made his three daughters partners. Founded in 1914 by immigrant Joel Russ (he got his start selling herring out of a barrel on Orchard Street), it's still in the family, and a fascinating place to duck into, even if you're not in

Russ & Daughters deli.

the market for the best smoked salmon on earth. Nearby is a fab cafe of the same name, created by the family. *179 E. Houston (at Orchard St.). www.russanddaughters. com.* ☎ *212/475-4880.*

⓱ ★ New Museum. The seven stories of the New Museum of contemporary art, designed by Tokyo–based architects Kazuyo Sejima and Ryue Nishizawa (aka SANAA), rise above the tenement buildings of the Lower East Side like boxes haphazardly piled upon one another. The offbeat exterior reflects the character of the exhibitions inside by new and emerging artists. ⏲ *1 hr. 235 Bowery (at Prince St.). www.newmuseum.org.* ☎ *212/219-1222. Admission $18 adults, $15 seniors, $12 students, free for children 18 and under; free for all Thurs 7–9pm. Wed and Fri–Sun 11am–6pm; Thurs 11am–9pm. Subway: 6 to Spring St.; N/R to Prince St.* ●

Shopping **Best Bets**

Best **Food Store**
Kalustyan's, *123 Lexington Ave.*
(p 95)

Best **Place to Deck Out Your Dream House**
ABC Carpet & Home, *881 and 888 Broadway (p 96)*

Best **Footwear**
Harry's Shoes *2299 Broadway*
(p. ###)

Best **All-Around Department Store**
Bloomingdale's, *1000 Third Ave.*
(p 91)

Best **Browsing**
MoMA Store, *44 W. 53rd St. (p 95)*

Best **Toy Store**
CAMP, *110 Fifth Ave. (and at Hudson Yards) (p 98)*

Best **Men's Designer Clothes**

Bergdorf Goodman for Men,
745 Fifth Ave. (p 91)

Best **Women's Designer Clothes**
Bergdorf Goodman, *754 Fifth Ave.*
(p 91)

Best **Cheap & Trendy Clothes**
UNIQLO, *666 Fifth Ave. (p 94)*

Best **Vintage Jewelry**
Pippin, *72 Orchard St. (p 97)*

Best **Wine & Liquor**
Astor Wines, *399 Lafayette St.*
(p 94)

Best **Deals on Electronics**
B&H Photo-Video-Pro Audio,
420 Ninth Ave. (p 92)

Best **Beauty Products**
C. O. Bigelow, *414 Sixth Ave.*
(p 90)

Sales-Tax Lowdown

The sales tax in New York City is 8.875% (4.5% for city sales tax, 4% for New York State tax, plus an additional surcharge). **No sales tax at all is charged for clothing and footwear purchases under $110.** If you have an item shipped, be sure to get proper documentation of the sale and keep the receipts handy until the merchandise arrives at your door.

Previous page: The swimwear section of Nordstrom's (see p. 92)

Downtown Shopping

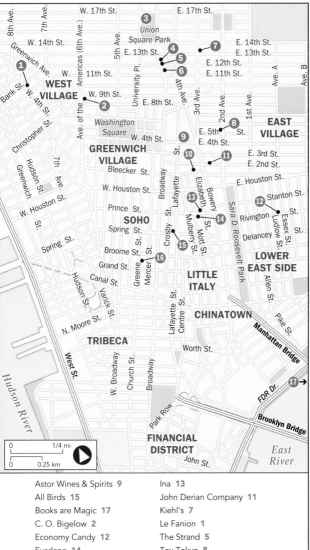

Astor Wines & Spirits **9**
All Birds **15**
Books are Magic **17**
C. O. Bigelow **2**
Economy Candy **12**
Everlane **14**
Flight Club **6**
Forbidden Planet **4**
Gudrun Sjödén **16**

Ina **13**
John Derian Company **11**
Kiehl's **7**
Le Fanion **1**
The Strand **5**
Toy Tokyo **8**
Ulla Johnson **10**
Union Square Greenmarket **3**
Whisk **17**

Midtown & Uptown Shopping

Upper West Side

ABC Carpet & Home 12
The Apple Store 27
B&H Photo & Video 7
Barnes & Noble
  Union Square 11
Bergdorf Goodman 26
Bloomingdale's 29
Book Culture 1
Books of Wonder 9
Camp 10
Camper 22
The Diamond District 19
Eataly 15
FAO Schwartz 21
Fine and Dandy 6
Fishs Eddy 13
Greenstones 3
Harry's Shoes 2
Harry Potter NY 14
Kalustyan's 17
Macy's 18
Manhattan Art and
  Antiques Center 28
Metropolitan Museum
  of Art Store 30
MoMA Store 23
Nordstrom's 5
Pippin Vintage Jewelry 8
Rizzoli 16
Saks Fifth Avenue 20
Tiffany & Co. 25
Uniqlo 24
Zabar's 4

UPPER EAST SIDE

E. 66th St.
E. 65th St.
E. 64th St.
E. 63rd St.
E. 62nd St.
E. 61st St.
Roosevelt Island Tram
E. 60th St.
E. 59th St.
E. 58th St.
E. 57th St.
E. 56th St.
E. 55th St.
E. 54th St.
E. 53rd St.
E. 52nd St.
E. 51st St.
E. 50th St.
E. 49th St.
E. 48th St
E. 47th St.
E. 46th St.
E. 45th St.
E. 44th St.
E. 43rd St.
E. 42nd St.
E. 41st St.
E. 40th St.
E. 39th St.
E. 38th St.
E 37th St.
E 36th St.
E. 35th St.
E. 34th St.
E. 33rd St.
E. 32nd St.
E. 31st St.
E. 30th St.
E. 29th St.
E. 28th St.
E. 27th St.
E. 26th St.
E. 25th St.
E. 24th St.
E. 23rd St.
E. 22nd St.
E. 21st St.
E. 20th St.
E. 19th St.
E. 18th St.
E. 17th St.
E. 16th St.
E. 15th St.
E. 14th St.

Queensboro Bridge

Queens-Midtown Tunnel

East River

PETER COOPER VILLAGE

STUYVESANT TOWN

St. Patrick's Cathedral

MIDTOWN EAST

ROCKEFELLER CENTER

Grand Central Terminal

Bryant Park
New York Public Library

MURRAY HILL

UNITED NATIONS

Empire State Building

Madison Square Park
Flatiron Building

FLATIRON DISTRICT

Gramercy Park
GRAMERCY PARK

Union Square

PARK
The Pond

Center Drive
East Drive
Fifth Ave.

Fifth Avenue
Madison Ave.

York Ave.

Sutton Pl. South Sutton Pl.

Beekman Place

Mitchell Place

FDR Drive

First Ave.
Second Ave.

Sixth Ave. (Ave. of the Americas)
Fifth Ave.
Madison Ave.
Vanderbilt Ave.
Park Ave.
Lexington Ave.
Third Ave.

Broadway
W 32nd St.

Park Ave. S.

Lexington Ave.

Asser Levy Pl.
Ave. C

N.D. Perlman Pl.
Irving Pl.
Union Sq. E.
Union Sq. W.

0   1/4 mi
0   0.25 km

Shopping A to Z

C. O. Bigelow, the nation's oldest apothecary shop.

Beauty/Apothecary

★★ **C. O. Bigelow** GREENWICH VILLAGE Its motto—"If you can't get it anywhere else, try Bigelow's"—is right on the money. This 182-year-old apothecary, oldest in the nation, carries unusual brands, plus its own great line of personal-care products. *414 Sixth Ave. (btw. 8th and 9th sts.). www.bigelowchemists.com.* ☎ *212/533-2700. AE, DISC, MC, V. Subway: A/C/E/F/M to W. 4th St.*

★ **Kiehl's** EAST VILLAGE This 150-plus-year-old firm's skin- and hair-care products have a cult following, and the store's free product samples add to its quirky charm. This is the now-chain's original location. *109 Third Ave. (btw. 13th and 14th sts.). www.kiehls.com.* ☎ *212/677-3171. AE, DC, MC, V. Subway: 4/5/6 to Union Sq.*

Books

★★ **Barnes & Noble Union Square** UNION SQUARE This red-brick, terra-cotta relic from 1881 holds one of the chain's most impressive Manhattan stores. *Century* magazine was published here in the late 19th century. Other branches are at Fifth Ave. and 45th St. and Broadway and 82nd St. *33 E. 17th St. (btw. Broadway and Park Ave.). www.bn.com.* ☎ *212/253-0810. AE, DC, DISC, MC, V. Subway: 4/5/6 to Union Sq.*

★★ **Book Culture** UPPER WEST SIDE A friendly, independent store with a wide range of books and a wonderfully knowledgeable staff. *2915 Broadway (at 114th St.).*

Antique Districts

If you're into antiquing, the best strategy is to head for areas where such stores tend to cluster. One of the best areas is Greenwich Village, particularly **10th Street between Broadway and University Place** (take the 4/5/6, N/Q/R, or L subways to Union Sq.); stores on the block specialize in Scandinavian antiques, French Art Deco, Mid-Century Modern, Neoclassical furnishings, and those from the Biedermeier school. There's also a flock of antique stores near the massive **Manhattan Art and Antiques Center** (1050 Second Ave. btw. 55th and 56th; subways 4/5/6 or N/Q/R to 59th St.). Best pickings are near Second Avenue on 59th, 60th, and 61st streets.

Refined book-browsing at Rizzoli.

www.bookculture.com. ☎ 646/403-3000. AE, DC, DISC, MC, V. Subway: 1 to 116th St.

★★ **Books Are Magic** BROOKLYN Founded by best- selling author Emma Straub, the store is smartly curated and has a stellar reading series. *225 Smith St., Cobble Hill.* www.booksaremagic.net. ☎ 718/246-2665. AE, MC, V. Subway: F/G to Bergen St.

★★ **Rizzoli** FLATIRON DISTRICT This gorgeous bookstore is an atmospheric place to browse for high-end visual art and design books, plus quality fiction and

gourmet cookbooks. *1133 Broadway (at 26th St.).* www.rizzolibookstore.com. ☎ 212/759-2424. AE, MC, V. Subway: N/R to 28th St.

★★★ **The Strand** UNION SQUARE This local legend is worth a visit for its staggering "18 miles of books," new and used titles at up to 85% off list price. *828 Broadway (at 12th St.).* www.strandbooks.com. ☎ 212/473-1452. AE, DC, DISC, MC, V. Subway: L/N/R/4/5/6 to Union Sq.

Department Stores
★★ **Bergdorf Goodman** MIDTOWN The place for ladies who lunch and anyone who reveres fashion and clothes built to last. The **men's store** across the street (745 Fifth Ave.) has a great selection. *754 Fifth Ave. (at 58th St.).* www.bergdorfgoodman.com. ☎ 800/558-1855. AE, DC, MC, V. Subway: E/F to Fifth Ave.

★★ **Bloomingdale's** MIDTOWN EAST Packed to the gills with goods, Bloomie's is more accessible and affordable than Nordstrom's, Bergdorf, or Saks. There's a SoHo outpost too, at 504

Bergdorf Goodman's iconic awning.

Broadway. *1000 Third Ave. (Lexington Ave. at 59th St.). www.bloomingdales.com.* ☎ *212/705-2000. AE, MC, V. Subway: 4/5/6 to 59th St.*

Macy's HERALD SQUARE The size is unmanageable and the service is clueless, but they do sell *everything.* And *everything* goes on sale, at some point or another. *151 W. 34th St. (at Broadway). www.macys.com.* ☎ *212/695-4400. AE, MC, V. Subway: B/D/F/N/Q/R/1/2/3/ to 34th St.*

★★ Nordstrom's MIDTOWN In 2019, Nordstrom opened its largest store—a whopping 320,000 square feet of luxury goods. It's also its most pampering outlet, with a martini bar in the shoe department and several eateries that will deliver food on chinaware anywhere in the store. *225 W. 57th St (near Broadway). www.shop.nordstroms.com.* ☎ *877/310-8537. AE, DISC, MC, V. Subway: A/B/C/D/1 to Columbus Cir.*

★ Saks Fifth Avenue MIDTOWN This legendary flagship store stocks big-name designers in fashion and accessories, with price tags to match. Look for smart house brands on the fourth and fifth floors. The make-up selection is the most wide-ranging in the city, with many European brands. *611 Fifth Ave. (btw. 49th and 50th sts.). www.saksfifthavenue.com.* ☎ *212/753-4000. AE, DC, DISC, MC, V. Subway: B/D/F/Q to 47th–50th sts./ Rockefeller Center; E/F to Fifth Ave.*

Electronics

★ The Apple Store MIDTOWN You know the drill: lots of tech, all laid out on tables for you to play with. But what's special about this store is its stunning architecture: Its glass cube top is the most photographed shop in the city. *767 Fifth Ave. (at 59th St.). www.apple.com.* ☎ *212/336-1440. AE, DISC, MC, V. Subway N/R to Fifth Ave.*

★★★ B&H Photo-Video-Pro Audio GARMENT DISTRICT The best place on the East Coast for deep discounts on cameras, TV's, computers, and other electronics. With 50% of their sales now online, service has become much less rushed (the salespeople are real experts). *Note:* Closed Saturdays. *420 Ninth Ave. (at 34th St.).*

Brooklyn Artisans and Outlets

For sheer, unadulterated shopping fun, it's hard to beat **Industry City.** Set on 35 riverside acres in Brooklyn, this campus of 16 former factory buildings has artisans of all sorts creating goods upstairs; on the ground floor, massive discount outlets from top home goods stores (**Design Within Reach, ABC Carpet & Home, West Elm**); a bogglingly big international food shop (**Sahadis**) and Japanese food court; and dozens of adorable boutiques, restaurants, breweries, and food counters, some of which spill out into art-adorned courtyards and lawns. In winter there's an ice-skating rink, in summer concerts galore, mini-golf, playgrounds, and festivals. Check the website for special events, especially frequent dates when artisans open their studios to the public. *From 30th street to 29th street, and from the Gowanus Expressway to the river. industrycity.com. No phone. Subway: D, N, R to 36th St.*

Happy outfit hunting at Gudrun Sjödén.

www.bhphotovideo.com. ☎ 800/
606-6969. AE, DISC, MC, V. Subway:
A/C/E to 34th St.

Fashion

★★ Everlane SOHO Ethically
created, very affordable basics at
one of the only bricks-and-mortar
outlets for this Internet phenom. *28
Prince St. (btw. Mott and Elizabeth
sts). www.everlane.com.* ☎ *212/
475-2470. AE, MC, V. Subway: N/Q/
R/W to Prince St. or 6 to Spring.*

★★★ Fine and Dandy
MIDTOWN This specialist in
men's accessories makes 80% of
the natty bowties, neckties, silky
socks, pocket squares, fedoras, and
other items of male glamor sold
here. They endow the wearer with
instant élan. *445 W. 49th St. (off
Tenth Ave.). fineanddandyshop.com.*
☎ *212/247-4847. AE, MC, V. Subway: Subway: C, E to 50th St.*

★★ Gudrun Sjödén SOHO No
shade of the rainbow is off limits, as
this eponymous Swedish designer
uses both subtle pastels and neon
hues in striking patterns for women's
clothing and homewares. Beyond
the jubilant palette, the brand is
known for eco-conscious practices,
fair pricing, and cuts that flatter all

sizes, including plus size. *50 A
Green Street (near Broome St.). www.
gudrunsjoden.com.* ☎ *212/219-
2510. MC, V. Subway: 6 to Spring St.
or N, Q, R, W to Canal St.*

★★ Ina NOLITA This consignment shop is so chic, the Sex In the
City costume designer resold clothing from that show here back in the
day. There's also a men's store next
door. *21 Prince St. (off Elizabeth St.).
www.inanyc.com.*
☎ *212/334-9048. AE, MC, V. Subway: 5, 6 to Spring St. or N, R, W to
Prince St.*

★★ Ulla Johnson NOHO
Handmade fabrics from around the
globe go into these casually elegant
boho threads, created by a born-
and-bred NYC designer. They're
pricey, but the microfloral dresses,
especially, are wonderfully whimsical. *15 Bleecker St. (at Elizabeth St.).
ullajohnson.com.* ☎ *965-0144. AE,
MC, V. Subway: 6 to Bleecker St.*

★ UNIQLO MIDTOWN The
largest UNIQLO on the planet
(there are also outposts in Soho, on
34th and 53rd sts.). Known as
Japan's answer to the Gap,
UNIQLO specializes in smartly constructed basics, like the perfect
black cotton V-neck shirt. *666 Fifth*

Midtown's UNIQLO is the chain's largest store.

Ave. (at 53rd St.). ☎ 917/237-8800. AE, DC, DISC, MC, V. Subway: N/R to Prince St.; 6 to Spring St.

Food & Wine
★★ Astor Wines & Spirits
EAST VILLAGE   With a deep stock and great values, this spacious downtown institution not only features hard-to-find wines, but also has a vast collection of varied spirits at world-beating prices. *399 Lafayette St. (at E.4th St.). www.astorwines.com.* ☎ *212/674-7500. Subway: B/D/F/M to Broadway-Lafayette St.*

★★★ Eataly FLATIRON DISTRICT
Owned today by Joe and Lidia Bastianich (Mario Batali, a founder, was "Me Too'ed" out), Eataly is an Italian market on steroids. Aisle upon groaning aisle is stocked with imported pastas, olive oils and vinegars, fresh mozzarella, pastries, coffee, books, and more. You can buy, or dine in at six different on-site Italian eateries. It also has a Financial Center outlet (see p 16). *200 Fifth Ave. (at 23rd St.). www.eatalyny.com.* ☎ *212/229-2560. AE, MC, V. Market daily 10am–11pm. Restaurants daily lunch and dinner. Subway: N/R/6 to 23rd St.*

★★★ Economy Candy LOWER
EAST SIDE   All of the obscure candies you gorged on as a kid, plus superb halvah and dried fruits, all at, yes, economy prices. A trip back in time. *108 Rivington St. (btw. Delancey and Norfolk sts.).*

Astor Wines & Spirits.

Union Square Greenmarket.

www.economycandy.com. 📞 212/254-1531. AE, MC, V. Subway: F to Delancey St.

★★★ Kalustyan's MIDTOWN This 72-year-old international market just keeps growing. Not long ago, it added 6,500 square feet, but the aisles still feel cramped, crammed with goodies from all over the globe: Korean chili paste, candied violets, Sicilian pistachios, 100 different types of salt, and every type of spice known to man. *123 Lexington Ave. (btw. 28th and 29th sts.). www.kalustyans.com.* 📞 *212/685-3451.AE, MC, V. Subway: 6 to 28th St.*

★★★ Union Square Greenmarket UNION SQUARE At Manhattan's largest farmer's market, you'll find fresh produce from upstate and New Jersey farms, fish just off the boat from Long Island, artisanal cheeses, home-cured meats, plants, and organic herbs and spices. I've seen star chefs here with wheelbarrows in tow. Open daytime year-round on Monday, Wednesday, Friday, and Saturday. *In Union Sq. www.grownyc.org.*

📞 *212/788-7476. No credit cards. Subway: 4/5/6/N/Q/R/W to Union Sq.*

★★ Zabar's UPPER WEST SIDE The one-and-only Zabar's is the place to go for great smoked salmon and all the works—not to mention terrific prepared foods, gourmet edibles, coffees, cheeses, you name it. *2245 Broadway (at 80th St.). www. zabars.com.* 📞 *212/496-1234. AE, DC, MC, V. Subway: 1 to 79th St.*

Gifts

★ Forbidden Planet UNION SQUARE Know someone who lives in a fantasy world? This superstore of comics and manga holds a gift for them, whether it be an action figure, a rare graphic novel, or a costume. *832 Broadway (btw. 12th and 13th sts.). www.fpnyc.com.* 📞 *212/473-1576. AE, MC, V. Subway: L/N/R/4/5/6 to 14th St./Union Sq.*

★★ John Derian Company EAST VILLAGE Fabulous decoupage items, colorful candleholders handmade in Paris, and terra-cotta pottery are but a few of the delicious treats here. *10 & 6 E. 2nd St. (btw. Second Ave. and the Bowery). www.johnderian.com.* 📞 *212/677-3917. AE, MC, V. Subway: 6 to Bleecker St., F/M to Second Ave.*

★★ Le Fanion GREENWICH VILLAGE Beautiful French Country pottery in a charming Village shop. *299 W. 4th St. (at Bank St.). www. lefanion.com.* 📞 *212/463-8760. AE, MC, V. Subway: 1/2/3 at 14th St.*

★★ Metropolitan Museum of Art Store UPPER EAST SIDE Great for jewelry, china, books, toys, textiles, umbrellas, and objets d'art modeled on the Met's collection. See website for branch locations. *1000 Fifth Ave. (at 82nd St.). www.metmuseum.org/store.* 📞 *212/570-3894. AE, DISC, MC, V. Subway: 4/5/6 to 86th St.*

The gift shop at the Museum of Modern Art has fabulous design-forward gifts.

★★★ MoMA Store MIDTOWN
The Museum of Modern Art store stocks fabulous, unique gifts, from silk scarves with Frank Lloyd Wright designs to Eames chairs. The Christmas ornaments are gorgeous. See website for branch locations. *44 W. 53rd St. (btw. Fifth and Sixth aves.). www.momastore.org. ☎ 212/767-1050. AE, DISC, MC, V. Subway: E/M to Fifth Ave./53rd St.*

Home Design & Housewares
★★★ ABC Carpet & Home
FLATIRON DISTRICT This magical (and costly) two-building emporium is the ultimate home fashions and furnishings store, with everything from zillion-thread-count sheets to enchanting children's furniture. *881 and 888 Broadway (at 19th St.). www.abchome.com. ☎ 212/473-3000. AE, DISC, MC, V. Subway: L/N/R/4/5/6 to 14th St./Union Sq.*

★ Fishs Eddy FLATIRON
DISTRICT Come here for vintage and reproduction dishes, flatware, and glasses. *889 Broadway (at 19th St.). www.fishseddy.com. ☎ 212/420-9020. AE, MC, V.*

Subway: L/N/R/4/5/6 to 14th St./Union Sq.

★★ Whisk BROOKLYN
The best kitchenware store in the city, it has every gadget, pot, and pan you'd ever need—and plenty you didn't *know* you needed until you walked in. Also in Brooklyn. *197 Atlantic Ave. (btw. Clinton and Court Sts.). www.whisknyc.com. ☎ 718/852-2665. AE, MC, V. Subway: 4, 5 to Borough Hall.*

Jewelry & Precious Stones
The Diamond District MID-
TOWN This is the heart of the city's diamond trade, although many merchants deal in semiprecious stones, too. If you know your four C's, it's a great place to get a deal on diamonds; if you don't, stick to window-shopping. Most shops open Monday to Friday only. *47th St. (btw. Fifth and Sixth aves.). Subway: B/D/F/M to Rockefeller Center.*

★ Pippin Vintage Jewelry
CHELSEA From stately pearls to funky Bakelite, this gem of a shop carries it all. Also check out Pippin

ABC Carpet & Home.

Fishs Eddy's New York–centric designs.

Home, a small shop selling antiques and home furnishings, behind the jewelry store. *112 W. 17th St. (btw. Sixth and Seventh aves.). www.pippinvintage.com.* ☎ *212/505-5159. AE, MC, V. Subway: A/E to 14th St.*

★★ **Tiffany & Co.** MIDTOWN Deservedly famous, this iconic multilevel store carries jewelry, watches, tableware, stemware, and a variety of gift items. The store is currently engaging in a multi-year renovation, so check the website for closings before heading over. *727 Fifth Ave. (at 57th St.). www.tiffany.com.* ☎ *212/755-8000. AE, DC, DISC, MC, V. Subway: N/R to Fifth Ave.*

Shoes
★★ **All Birds** SOHO One of the first stores for the Internet's wildly comfy wool shoe brand. *73 Spring St. (at Crosby St.). www.allbirds.com.* ☎ *917/985-6646. AE, MC, V. Subway: 6 to Spring St.*

★★★ **Camper** MIDTOWN Chic chunky footwear, soothing to the sole, in a range of cool colors: These are the hallmarks of the men's and women's shoes made by this Spanish chain. *60 W. 50th St. (Rockefeller Center). www.camper.com.* ☎ *212/339-0078. AE, DISC, MC, V. Subway: N/Q/R to 49th St.*

★★ **Flight Club** GREENWICH VILLAGE Sneaker freaks looking for limited edition and vintage kicks come here. Part consignment and part new goods, each pair of shoes is displayed like a Van Gogh. A fascinating place to browse. *812 Broadway (btw. 11th and 12th sts). www.flightclub.com.* ☎ *888/937-8020. AE, MC, V. Subway: 4,5,6, N, Q,R,W, L to Union Sq.*

★ **Harry's Shoes** UPPER WEST SIDE This old-school store doesn't sell sex, it sells shoes. Great selection of comfortable styles. **Harry's Shoes for Kids** is a half-block away at 2315 Broadway. *2299 Broadway (at 83rd St.). www.harrys-shoes.com.* ☎ *866/442-7797. AE, DISC, MC, V. Subway: 1 to 79th St. or 86th St.*

Toys, Children's Books & Clothing
★★ kids **Books of Wonder** UNION SQUARE Remember the

charming bookstore in the Meg Ryan rom-com *You've Got Mail*? It was inspired by Books of Wonder, and the real thing is just as magical (and jam-packed with great kiddie reads). *18 W. 18th St. (btw. Fifth and Sixth aves.). www.booksofwonder. com.* ☎ *212/989-3270. AE, MC, V. Subway: L/N/R/4/5/6 to 14th St./ Union Sq.*

★★★ **CAMP** UNION SQUARE Now here's a concept: a toy store that's as much play-space as store. Come here with your tot and you'll while away hours doing sing-alongs, pretending to drive a life-size truck, and more. You may not even have to buy anything to keep the kid happy! *110 Fifth Ave. (btw. 17th and 18th sts.). Also at Hudson Yards. https://camp.com.* ☎ *917/997-0439. AE, MC, V. Subway: 4/ 5 6/N/Q/R/L to Union Sq.*

★★ **F.A.O. Schwartz** ROCKEFELLER CENTER The classic store is back, whimsy intact, with a wide range of stuffed animals, art supplies, customizable toy cars, and games of all sorts. Test the goods at stations around the shop. *30 Rockefeller Plaza (near the ice skating rink). www.faoschwartz.com. Subway: B/D/F/M to Rockefeller Center.*

★ **Greenstones** UPPER WEST SIDE Greenstones has a wide variety of trendy but tasteful clothing for newborns through tweens. *454 Columbus Ave. (at 84th St.). www. greenstonesnyc.com.* ☎ *212/580-4322. AE, MC, V. Subway: B/C to 81st St.*

★ **Harry Potter NY** FLATIRON DISTRICT One wand's length away from being a full-fledged indoor amusement park, the boy wizard's first flagship store has virtual reality experiences, interactive wand duel stations, a butterbeer bar, a scavenger hunt (exploring displays of actual props and costumes from the movies), and tons of merch. Collectors take note: Anything marked "New York" is exclusive to this location. *935 Broadway (at 22nd St.). www.harrypotterstore.com. AE, MC, V. Subway: N, R to 23rd St.*

★★★ kids **Toy Tokyo** EAST VILLAGE Action figures, oddball board games, and hundreds of fist-sized or smaller toys (great stocking stuffers) are just a few of the temptations here. And yes, there are a ton of Japanese toys. *91 Second Ave. (btw. 5th and 6th sts.). www. toytokyo.com.* ☎ *212/673-5424. AE, MC, V. Subway: 6 to Astor Place.* ●

Action figures galore at Toy Tokyo.

6 The Great Outdoors

Central Park

1. Harlem Meer
2. Conservatory Garden
3. The Reservoir
4. The Obelisk
5. The Great Lawn
6. The Ramble
7. The Lake
8. The Loeb Boathouse
9. Bethesda Terrace
10. The Mall
11. The Carousel
12. Wollman Rink
13. The Arsenal
14. Central Park Zoo

```
0              1/4 mi
0      0.25 km
```

Douglass Circle · Central Park North · Frawley Circle
E. 110th St.
E. 109th St.
E. 108th St.
Lasker Rink & Pool
Harlem Meer
E. 107th St.
E. 106th St.

The Great Hill
Conservatory Garden
Museum of the City of New York
E. 102nd St.

West Dr.
East Dr.

The Pool
North Meadow
East Meadow

Central Park West
5th Ave.
Madison Ave.
Park Ave.

Mt. Sinai Hospital

CENTRAL
97th St. Transverse Rd.
E. 97th St.
E. 96th St.
E. 95th St.

PARK
E. 94th St.
E. 93rd St.

Tennis Courts
E. 92nd St.
E. 91st St.
E. 90th St.

Jacqueline Kennedy Onassis Reservoir
Cooper-Hewitt Museum
W. 91st St.
W. 90th St.
W. 89th St.
E. 89th St.
E. 88th St.

Guggenheim Museum
E. 87th St.

W. 88th St.
W. 87th St.
W. 86th St.
E. 86th St.
E. 85th St.

Central Park West
Columbus Ave.
Amsterdam Ave.

UPPER WEST SIDE
W. 85th St.
W. 84th St.
W. 83rd St.
W. 82nd St.
W. 81st St.
W. 80th St.

86th St Transverse Rd.

GREAT LAWN

Metropolitan Museum of Art
E. 84th St.
E. 83rd St.
E. 82nd St.
E. 81st St.
E. 80th St.

West Dr.
West End Ave.
Broadway

Belvedere Lake
Delacorte Theater

UPPER EAST SIDE

W. 79th St.
W. 78th St.
79th St Transverse Rd.

American Museum of Natural History

W. 77th St.
W. 76th St.
W. 75th St.
W. 74th St.

CENTRAL PARK
The Ramble
Conservatory Pond
E. 75th St.

New York Historical Society

5th Ave.
Madison Ave.

The Lake

W. 73rd St.
W. 72nd St.
W. 71st St.
W. 70th St.

Dakota Apartments
Strawberry Fields
Bandshell

The Frick Collection
E. 72nd St.
E. 71st St.
E. 70th St.

W. 69th St.
W. 68th St.
W. 67th St.
W. 66th St.

Sheep Meadow
The Mall
East Green
E. 69th St.
E. 68th St.
E. 67th St.
E. 66th St.

West End Ave.
Central Park West

W. 65th St.
W. 64th St.
W. 63rd St.
W. 62nd St.

65th St. Transverse Rd.
Zoo
E. 65th St.
E. 64th St.
E. 63rd St.
E. 62nd St.

LINCOLN CENTER

Heckscher Playground

The Pond

E. 61st St.
E. 60th St.
E. 59th St.

FORDHAM UNIV.
W. 60th St.
W. 59th St.
Broadway
Columbus Circle · Central Park South
Grand Army Plaza

Previous page: Walking on a spring day on the Mall in Central Park.

Central Park serves as the city's backyard, its concert hall, its daytime pick-up bar, its outdoor gym, and, in summer, when dozens don bathing suits to soak up the rays, its green beach. The marvel of the park, beside its size (843 acres, a full 6% of Manhattan's total area), is the fact that none of it is "natural" in the usual sense. This park was created in the 1850s by landscape architects Frederick Law Olmstead and Calvert Vaux out of swampland, farms, and suburban towns. Every tree, every shrub, every lake, and most of the rolling hills were designed, planted, and blasted into existence by these two geniuses.

1 Harlem Meer. This 11-acre *meer* (the Dutch word for lake) wasn't part of the original Central Park. Added in 1863, it has a natural, rugged shoreline and a community of swans. The **Charles A. Dana Discovery Center**, on the northern shore, contains a year-round visitor center and hosts Central Park Conservancy seasonal exhibitions. *Fifth Ave. from 106th–110th sts.*

2 ★★ Conservatory Garden. Commissioned by the WPA (Work Projects Administration) in 1936, this formal garden has many showpieces: an elegant Italian garden with a classical fountain, a mazelike English garden, a bronze statue of the children from the novel *The Secret Garden* in a reflecting water-lily pool. To reach the Reservoir (below) from here, walk south through the park or, to save a mile of walking, take a bus down Fifth Avenue to 86th Street. *Fifth Ave. and 105th St.*

3 The Reservoir. Created in 1862 as part of the Croton Water

The Secret Garden statue in the Conservatory Garden.

System, the Reservoir was in use until 1994. Occupying 106 acres, it is surrounded by bridle and running paths. Many a celebrity and civilian has jogged along the 1.6-mile (2.6km) upper track, which overlooks the water and affords great skyline views. The reservoir holds a billion gallons of water and is 40

A Word on Playgrounds

With a few exceptions, most of the park's playgrounds are located on the rim of the park, near the entrances. They pop up every 6 blocks or so. Adults are not supposed to enter them without children in tow.

feet (12m) at its greatest depth, but these days it is only used as an emergency backup water supply. *Midpark from 85th–96th sts.*

④ ★★ The Obelisk. This 71-foot (21m) artifact from Ancient Egypt was an 1881 gift to the U.S. from the khedive of Egypt. *See p 12.*

⑤ ★ The Great Lawn. Expansive enough for simultaneous games of softball, volleyball, or soccer, the Great Lawn is also a plum spot for a picnic—especially on those warm summer nights when the New York Philharmonic or Metropolitan Opera performs for free (p 143). Bring along picnic fare from nearby gourmet grocery **Zabar's** (p 95). At the southern end, ★ **Belvedere Castle** (p 12) and its surrounding duck pond are particularly picturesque. *Midpark from 79th–85th sts.*

⑥ ★ The Ramble. Designed to mirror untamed nature, Olmstead called this 38-acre stretch his "wild garden." The Ramble has a seedy reputation after dark, but during the day it's wonderful to explore. The inviting paths that curve through the wooded area offer some of the best scouting ground for bird-watchers in the city—some 230 species have been spotted here. A statue of a crouching cougar overlooks the East Drive between 76th and 77th streets. *Midpark from 73rd–79th sts.*

⑦ ★★ The Lake. By far the most beautiful body of water in the park, this idyllic lake was once a swamp. Rent a rowboat ($15 for the first hour) at the Loeb Boathouse (see below) and take your sweetie for a turn around the lake—the views from the water are superb. (At certain times of a year, a singing gondolier also plies the lake, but at $45/hour we're not sure it's worth the outlay.) *Midpark from 71st–78th sts.*

⑧ ★ The Loeb Boathouse. At the eastern end of the Lake is the Loeb Boathouse, where you can rent boats and bikes as well as dine—and dine well. The upscale Lakeside Restaurant (lunch/brunch year-round; dinner Apr–Nov) is a lovely fine-dining space with alfresco lakeside seating under a white canopy. The menu is contemporary American. The casual Express Café serves breakfast, burgers, salads, and sandwiches (year-round 8am–5pm daily). *Fifth Ave. (btw. 74th and 75th sts.).* www.thecentralparkboathouse.com. ☎ 212/517-2233. $–$$$.

⑨ ★★ Bethesda Terrace. The architectural heart of the park, this extraordinarily lovely area is filled with art. If you approach it from the Mall, you'll come to a ravishing carved gate, with symbols representing "day" and "night" (the witches on brooms). The fountain celebrates the opening of the Croton Aqueduct, which finally solved NYC's water problems in 1842. The *Angel Bethesda* was sculpted by Emma Stebbins, the first woman ever to receive this sort of commission from the city. *Midpark at 72nd St.*

⑩ ★★ The Mall. This beguiling promenade is shaded by a curving canopy of American elms—a favorite tree of the park's designers. At the south end of the Mall is the **Literary Walk,** flanked by statues of Shakespeare, Robert Burns, Sir Walter Scott, and other historic and literary figures. *Midpark from 66th–72nd sts.*

⑪ ★★ kids The Carousel. The original carousel was built in 1871; fires destroyed it and its successor. Park officials searched high and low for a replacement, only to discover this treasure abandoned in an old trolley building on Coney Island. Its

On the Reservoir jogging path.

58 colorful steeds—among the largest carousel ponies in the world—were hand-carved by Russian immigrants Solomon Stein and Harry Goldstein in 1908. *Midpark at 64th St.* ☎ *212/439-6900, ext. 12. $3.25 ride. Apr–Oct daily 10am–6pm; Nov–Mar call.*

⑫ kids **Wollman Rink and Victorian Gardens Amusement Park.** Remember the flick *Love Story?* This is where he skated right before she died. In summer, the spot is home to the immaculate Victorian Gardens Amusement Park, geared toward young children. *Fifth Ave. (btw. 62nd and 63rd sts.). Rink: www.wollmanskatingrink. com.* ☎ *212/439-6900. Mon–Tues 10am–2:30pm, Wed–Thurs 10am– 10pm, Fri–Sat 10am–11pm, Sun 10am–9pm. Admission $12–$16 adults, $6 children 11 and under; skate rental $10. Victorian Gardens: www.victoriangardensnyc.com.* ☎ *212/982-2229. Daily 11am–7pm. Admission w/unlimited rides $20.*

⑬ **The Arsenal.** Predating the park, this Gothic Revival building looks like a fortress—which it briefly was, when it lodged troops in the Civil War. It was later the original site of the American Museum of Natural History (p 50) and even home to some of P. T. Barnum's circus animals, from a black bear to white swans. Today, it holds the park headquarters and a third-floor art gallery. *Fifth Ave. and 64th St.* ☎ *311 in New York City or 212/ NEW-YORK.*

⑭ ★★ kids **Central Park Zoo.** The Central Park Zoo was built in 1988 to replace a 1934 WPA-built structure that had become cramped and outdated. Today the zoo's 5½ acres house more than 400 animals. Watch sea lions cavorting in the Central Garden pool, polar bears splashing around their watery den, or penguins being fed in the chilly "Polar Circle." A favorite of all ages: the **Delacorte Clock,** a timepiece with six clock-work bronze animals twirl to music on the hour and half-hour. In the small **Tisch Children's Zoo,** kids can feed and pet tame farm animals. ⏱ *75 min. Fifth Ave. (btw. 63rd and 66th sts.). www.centralpark zoo.com.* ☎ *212/861-6030. Admission $20 adults, $17 seniors, $15 children 3–12, free for kids 2 and under. Daily 10am–4:30pm (extended hours for weekends, holidays, and spring/summer).*

Feeding the sheep at the Central Park Children's Zoo.

Little Island & The High Line

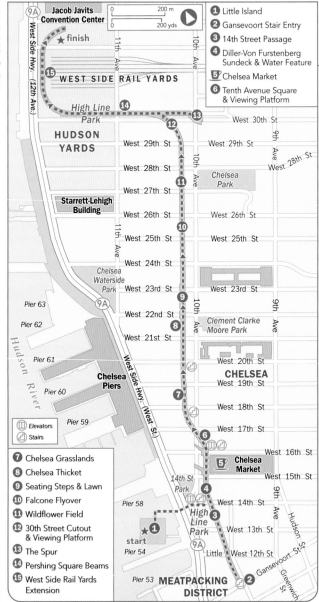

Jacob Javits Convention Center

★ finish

WEST SIDE RAIL YARDS

High Line Park

HUDSON YARDS

West 29th St

West 28th St

West 27th St

Starrett-Lehigh Building

West 26th St

West 25th St

West 24th St

Chelsea Waterside Park

West 23rd St

West 22nd St

West 21st St

Pier 63

Pier 62

Hudson River

Pier 61

Chelsea Piers

Pier 60

Pier 59

West Side Hwy. (West St.)

West Side Hwy. (12th Ave.)

11th Ave

10th Ave

West 30th St

West 29th St

West 28th St

9th Ave

Chelsea Park

West 26th St

West 25th St

West 23rd St

10th Ave

Clement Clarke Moore Park

West 20th St

CHELSEA
West 19th St

West 18th St

West 17th St

9th Ave

West 16th St

Chelsea Market

West 15th St

West 14th St

9th Ave

Hudson St

Gansevoort St

Greenwich St

14th St Park

Pier 58

High Line Park

West 13th St

West 12th St

Little

MEATPACKING DISTRICT

Pier 53

Pier 54

★ start
Pier 54

0   200 m
0   200 yds

❶ Little Island
❷ Gansevoort Stair Entry
❸ 14th Street Passage
❹ Diller-Von Furstenberg Sundeck & Water Feature
🄯 Chelsea Market
❻ Tenth Avenue Square & Viewing Platform

🅙 Elevators
🄯 Stairs

❼ Chelsea Grasslands
❽ Chelsea Thicket
❾ Seating Steps & Lawn
❿ Falcone Flyover
⓫ Wildflower Field
⓬ 30th Street Cutout & Viewing Platform
⓭ The Spur
⓮ Pershing Square Beams
⓯ West Side Rail Yards Extension

Two trailblazing parks! Little Island, which opened in 2021, has been praised for its luxuriant green spaces and the surreal way it rises from the Hudson River. The High Line, an abandoned elevated rail line smartly reinvented as an urban park, has spawned imitators around the globe. Combine this tour with "Chelsea, the High Line & Hudson Yards" (p. ###) for a leisurely day.

Visitors entering Little Island.

❶ ★★ Little Island. Created by Thomas Featherwick (of The Vessel, p. 67), paid for by mogul Barry Diller ($260 million), and extravagantly landscaped by Signe Nielson ($5 million alone was spent on the 350 different species of plants and flowers), this is the hilly green yin to the city's flat and gray yang. Admire first the 132 concrete "tulips", each of different height, which hold up the island. Then head onto the island to play on interactive musical instruments, snap photos of the views, and lounge on the grass. It's a bewitching addition to the city. *Hudson River btw. 13th and 14th sts.*

❷ Gansevoort Stair Entry. The foliage in the **Gansevoort Woodland,** at the top of the stairs, changes with the seasons. In autumn, aromatic aster, smokebush, and winterberry holly dust the paths in purple and red hues. In spring, walkways are pillowed in creamy white serviceberry blossoms. The old track's rusted rails are integrated into the landscaping. *Btw. Gansevoort and Little W. 12th sts.*

❸ ★★★ 14th Street Passage. You're walking through the only building that shares a support system with the original tracks. This was once a meat storage and packing facility; in fact, architects working on the High Line found 60 vats

Practical Matters

Both the Highline and Little Island are free to enter but require advance tickets for busy periods (weekends for The High Line, noon to 8pm for Little Island). Little Island is open 6am to 1am, the Highline 7am to 9pm. Both are wheelchair accessible; the High Line has elevators at 14th, 16th, 23rd and 30th streets. Go to www.thehighline.org or littleisland.org for info and tickets.

of animal carcasses in the basement here when they began their work. *At 14th St.*

④ ★★★ **Diller–Von Furstenberg Sundeck & Water Feature.** Grab yourself a wooden chaise and admire the river views. Dip your toes in the scrim of water—a flattened waterfall, if you will—running the length of the sundeck. The bubbling almost drowns out the noise of the traffic. *Btw. 14th and 15th sts.*

⑤ ★★ **Chelsea Market.** The city's most exciting food court not only has fab food and drink, it's become a major shopping venue thanks to the addition of **Pearl River Mart** (Asian goods) and **Artists and Fleas** (a maker market). Tons of fun! (p. 119) *See p 117.*

⑥ ★ **Tenth Avenue Square & Viewing Platform.** Crowds flock to these tiered wooden bleachers plunked virtually on top of Tenth Avenue. You can stare down the traffic on Tenth through the big picture window. *At 17th St.*

⑦ ★ **Chelsea Grasslands.** Spring sees daffodils and hundreds of pink-and-white Lady Jane tulips. By late summer, prairie grasslands bend in the breeze. To the east, you'll spot the needle spire of the Empire State Building. To the west (btw. 18th and 19th sts.) is Frank Gehry's fanciful IAC office building (p 65). Across Eleventh Avenue is the Chelsea Piers sports complex, with a golf driving range atop a Hudson River pier. *Btw. 17th and 19th sts.*

⑧ ★ **Chelsea Thicket.** This dense planting of flowering shrubs and small trees includes hollies, winterberry, and redbud. *Btw. 20th and 21st sts.*

⑨ **Seating Steps & Lawn.** Here, where extra tracks once served as loading decks for adjacent warehouses, is a 4,900-square-foot swath of turf for sunbathing and picnicking. Stepped seating made of reclaimed teak anchors the southern end. At the northern

What Was the High Line?

The railroad built America's Wild West, but it also helped build downtown Manhattan, where street-level freight trains chugged along the city's gritty West Side in the mid-1800s. Alas, as street traffic increased, Tenth Avenue became known as "Death Avenue" for its glut of gruesome accidents. Still, it wasn't until 1929 that the city did something about the problem, elevating miles of railroad track above the fray. The High Line opened in 1934, running from 34th Street to Spring Street. Eventually competition from trucking put it out of business, and in 1980 the last train still using the track was shut down. In 1999, the preservation of the old rail line entered the collective consciousness when the Friends of the High Line was founded by two neighborhood residents. Ten years later, the first section opened to the public.

Strolling along the High Line's landscaped walkway.

end, a rise in the lawn lifts visitors above the walkway, with views of Brooklyn to the east and the Hudson River to the west. *Btw. 22nd and 23rd sts.*

⑩ ★★ Philip A. and Lisa Maria Falcone Flyover. A dense grove of tall shrubs and trees once grew between the tracks here when the trains stopped running. Today, a metal walkway rises 8 feet above the High Line's path, carrying visitors through a leafy sumac-and-magnolia tree line. *Btw. 25th and 26th sts.*

⑪ ★★ Wildflower Field. A landscape dominated by tough drought-resistant grasses and wildflowers took root on the High Line when trains stopped running. The modern-day landscape is planted not only with a variety of blooms, but also with many of the same native species that survived. *Btw. 26th and 29th sts.*

⑫ ★★ 30th Street Cutout & Viewing Platform. This viewing platform allows visitors to peer down through the grid of steel beams and girders to the traffic passing below on 30th Street. *At 30th St.*

⑬ ★★ The Spur. Jutting over Tenth Avenue, the plinth here houses monumental contemporary artworks. *At 30th St. and Tenth Ave.*

⑭ ★★ Pershing Square Beams. What's a park without a playground? In this section over the rail yards, the viaduct's original beams were exposed and coated with rubber to create a jungle gym. *At 31st St.*

⑮ ★★★ West Side Rail Yards extension. This stretch makes a wide U because locomotives pulling heavy boxcars needed extra room to climb from street level up to the elevated tracks. It's a little wilder than other areas. On one side you get views of still-working train tracks on the other side you get the closest river views that the High Line affords. *Btw. 31st and 34th sts.*

Green-Wood Cemetery

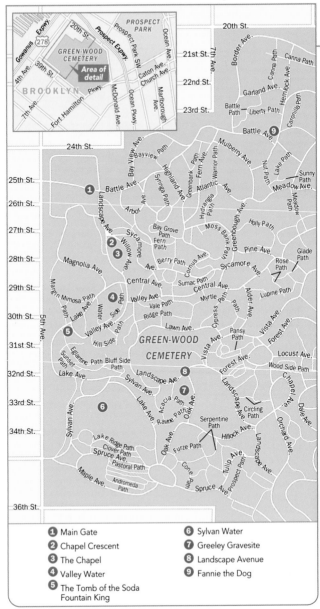

1 Main Gate

2 Chapel Crescent

3 The Chapel

4 Valley Water

5 The Tomb of the Soda Fountain King

6 Sylvan Water

7 Greeley Gravesite

8 Landscape Avenue

9 Fannie the Dog

"It is the ambition of the New Yorker to live upon Fifth Avenue, to take his airings in the Park, and to sleep with his fathers in Green-Wood." So declared the *New York Times* in 1866. Today, Brooklyn's 1838 Green-Wood Cemetery is a great place to revel in the outdoors, with 438 scenic acres and countless ornate mausoleums.

❶ **★★ Main Gate.** Green-Wood has five entrances, but this Gothic gate with spires that stretch church-like into the sky is by far the most spectacular. A New York City Historic Landmark, it was built from 1861 to 1865 by architect Richard M. Upjohn. At the information booth inside, you can pick up a free map of the grounds. It lists the many famous (and infamous) residents—some 600,000 in all. These include Samuel Morse, Henry Ward Beecher, Leonard Bernstein, Boss Tweed, Nathaniel Currier and James Ives, Jean-Michel Basquiat, and hundreds of Civil War soldiers. A self-guided walking tour app is free. The cemetery also hosts excellent trolley tours. ⏱ *2 hr. 500 25th St. (at Fifth Ave.), Brooklyn. www. green-wood.com.* ☎ *718/768-7300. Daily 8am–5pm (extended hours in summer). Trolley tours $20. Subway: N/R to 25th St. in Brooklyn.*

❷ **★ Chapel Crescent.** Green-Wood's grand chapel (see below) is surrounded by stunning tombs. The B. Stephens tomb is shaped like a small Egyptian pyramid. The Chambettaz tomb has an angel statue overlooking the crescent as well as symbols from the secret society of the Freemasons.

❸ **★★★ The Chapel.** A few minutes' walk from the main gates is Green-Wood's crowning glory. The 1911 chapel is a relatively recent arrival, its design inspired by Tom Tower at Oxford's Christ Church College, a 17th-century work by architect Christopher Wren. The multi-domed structure is built entirely of Indiana limestone.

The stately Chapel in Green-Wood Cemetery.

The small interior frequently hosts readings and special exhibits that explore funerary art. Check **www. green-wood.com** for a calendar of events.

❹ **Valley Water.** Some of Green-Wood's ponds have been filled in to create new burial plots, but happily this stunning one remains. The avenue that curves around Valley Water is a treasure trove of 19th-century sculpture. Many of the monuments are partially draped by a carved "cloth." This popular Victorian Resurrectionist style reflected a belief that the body in the grave would rise on Judgment Day, when the cloth would fall away as if pulled back by the hand of God.

❺ **★ The Tomb of the Soda Fountain King.** This towering work of sculpture is really just one

An outdoor movie night on Governors Island.

giant tombstone: In 1870, it won the Mortuary Monument of the Year award. (Didn't know there was such a thing, did you?) This is the resting place of John Matthews, the man who invented the soda fountain—and that information is about the only thing not carved into it. Gargoyles, members of the Matthews family, and Matthews himself are all here.

6 Sylvan Water. The largest body of water in Green-Wood. Sylvan Water is surrounded by a series of tombs, some of which look large enough to house a (living) family.

7 ★ Greeley Gravesite. Horace Greeley was an antislavery advocate who founded the *New York Tribune* and was a national figure. ("Go West, young man" is one of his famous aphorisms.) The views from his family plot are lovely.

8 Landscape Avenue. This winding avenue offers memorable vistas and some great statuary.

9 Fannie the Dog. Anyone who has ever loved a pet will relate to the engraving on the headstone of Fannie, sewing-machine inventor Elias Howe's pooch: "FROSTS OF WINTER NOR HEAT OF SUMMER / COULD MAKE HER FAIL IF MY FOOTSTEPS LED / AND MEMORY HOLDS IN ITS TREASURE CASKET / THE NAME OF MY DARLING WHO LIES DEAD."

Governors Island

A military base for 200 years, this 172-acre island—just a short (free) ferry ride from lower Manhattan—became a public park soon after being decommissioned in 1996. Visitors can explore the island's historic district, including a national monument centered around two 1812 fortresses. But most come to the beguiling automobile-free island for concerts, performances and exhibits, table-tennis championships, kite flying, views, and free walking tours. Info at ☎ 212/440-2200 or **www.govisland.com**. Ferries depart from Battery Maritime Building, Slip #7. Subway: 1 to South Ferry.

Observation Decks

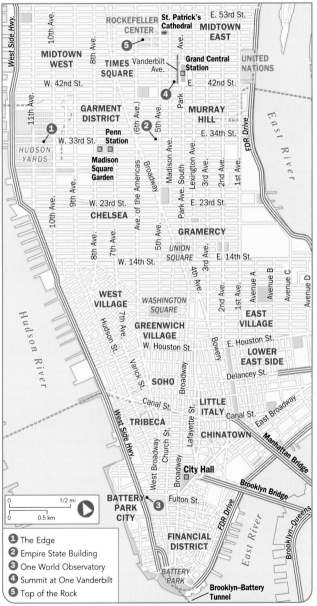

ROCKEFELLER CENTER
St. Patrick's Cathedral
E. 53rd St.
MIDTOWN EAST
UNITED NATIONS
MIDTOWN WEST
TIMES SQUARE
Vanderbilt Ave.
Grand Central Station
GARMENT DISTRICT
W. 42nd St.
E. 42nd St.
(6th Ave.)
5th Ave.
MURRAY HILL
E. 34th St.
Penn Station
W. 33rd St.
HUDSON YARDS
Madison Square Garden
Broadway
Madison Ave.
Park Ave. South
Lexington Ave.
3rd Ave.
2nd Ave.
1st Ave.
FDR Drive
East River
W. 23rd St.
Ave. of the Americas
E. 23rd St.
CHELSEA
5th Ave.
GRAMERCY
UNION SQUARE
4th Ave.
3rd Ave.
2nd Ave.
1st Ave.
W. 14th St.
E. 14th St.
Avenue A
Avenue B
Avenue C
Avenue D
WEST VILLAGE
WASHINGTON SQUARE
EAST VILLAGE
7th Ave.
Hudson St.
GREENWICH VILLAGE
W. Houston St.
E. Houston St.
LOWER EAST SIDE
Bowery
Hudson River
Varick St.
SOHO
Broadway
Delancey St.
West Side Hwy.
Canal St.
LITTLE ITALY
Canal St.
East Broadway
TRIBECA
West Broadway
Church St.
Lafayette St.
CHINATOWN
Manhattan Bridge
City Hall
BATTERY PARK CITY
Fulton St.
Brooklyn Bridge
West Side Hwy.
FDR Drive
FINANCIAL DISTRICT
East River
Brooklyn–Queens
BATTERY PARK
Brooklyn–Battery Tunnel

0   1/2 mi
0   0.5 km

❶ The Edge
❷ Empire State Building
❸ One World Observatory
❹ Summit at One Vanderbilt
❺ Top of the Rock

10th Ave.
8th Ave.
11th Ave.
9th Ave.
7th Ave.
8th Ave.

Recently, going outdoors in Gotham has meant getting up high, where the wind can whip your hair and the view will take your breath away. But with so many observation decks debuting in the last decade or so, choosing the right one has become complicated yet essential—they're pricey, and it's an experience you likely want just once per trip. Here's a quick look at the top contenders.

Visitors to The Edge at Hudson Yards.

★★ The Edge.

Part of the Hudson Yards complex, The Edge juts out from its skyscraper, making it the tallest "sky deck" in the Western Hemisphere. Part of that deck is a thick see-through glass panel that visitors can lie on for a "floating" photo (many do so with a flute of champagne from the deck's bar). On the floor above, the restaurant **Peak** (peaknyc.com) has gourmet American food that's better than it needs to be with these splendid views. The "experience" leading to the view includes exhibits on the engineering and environmental innovations at Hudson Yards. See p. 6 for more.

★★★ Empire State Building.

This oldie is not just a goodie, it's still the bestie, thanks to how the history of this storied structure is presented. Before you even come close to the views, you'll pass through excellent exhibits about the building's remarkably brisk construction, and its place in the American zeitgeist. By the time you get to the top, you realize that you too are part of the building's noble story—a thrill. A word on costs: this can be either the priciest view on this list (if you buy tickets to the indoor 102nd floor, an extra charge) or the least pricey, if you buy a CityPass (www.CityPass.com). For full details go to p. 7.

One World Observatory.

Just next to the 9/11 Memorial and Museum, One World is probably the least satisfying viewpoint because it doesn't have outdoor space, and its location far downtown means it feels like you're looking at the heart of the city through the wrong end of a telescope. See p. 17 for more.

★★ Summit at 1 Vanderbilt.

New in 2021, Summit is in the thick of midtown, so, like the Empire State Building, it has pulsing life all around it and superb views of the iconic Chrysler Building. But what will draw visitors are its thrills: an all-glass elevator (including the floor) that crawls up the side of the building, plus glass-floored areas that jut out for a dizzying view down. It also takes a bit of a psychedelic turn, with mirrored walls and ceilings, floating orbs, sculptures, and light shows. *Entrance in Grand Central Station (42nd St., near Vanderbilt Ave). www.summitov. com. ☎ 877-682-1401. $38 basic entry. Subway: 4/5/6/S to 42nd St.*

★ Top of the Rock.

Mimicking the look of the deck on a 1930's-era passenger liner, Rockefeller Center's apex is a classy place to gaze. While not as tall as the others on this list, at "just" 70 stories, it's the closest to Central Park, giving it a grand view of that expansive swatch of green, as well as midtown Manhattan. To save money consider getting the New York City Pass, which bundles this attraction with several others, at a good overall cost. More info on TOTR on p. 8. ●

Dining Best Bets

Best Places for a Carnivore
Keens $$$ *72 W. 36th St.* (p 124)

Best Vegetarian
Eleven Madison Park $$$ (p. 121)
Eleven Madison Ave.

Best French
Le Bernardin $$$$ *55 W. 51st St.*
(p 125)

Best Cheap Eats
Xian Famous Foods $ *37 W. 43rd
St. and other locations* (p 128) and
Los Tacos No. 1 $ *229 W. 43rd St.*
(p 125)

Best Chinese
Hao Noodle $$ *343 W. 14th St.*
(p 123)

Best Party
Berimbau $$ *47 Carmine St.* (p. 118)

Best Fusion Cuisine
Mokyo $$ *109 St. Marks Place*
(p. 126)

Best Delis
Barney Greengrass $ *541 Amster-
dam Ave.* (p 118) and Katz's $ *205
E. Houston St.* (p 124)

Best Seafood
Le Bernardin $$$$ *55 W. 51st St.*
(p 125)

Best Splurge
Blue Hill $$$$ *74 Washington Place*
(p. 119)

Best Italian
Via Carota $$$ *51 Grove St.* (p 128)

Best New Restaurant
Iris $$$ *1740 Broadway* (p. 123)

Best for Families
Gyu Kaku $ *321 W. 44th St.* (p 123)

Restaurant Week: Prix-Fixe Dining

Everyone loves a deal, and Restaurant Week is one of New York's best. It started more than a decade ago, when some of the city's best dining spots began to offer three courses for a fixed low price at lunch ($29) and dinner ($42). Now it's an institution that lasts for several weeks in January and July/August. Check out **www. opentable.com** or **www.nycvisit.com** for more info on participating restaurants.

Previous page: Outdoor dining at The Fulton overlooks the Brooklyn Bridge.

Downtown Dining

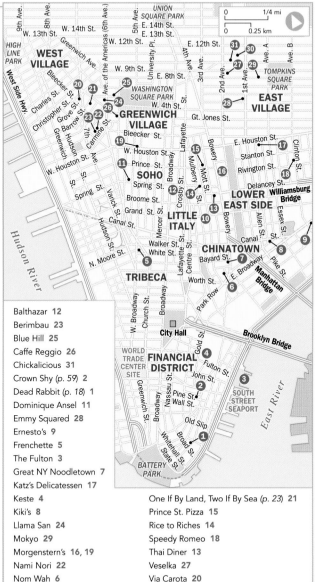

Balthazar **12**

Berimbau **23**

Blue Hill **25**

Caffe Reggio **26**

Chickalicious **31**

Crown Shy (*p. 59*) **2**

Dead Rabbit (*p. 18*) **1**

Dominique Ansel **11**

Emmy Squared **28**

Ernesto's **9**

Frenchette **5**

The Fulton **3**

Great NY Noodletown **7**

Katz's Delicatessen **17**

Keste **4**

Kiki's **8**

Llama San **24**

Mokyo **29**

Morgenstern's **16, 19**

Nami Nori **22**

Nom Wah **6**

Nyonya **10**

One If By Land, Two If By Sea (*p. 23*) **21**

Prince St. Pizza **15**

Rice to Riches **14**

Speedy Romeo **18**

Thai Diner **13**

Veselka **27**

Via Carota **20**

Venieros **30**

Midtown & Uptown Dining

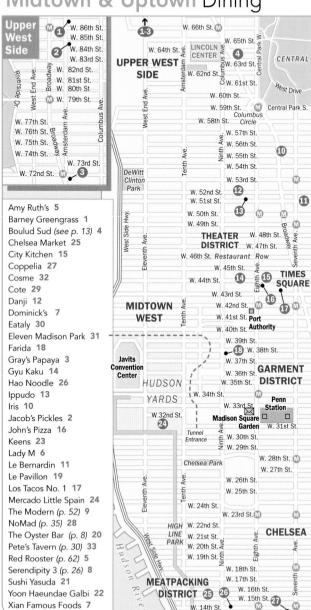

Amy Ruth's **5**
Barney Greengrass **1**
Boulud Sud (see p. 13) **4**
Chelsea Market **25**
City Kitchen **15**
Coppelia **27**
Cosme **32**
Cote **29**
Danji **12**
Dominick's **7**
Eataly **30**
Eleven Madison Park **31**
Farida **18**
Gray's Papaya **3**
Gyu Kaku **14**
Hao Noodle **26**
Ippudo **13**
Iris **10**
Jacob's Pickles **2**
John's Pizza **16**
Keens **23**
Lady M **6**
Le Bernardin **11**
Le Pavillon **19**
Los Tacos No. 1 **17**
Mercado Little Spain **24**
The Modern (p. 52) **9**
NoMad (p. 35) **8**
The Oyster Bar (p. 8) **20**
Pete's Tavern (p. 30) **33**
Red Rooster (p. 62) **5**
Serendipity 3 (p. 26) **8**
Sushi Yasuda **21**
Yoon Haeundae Galbi **22**
Xian Famous Foods **7**

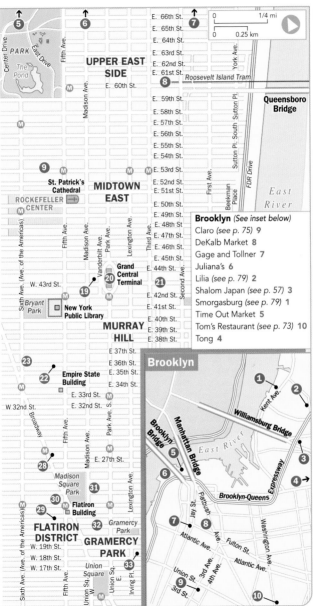

UPPER EAST SIDE

PARK
The Pond
Center Drive
East Drive

E. 66th St.
E. 65th St.
E. 64th St.
E. 63rd St.
E. 62nd St.
E. 61st St.
Roosevelt Island Tram

York Ave.
Fifth Ave.
Madison Ave.

E. 60th St.
E. 59th St.
E. 58th St.
E. 57th St.
E. 56th St.
E. 55th St.
E. 54th St.
E. 53rd St.
E. 52nd St.
E. 51st St.
E. 50th St.
E. 49th St.
E. 48th St
E. 47th St.
E. 46th St.
E. 45th St.
E. 44th St.
E. 43rd St.
E. 42nd St.
E. 41st St.
E. 40th St.
E. 39th St.
E. 38th St.

Queensboro Bridge

Sutton Pl. South Sutton Pl.
First Ave.
Beekman Place
FDR Drive

East River

St. Patrick's Cathedral
ROCKEFELLER CENTER
MIDTOWN EAST

Fifth Ave. (Ave. of the Americas)
Madison Ave.
Park Ave.
Vanderbilt Ave.
Lexington Ave.
Third Ave.
Second Ave.

Grand Central Terminal

W. 43rd St.
Bryant Park
New York Public Library

MURRAY HILL

Brooklyn *(See inset below)*
Claro *(see p. 75)* 9
DeKalb Market 8
Gage and Tollner 7
Juliana's 6
Lilia *(see p. 79)* 2
Shalom Japan *(see p. 57)* 3
Smorgasburg *(see p. 79)* 1
Time Out Market 5
Tom's Restaurant *(see p. 73)* 10
Tong 4

E 37th St.
E. 36th St.
E. 35th St.
E. 34th St.
E. 33rd St.
E. 32nd St. S.

Empire State Building

W 32nd St.
Broadway
Fifth Ave.
Madison Ave.
Park Ave.

E. 27th St.

Madison Square Park

Flatiron Building

FLATIRON DISTRICT
W. 19th St.
W. 18th St.
W. 17th St.
Sixth Ave. (Ave. of the Americas)
Fifth Ave.

Gramercy Park
GRAMERCY PARK

Union Square
Union Sq. W.
Union Sq. E.
Irving Pl.

Brooklyn

Kent Ave.
Williamsburg Bridge
Brooklyn Bridge
Manhattan Bridge
East River
Brooklyn-Queens Expressway
Washington Ave.
Flatbush Ave.
Jay St.
Atlantic Ave.
Fulton St.
3rd Ave.
4th Ave.
Union St.
3rd St.

0   1/4 mi
0   0.25 km

Restaurants A to Z

Adda Indian Canteen draws foodie crowds to Queens.

★★★ Adda Indian Canteen

QUEENS *INDIAN* No punches are pulled spice-wise at this wonderfully authentic newcomer, which brings foodie crowds to this obscure but easy-to-get-to corner of Queens. Star dishes: goat *biriyani* encased in *naan* dough, and *saag paneer* made with seasonal greens and house-made cheese. Named one of the best new U.S. restaurants by several prominent magazines. *31–31 Thomson Ave. www.addanyc.com.* ☎ *718/433-3888. Entrees $12–$25. AE, DC, DISC, MC, V. Lunch and dinner Mon–Sat. Subway: E/M/R Queens Plaza.*

★ Amy Ruth's HARLEM

AMERICAN The best soul food uptown—the chicken and waffles are topped with honey from an apiary on the roof. *113 W. 116th St. www.amyruthsharlem.com.* ☎ *212/280-8779. Main courses $10–$20. AE, DC, MC, V. Breakfast, lunch, and dinner daily. Subway: 2, 3, B, C to 116th St.*

★ Balthazar SOHO *FRENCH*

The quintessential Parisian-style brasserie. Not only does Balthazar look picture-perfect, with its zinc bar, smoked mirrors, soaring ceiling, and serious, vest-wearing waiters, the food hits the mark as well. *80 Spring St. (btw. Broadway and Crosby St.). www.balthazarny.com.* ☎ *212/965-1414. Main courses $11–$43. AE, DC, DISC, MC, V. Breakfast, lunch, dinner, and late-night dining. Subway: 6 to Spring St, N/R to Prince St.*

★ Barney Greengrass UPPER

WEST SIDE *DELI* The Sturgeon King has been selling lox and bagels for a century at this favorite weekend brunch spot. The vintage counters and dairy case are beautiful. *541 Amsterdam Ave. (btw. 86th and 87th sts.). www.barney greengrass.com.* ☎ *212/724-4707. Main courses $5–$22, smoked-fish platters $34–$56. AE, MC, V. Breakfast and lunch (or brunch) Tues–Sun. Subway: 1/9 to 86th St.*

★★ Berimbau GREENWICH

VILLAGE *BRAZILIAN* Meals here are a party, thanks to a boppy soundtrack and creative caipirinha menu. Berimbau's coconut-laced entrees, while new to most diners,

Balthazar Restaurant.

Foodie Food Halls

Forget Aunt Annie's pretzels. Gotham's food courts are dazzling displays, with food from every corner of the globe and almost every star chef in the city. My faves include the all-Iberian **Mercado Little Spain** (Hudson Yards, see p 67) and **Eataly** (see p 94), for Italian delights. Other halls mix cuisines from different cultures, such as **Chelsea Market** (75 Ninth Ave. between 15th and 16th sts., Chelsea; www.chelseamarket.com), known for Jamaican jerk chicken, halvah, and Mexico City–style burritos; **Dekalb Market** (at 445 Albee Sq. W. in downtown Brooklyn; www.dekalbmarkethall. com), which has the only Katz Deli offshoot and great Hong Kong cuisine; **Time Out Market** (55 Water St. in Dumbo, Brooklyn; www. timeoutmarket.com) which is half cocktail bars, half ethnic food; and **City Kitchen,** just off Times Square, for fab ramen, gourmet donuts, and Persian sandwiches (it's at 700 Eighth Ave at 44th St., 2nd floor; http://citykitchen.rownyc.com). **Smorgasburg** in Brooklyn (p 79) is as much of a weekend event as it is a place to get grub.

are comforting rather than wildly spicy or challenging. *43 Carmine St. (btw Bedford and Bleecker Sts.) www.berimbaunyc.com.* ☎ *212/206-6900. Entrees $21-$28. AE, MC, V. Lunch, brunch (weekends) and dinner daily. Subway: A/C/E/B/D/F to West 4th St.*

★★★ Blue Hill GREENWICH VILLAGE *AMERICAN* This soothing, understated Village townhouse space quietly goes about its business serving some of the most delicious food in town, with an admirable sustainable-foods philosophy. Chef Dan Barber coaxes the

Berimbau's sidewalk cabin, for indoor/outdoor dining.

best out of the best ingredients. Even lowly brussels sprouts become irresistible. *75 Washington Place (btw. Sixth Ave. and Washington Sq. W.). www.bluehillfarm.com.* ☎ *212/539-1776. Tasting menu $95–$108. AE, DC, MC, V. Dinner daily. Subway: B/D/F/M/A/C/E to W. 4th St.*

★ **Coppelia** CHELSEA *LATIN AMERICAN* Diner-like on the outside, inside is another world. Coppelia's soundtrack is salsa, its decor is tropical, and the menu ranges across the Caribbean and Latin America, offering up perfect renditions of *lomo saltado* (Peruvian tomato and ginger beef stir-fry), Cuban roast pork with *chicharons,* and Brazilian sweet-corn *empanadas. 207 W. 14th St. (near Seventh Ave.). https://ILoveCoppelia.com.* ☎ *212/858-5001. Main courses $7–$18. AE, DC, DISC, MC, V. Daily 24 hr. Subway: 1/2/3 to 14th St.*

★★★ **Cosme** MIDTOWN EAST *MEXICAN* Cosme was the first U.S. restaurant from Enrique Olvera, owner of Mexico City's iconic Pujol Restaurant (named the 20th best restaurant in the world by the Diner's Club Academy). It brings to New York the kind of contemporary, deeply luxurious Mexican food that it had yet to experience. *Tip:* If you can't get a reservation, go anyway. There's a lot of seating for walk-ins at the front. *35 E. 21st St. (btw. Broadway and Park Ave. South). www.cosmenyc.com.* ☎ *212/913-9659. Main courses $28–$59. AE, DC, DISC, MC, V. Lunch and dinner daily. Subway: 6/N/R to 23rd St.*

★★★ **Cote** FLATIRON DISTRICT *STEAK* Yes, the city's best new steakhouse is Korean. The meat cuts like butter, and the waiters cook it at a grill in your table. *16 W. 22nd St. (off Fifth Ave.). www.cote nyc.com.* ☎ *212/401-7986. Meals*

Eleven Madison Park.

$47 and up. AE, MC, DC, V. Dinner daily. Subway: 6/N/R to 23rd St.

★★ **Danji** THEATER DISTRICT *KOREAN* Danji reinvents Korean classics in odd but very tasty ways. That might mean a kimchee, bacon, and Spam paella, or tofu infused with ginger before being flash-fried. Young chef Hooni Kim got his chops cooking for such master chefs as Daniel Boulud. *Warning:* The flavors are big here, but the space is tiny, so you *will* get to know your neighbor. *346 W. 52nd St. (btw. Eighth and Ninth aves.). www.danjinyc.com.* ☎ *212/586-2880. Main courses $13–$26, with most in the teens. AE, MC, V. Lunch and dinner Mon–Sat. Subway: C/E to 50th St.*

★★ **Dominick's** THE BRONX *ITALIAN* The dining room is all shared tables, topped with oilcloth, and the wait can be long on weekend evenings. But hang in and you'll be well taken care of by the gruff but friendly waitstaff at this legendary spot, which has no menus and no checks. You want some clams to start? A salad or a seafood pasta maybe? Yes, yes, and yes. *2335 Arthur Ave. (btw. 187th St. and Crescent Ave.).* ☎ *718/733-2807. Entrees $10–$25. Cash only. Lunch and dinner Wed–Mon. Take a taxi/Uber (subway very far away).*

★★★ Eleven Madison Park

FLATIRON DISTRICT *VEGAN* Chef Daniel Humm has won every award in the book (including a James Beard award—the culinary world's Oscar—for best in the U.S.). In 2021, he made headlines by taking this iconic restaurant vegan. But with the splendid Art Deco setting and the level of gastronomic artistry going on here, most diners won't miss the meat, fish and dairy. *11 Madison Ave. (at 24th St.). www.elevenmadisonpark.com.* ☎ *212/889-0905. Tasting menu $335. AE, DC, DISC, MC, V. Lunch Mon–Sat, dinner daily. Subway: N/R/6 to 23rd St.*

★★★ Ernesto's

LOWER EAST SIDE *SPANISH* Ernest Hemingway, the restaurant's namesake, would feel right at home in this Art Nouveau gem, tucking into the type of hearty Basque fare served at taverns in San Sebastian. The

Enjoying octopus salad and a cocktail at one of Ernesto's sidewalk tables.

waiters will push you to over-order: don't. *259 E. Broadway (at Montgomery St.) www.ernestosnyc.com.* ☎ *646/692-8300. Entrees $16-$40. AE, MC, V. Dinner Tues–Sat. Subway: F to East Broadway.*

★ Farida

MIDTOWN WEST *CENTRAL ASIAN* "Very nice!" That's the review we could see Borat giving this hole-in-the-wall eatery, which serves the dumplings, kebabs, and pilafs of Kazakhstan and Uzbekistan. You dine on this fresh, tasty fare in a cozy room adorned

Authentic Uzbek plov (pilaf) sided by beet salad, at Farida.

Sweets for the Sweet

When it comes to desserts, the Big Apple has definite polish. Here are just a few places where you can destroy your diet with glee. Downtown **Morgenstern's** (88 West Houston and 2 Rivington sts.; www.morgensternnyc.com) serves the finest ice cream known to man (especially the Vietnamese Coffee). **Chikalicious** (203 E. 10th St., off Second Ave.; www.chikalicious.com) is a dessert-only restaurant where all customers get a marvelous three-course tasting menu for $19, while nearby **Venieros** (342 E. 11th St. at First Ave.; www.venierospastry.com) is a beloved Italian bakery in business since 1894. SoHo's **Dominique Ansel** (189 Spring St., btw. Thompson and Sullivan sts.; www.dominqueansel.com) sells not just Ansel's famous "cronuts," but also wonderful and very French pastries of all sorts. A few blocks east, **Rice to Riches** (37 Spring St., btw. Mott and Mulberry sts.; www.ricetoriches.com; ☎ 212/274-0008) is a delightful one-trick pony—it serves only rice pudding, but tarted up with all sorts of exotic flavorings. **Lady M Cake Boutique** (41 E. 78th St. near Madison Ave. and other locations; www.ladym.com) whips up crepe cakes to die for.

with homeland knick-knacks (a lot of which are weapons, oddly). *498 Ninth Ave. (btw. 37th and 38th sts). www.farida.us.* ☎ *646/863-2020. Entrees $14-$32. AE, MC, V. Lunch and dinner daily. Subway: A/C/E to 42nd St.*

★★ Frenchette TRIBECA *FRENCH* Taking a cue from the *neo-bistros* of Paris (traditional-looking places that put a creative spin on Gallic fare), Frenchette has become Manhattan's top date place. Just getting a reservation impresses, and then the cozy booths, perfectly lit by yellowed globe lights, up the romance quotient. The food, too, is sexy, like the softly scrambled eggs with escargot. And if picking up the hefty check here doesn't say "I love you," I don't know what does. *241 W. Broadway (btw. Walker and White sts.). www.frenchettenyc.com.* ☎ *212/334-3883. Main courses $34–$64. AE, DC, DISC, MC, V. Lunch and*

dinner Mon–Fri, brunch and dinner Sat–Sun. *Subway: 1 to Franklin St.*

★★ The Fulton SEAPORT DISTRICT*SEAFOOD* Eye-popping Brooklyn Bridge and river views, plus fresh fish cooked by master chef Jean Georges Vongrichten, have made The Fulton one of the city's top "special occasion meal" choices. *89 South St. (on Pier 17). www.thefulton.com.* ☎ *212/838-1200. Main courses $21–$50, AE, MC, V. Dinner daily. Subway: A/C/E/F/B/D to 4th St.*

★★★ Gage & Tollner BROOK-LYN *AMERICAN* From 1879 to its closing in 2004, this was one of the finest chop and oyster houses in Brooklyn. This re-do brings back the glorious Belle Epoque trappings and many of the recipes—she-crab soup, oysters Rockefeller, baked Alaska. It's a splendid, fun time machine. *372 Fulton St. (at Smith St.) www.gageandtollner.com.*

☎ 347-689-3677. Entrees $27–$58.
AE, DISC, MC, V. Dinner Wed-Sun.
A/C/F/N/R to Jay St.

Gray's Papaya UPPER WEST
SIDE *HOT DOGS*   Gray's Papaya
serves the best—and cheapest—
dogs in the city. Open 24 hours,
the Gray's outpost on the Upper
West Side is an institution. *2090
Broadway (at 72nd St.).* ☎ *212/799-
0243. Hot dogs $2. Cash only. Sub-
way: 1/2/3 to 72nd St.*

★★ Great NY Noodletown
CHINATOWN *CHINESE*   Don't be
fooled by the run-down diner
appearance; the food here may be
the best in Chinatown. The salt-
baked shrimp is as good as you'll
find anywhere, and the platters of
roast pig, roast pork (yes, there is a
difference), and spareribs on rice
are irresistible. Whatever you order
is very easy on the wallet, adding to
Noodletown's immense appeal. *28
Bowery (at Bayard St.). www.greatny
noodletown.com.* ☎ *212/349-0923.
Platters/soups $6–$16. Cash only.
Breakfast, lunch, and dinner daily.
Subway: N/R/6 to Canal St.*

★ kids Gyu-Kaku THEATER
DISTRICT *JAPANESE BBQ*   Think
Benihana, but with *you* as the chef.
Diners choose proteins and veg-
gies, and then cook them them-
selves on a sizzling metal tabletop,
dipping them in three splendid
sauces. It's great fun, delicious, and
kids love it. *321 W. 44th St. (btw.
Eighth and Ninth aves.). www.gyu-
kaku.com.* ☎ *646/692-9115. Average meal $17–$21. AE, DC, DISC,
MC, V. Lunch and dinner daily. Subway: A/C/E to 42nd St.*

★★ Hao Noodle CHELSEA
CHINESE   NYC is experiencing a
Chinese food renaissance, with
some of that country's most cele-
brated chefs opening offshoots in
Gotham. Hao is among the

choicest of them, serving mostly
Shanghai cuisine, from deliciously
fiery *lan shan* chicken to ambrosial
pea shoots sautéed in wine and
garlic. *343 W. 14th St. (near Ninth
Ave.). https://haonoodle.com.*
☎ *646/882-0059. Entrees $9–$22.
AE, MC, V. Lunch and dinner daily.
Subway: A/C/E/L to 14th St.*

★★★ Ippudo THEATER DISTRICT
JAPANESE   Ramen can be life-
changing. That may sound hyper-
bolic, but try the silky soups here,
made from the finest Berkshire pork
and filled with toothsome noodles,
and you'll see I'm right. Also at 65
Fourth Ave. *321 West 51st St. (btw.
Eighth and Ninth aves). www.ippudo
ny.com.* ☎ *212/974-2500. Main
courses $15–$18. AE, MC, V. Lunch
and dinner daily. Subway: C/E to
51st St.*

★★★ Iris MIDTOWN WEST
GREEK   Our top pick for a cele-
bratory pre-Broadway show meal,
Iris has a sleek, ultra-modern look
that belies the passionate cooking
Chef John Fraser is doing here. Get

Ramen at Ippudo.

Katz's Deli.

ready for a rapturously rich, surprising meal, one that goes deep into authentic Greek and Turkish recipes using mastic, sorrel, purslane, and other unusual ingredients in its spreads, lamb, and fish offerings. Primo cocktails, too. *1740 Broadway (at 55th St.). www.irisrestaurant.nyc. No phone. Entrees $26-$48. AE, MC, V. Tues-Sun 5-9:45pm. Subway: N, Q, R, W to 57th or B, D to Seventh Ave.*

★ **Jacob's Pickles** UPPER WEST SIDE *AMERICAN* Pickles, pickups, and artisanal beers: Those are the holy trinity at this buzzy tavern. It's become THE place for the neighborhood's singles, who scope one another out over some of the finest comfort food in town, like fried chicken atop huge, flaky biscuits, and creamy grits with head-on shrimp. *509 Amsterdam Ave. (btw. 84th and 85th sts.). www.jacobs pickles.com. ☎ 212/470-5566. AE, DISC, MC, V. Brunch (starting at 10am) through late night daily. Subway: 1, B, C to 86th St.*

★ **Katz's Delicatessen** LOWER EAST SIDE *DELI* Founded in 1888, this homely, cacophonous space is one of the city's last great old-time delis. No one makes a better pastrami sandwich. Plus, you can see the spot where Meg Ryan performed her famous scene in *When Harry Met Sally*. *205 E. Houston St. (at Ludlow St.). www.katzdeli.com. ☎ 212/254-2246. Sandwiches $3–$10, other items $5–$18. AE, MC, V. Breakfast, lunch, and dinner daily. Subway: F to Second Ave.*

★★ **Keens** MIDTOWN WEST *STEAK* If you're searching for olde New York, look no further than this 1885 survivor tucked away on a side street near Madison Square Garden. The space has always been wonderful; now the food is its equal. *72 W. 36th St. (at Sixth Ave.). www.keens.com. ☎ 212/947-3636. Main courses $28–$64. AE, DC, DISC, MC, V. Lunch and dinner Mon–Fri, dinner Sat and Sun. Subway: 1/2/3/9 to 34th St./Penn Station.*

★★ **Kiki's** LOWER EAST SIDE *GREEK* Here's a unicorn: a sit-down restaurant in Manhattan with prices that seem slightly too *low* for the high-quality fare you'll be served (classic Greek dishes like

The tofu shrimp crispy rice at Llama San.

Los Tacos No, 1.

roasted whole fish, grilled octopus, spreads with pita). Oddly, its awning has only Chinese characters, so look for the number, not the name. *130 Division St. (at Orchard St.). No website.* ☎ *646/882-7052. Average entrees $10–$15. AE, MC, V. Lunch and dinner daily. Subway: F to East Broadway.*

★★★ **Le Bernardin** MIDTOWN WEST *FRENCH/SEAFOOD* Chef Eric Ripert is a giant on the NYC culinary scene and a master with seafood. The formal service is impeccable. *55 W. 51st St. (btw. Sixth and Seventh aves.). www. le-bernardin.com.* ☎ *212/489-1515. Prix-fixe dinner $165, tasting menu $228. AE, DC, DISC, MC, V. Lunch Mon–Fri, dinner Mon–Sat. Subway: N/R to 49th St.; 1/9 to 50th St.*

★★ **Le Pavillon** MIDTOWN EAST *AMERICAN* An oasis of serenity next to Grand Central Station, Chef Daniel Boulud's latest has pampering down pat. The staff treat each guest like a long-lost cousin, the food is superb, and the setting, with its soaring ceiling and indoor garden (including mature olive trees) is like a long exhale. The only sharp gasp? When you get the

check. *1 Vanderbilt (at 42nd St.). www.lepavillon.com.* ☎ *212/662-1000. $125 tasting menu, a la carte at the bar. AE, MC, V. Dinner Wed-Sat. Subway: 4/5/6/S to Grand Central.*

★★ **Llama San** GREENWICH VILLAGE *NIKKEI* In the late 19th century, a number of Japanese "gold-rushers" moved to Peru and created an exquisite hybrid cuisine featuring techniques and ingredients from both traditions. It's a match made in foodie heaven, especially the ceviches/sashimis. *359 6th Ave. (at Washington St.). www.llamasannyc.com.* ☎ *646/490-4422. Entrees $24–$36. AE, MC, V. Daily 5–11pm. Subway: A/B/C/D/E/F to West 4th St.*

★ **Los Tacos No. 1** TIMES SQUARE *MEXICAN* The Latin music blares as lines of office workers await their midday treat: the perfect taco or tortilla, blazing with flavor and heat, quickly prepared and quickly downed (there are no seats, just counters to stand at). A bona fide taste of Tijuana. *Tip:* If you're averse to spice, ask the cooks to make yours without salsa, and then add milder sauce at the

New York's Pizza Universe

A pizza place can be found on almost every city block, but many aren't worth the $3 advertised for a slice. While in NYC, stick to the standouts, of which there are many, of many different traditions. For **NEW YORK–STYLE** (round, thin crust, sweet sauce):

- **John's Pizza ★** (260 W. 44th St.; www.johnpizzerianyc.com)
- **Juliana's ★★** (19 Old Fulton St., Brooklyn; julianaspizza.com)
- **Prince Street Pizza ★★★** (27 Prince St.)—the pepperoni masters!

NEAPOLITAN STYLE (thin and tender crust, more complex sauce):
- **Totonno's ★★** (1524 Neptune Ave., Coney Island, Brooklyn; www.totonnosconeyisland.com)
- **Keste ★★★** (271 Bleecker St.; www.kestepizzeria.com)

OTHER STYLES:
- **Emmy Squared ★** Detroit-style square pizza, sometimes with ranch dressing (83 First Ave.; www.emmysquared.com)
- **Speedy Romeo ★** St. Louis–style, very yeasty and often with béchamel sauce (62 Clinton St.; www.speedyromeo.com)

Note: All of these are sit-down restaurants (except for Prince Street Pizza), and serve alcoholic beverages.

condiments station. *229 W. 43rd St. (off Times Square). www.lostacos1. com.* ☎ *212/574-4696. Tacos $3.50–$4. AE, MC, V. Lunch and dinner daily. Subway: 1/2/3/N/Q/R/S to Times Square. Also in Grand Central Station and Chelsea Market.*

Mokyo's paprika octopus stew.

★★ Mokyo EAST VILLAGE *FUSION* A science fiction meal. The influences and ingredients are so disparate here—a Korean version of gumbo, mascarpone with pop rocks, dumplings filled with Mexican-style corn–that they feel like they were created by a very talented ET. Did we mention cocktails come in plastic bags that light up? *109 St. Marks Place (btw First Ave. and Avenue A). www.mokyony.com.* ☎ *No phone. Plates $11-$18. AE, MC, V. Dinner Tues–Sun. Subway: L to First Ave.*

★★ Nami Nori GREENWICH VILLAGE *SUSHI* A sushi dinner, created by alums of the city's most prestigious Japanese restaurants, for less than $30? That's the lure here, as are creative temaki, featuring wonderfully fresh seafood, and such extras as XO sauce, gobo

Nami Nori's temaki kit is fun to use and absolutely delicious.

chips, and yuzu aioli. The vegan sushi options rock, too. *33 Carmine St. (btw Bedford and Bleecker Sts.).* naminori.nyc. ☎ *646/998-4588. Temaki set $28. AE, MC, V. Daily noon–10pm. Subway: A/C/E/B/D/F to West 4th St.*

★ **Nyonya** LITTLE ITALY *MALAYSIAN* Spacious, bustling, and inexpensive, Nyonya introduces diners to this wonderfully varied cuisine. Try the *roti canai* (a pancake with a curry chicken dipping sauce). *199 Grand St. (btw. Mulberry and Mott sts.). www.ilovenyonya. com.* ☎ *212/619-0085. Entrees $6–$23. Cash only. Lunch and dinner daily. Subway: 6 to Spring St.*

★★★ **Sushi Yasuda** MIDTOWN EAST *JAPANESE* Pure Japanese sushi, as it's been made for centuries (that is, no mayonnaise or other fusion touches), cut, dabbed with soy sauce, and patted into shape by master chefs. That's the zen formula here, and it can't be improved on. *Tip:* Go for the nigiri sushi rather than rolls; with fish this meltingly tender, you don't want it buried in a lot of rice. *204 E. 43rd St. (btw. Second and Third aves.).*

www.sushiyasuda.com. ☎ *212/972-2001. Sushi $5–$17 per piece, including gratuities. AE, MC, V. Lunch and dinner Mon–Sat. Subway: 4/5/6/7/S to 42nd St.–Grand Central.*

★★ **Thai Diner** NOLITA *THAI* Fun, kitschy decor belies the serious ambitions of the chef/owners, a married pair who met working at California's famed Per Se restaurant. Their version of Thai food is complex, toothsome, and often surprising, with many dishes the U.S. hasn't seen before; such standards as massaman curry and pad thai are stripped of cloying sweetness and endowed with a punch of spice. *186 Mott St. (at Kenmare St.). www. thaidiner.com.* ☎ *646/559-4140. Entrees $12–$25. AE, DISC, MC, V. Daily 11am–10pm. Subway: N/Q/R/6 to Canal St.*

★★ **Tong** BUSHWICK BROOKLYN *ISAN THAI* You come to NYC to have just this type of culinary experience: a deep dive into a cuisine rarely found in the U.S., in a groovy setting, among groovy people. The menu revolves around traditional kub klaem, "drinking snacks" like grilled chile octopus or beef

Chic, stylish Via Carota also wows with its Italian flavors.

tartare, which can be fiery (to encourage thirst) so alert the waiter if you're spice averse. *321 Starr St. (nr Cypress Ave.) www.tongbrooklyn. com.* ☎ *718/366-0586. Entrees $10–$23. AE, MC, V. Daily lunch and dinner. Subway: L to Jefferson St.*

Veselka EAST VILLAGE *UKRANIAN* When Veselka debuted in 1954, this neighborhood was awash in Ukrainian diners (and Ukrainians). As the area changed, the eateries disappeared, leaving this crowded, friendly place as the standard-bearer for borscht, pierogi, kielbasa, and other Eastern European staples. *144 Second Ave. (at 9th St.). www. veselka.com.* ☎ *212/228-9682. Entrees $10–$17. AE, DC, DISC, MC, V. Daily 24 hr. Subway: 6 to Astor Place.*

★★★ Via Carota GREENWICH VILLAGE *ITALIAN La dolce vita* comes to life here: beautiful people in a beautiful room eating beautiful foods. These include fluffy, herb-laden salads, pastas that would make your Italian *nonna* kvell, and stews that seem far too hearty for the models and millionaires who make this their unofficial canteen. Winner "Best Chef" in the 2019 James Beard Awards. *51 Grove St. (near Seventh Ave.). www.viacarota. com.* ☎ *212/475-5829. Main courses $17–$27. AE, DISC, MC, V. Lunch and dinner daily. Subway: 1 to Christopher St. No reservations.*

★★ Yoon Haeundae Galbi MIDTOWN WEST *KOREAN* Koreatown's best BBQ, especially if you get short ribs, which are served every which way here—grilled on your tabletop, or in dumplings, pancakes, stews and soups. *8 West 36th St. (nr Fifth Ave.). yoon-nyc.com.* ☎ *212/244-5345. AE, MC, V. Shared meal from $45 for two. Subway: B/D/ F/N/Q/R to 34th St.*

★★ Xian Famous Foods MIDTOWN WEST *CHINESE* With a laboratory-like white tiled space, Xian seems to be testing just how much spice the human tongue can take before it explodes. It does this in myriad delish noodle dishes, served counter-style. Very authentic, very fast. *37 W. 43rd St. and other locations. www.xianfamous foods.com.* ☎ *212/235-1098. Dishes $7–$13. AE, MC, V. Lunch and dinner daily. Subway: B/D/F/M to Rockefeller Center.* ●

Nightlife **Best Bets**

Best **Old-School Atmosphere**
King Cole Bar, *2 E. 55th St.* (p 136)

Best **Fake Old-School Atmosphere**
The Dead Rabbit, *30 Water St.* (p 18)

Best **Choice of Single-Malt Scotches**
d.b.a., *41 First Ave.* (p 135)

Best **Non-Alcoholic Intoxicants**
Kavasutra, *261 E. 10th St.* (p 136)

Best **Piano Bar**
Marie's Crisis, *59 Grove St.* (p 138)

Best **Cocktails**
Dante, *77 W. Houston St.* (p 134)

Best **Hotel Bar**
Bemelmans Bar, *the Carlyle, 35 E. 76th St.* (p 134)

Best **Museum Bar**
Roof Garden, *Metropolitan Museum of Art, 1000 Fifth Ave.* (p 134)

Best **Bar with a View**
Ophelia Lounge, *3 Mitchell Pl.* (p 135) or Westlight (p 137)

Best **Beer Garden**
Radegast Hall, *see below*

Best **Wine Bar**
Aldo Sohm, *151 W. 51st St.* (p 134)

Take the L Train: Billyburg Bars

Just over the bridge in Brooklyn, Williamsburg, is an arts and nightlife hub (see p 76 for more on the 'hood). To check out some of the city's freshest bars and clubs, take a short ride on the L train from 14th Street in Manhattan to Lorimer Street in Brooklyn. **Union Pool** (www.union-pool.com) is a welcoming bar with a large outdoor space, dance floor with live music, and a post-hipster crowd. **Radegast Hall & Biergarten** (http://radegasthall.com) is just what the name promises, and looks like it was airlifted from Munich. For some of Brooklyn's best indie bands, catch a show (usually without cover) at **Baby's All Right** (http://babysallright.com). For a more formal night of music (top bands, stellar sightlines), head to the **Music Hall of Williamsburg** (www.musichallofwilliamsburg.com)— a sister club to the Bowery Ballroom and Mercury Lounge in Manhattan. And for a romantic night out, choose **Westlight** (http://westlight.com), an indoor/outdoor rooftop bar at the acme of one of the tallest buildings in the neighborhood, the William Vale hotel. The views of the Manhattan skyline are jaw-dropping. Also hit **The Shanty** (p 77).

Previous page: The vintage neon sign of the Dublin House.

Downtown Nightlife

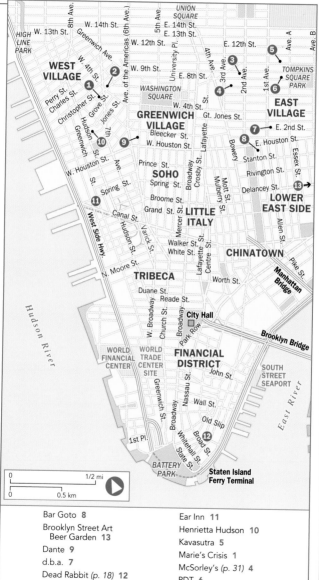

UNION SQUARE

W. 14th St.
W. 13th St.
8th Ave.
HIGH LINE PARK
Greenwich Ave.
W. 4th St.
W. 12th St.
W. 9th St.
W. 4th St.
University Pl.
5th Ave.
Ave. of the Americas (6th Ave.)
E. 14th St.
E. 13th St.
E. 12th St.
E. 8th St.
Ave. A
Ave. B

WEST VILLAGE
Perry St.
Charles St.
Christopher St.
Grove St.
Jones St.
Hudson St.
Greenwich
4th St.
WASHINGTON SQUARE

GREENWICH VILLAGE
Bleecker St.
W. Houston St.
Gt. Jones St.
4th Ave.
3rd Ave.
2nd Ave.
1st Ave.

TOMPKINS SQUARE PARK

EAST VILLAGE
E. 2nd St.
E. Houston St.
Stanton St.
Rivington St.
Delancey St.
Essex St.
Bowery

SOHO
Prince St.
Spring St.
Broome St.
Grand St.
W. Houston St.
Spring St.
Canal St.
Hudson St.
Mercer St.
Crosby St.
Broadway
Lafayette
Mott St.
Mulberry St.
Elizabeth St.

LITTLE ITALY

LOWER EAST SIDE
Allen St.

CHINATOWN
Walker St.
White St.
Worth St.
Lafayette St.
Centre St.
Pike St.
Manhattan Bridge

TRIBECA
West Side Hwy.
Varick St.
N. Moore St.
Duane St.
Reade St.
W. Broadway
Church St.
Park Row

City Hall

Brooklyn Bridge

WORLD FINANCIAL CENTER
WORLD TRADE CENTER SITE

FINANCIAL DISTRICT
John St.
Greenwich St.
Nassau St.
Broadway
Wall St.
Old Slip
Whitehall St.
State St.
Broad St.
1st Pl.

SOUTH STREET SEAPORT

Hudson River
East River

BATTERY PARK
Staten Island Ferry Terminal

0 — 1/2 mi
0 — 0.5 km

Bar Goto **8**

Brooklyn Street Art
   Beer Garden **13**

Dante **9**

d.b.a. **7**

Dead Rabbit (p. 18) **12**

Decibel **3**

Ear Inn **11**

Henrietta Hudson **10**

Kavasutra **5**

Marie's Crisis **1**

McSorley's (p. 31) **4**

PDT **6**

The Stonewall **2**

Midtown & Uptown Nightlife

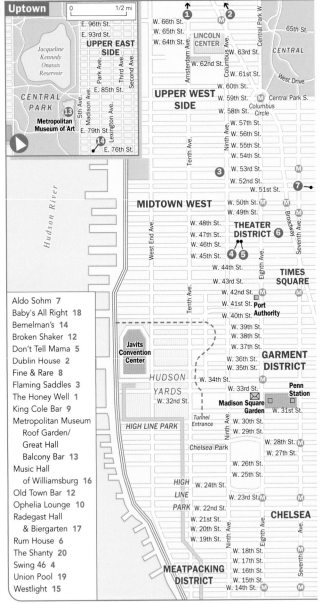

Uptown

0   1/2 mi

E. 96th St.
E. 93rd St.

UPPER EAST SIDE

Jacqueline Kennedy Onassis Reservoir

E. 85th St.

CENTRAL PARK

Park Ave.
Third Ave.
Second Ave.

13

Metropolitan Museum of Art

5th Ave.
Madison Ave.
Lexington Ave.

E. 79th St

14

E. 76th St.

Hudson River

W. 66th St. **1**
W. 65th St. **2**
W. 64th St.

LINCOLN CENTER

Amsterdam Ave.
Columbus Ave.
Central Park W

65th St.

W. 63rd St.

CENTRAL

W. 62nd St.

W. 61st St.

West Drive

W. 60th St.

UPPER WEST SIDE

W. 59th St.   Central Park S.

W. 58th St.   Columbus Circle

W. 57th St.
W. 56th St.
W. 55th St.
W. 54th St.
W. 53rd St.   **3**
W. 52nd St.
W. 51st St.   **7**

Ninth Ave.

MIDTOWN WEST

W. 50th St.
W. 49th St.

W. 48th St.   **THEATER**
W. 47th St.   **DISTRICT 6**
W. 46th St.
W. 45th St.   **4 5**
W. 44th St.

Broadway
Seventh Ave.

West End Ave.

Eighth Ave.

TIMES SQUARE

W. 43rd St.
W. 42nd St.
W. 41st St. **Port**
W. 40th St. **Authority**
W. 39th St.
W. 38th St.
W. 37th St.   **GARMENT**
W. 36th St.   **DISTRICT**
W. 35th St.

Tenth Ave.

Javits Convention Center

W. 34th St.
W. 33rd St.   **Penn Station**

HUDSON YARDS

W. 32nd St.   **Madison Square Garden**   W. 31st St.

Tunnel Entrance

W. 30th St.
W. 29th St.

Ninth Ave.

HIGH LINE PARK

Chelsea Park

W. 28th St.
W. 27th St.

W. 26th St.
W. 25th St.

HIGH LINE PARK   W. 24th St.

W. 23rd St.

CHELSEA

W. 22nd St.
W. 21st St.
W. 20th St.
W. 19th St.

Ninth Ave.
Eighth Ave.
Seventh Ave.

W. 18th St.
W. 17th St.
W. 16th St.

MEATPACKING DISTRICT   W. 15th St.
W. 14th St.

Aldo Sohm **7**
Baby's All Right **18**
Bemelman's **14**
Broken Shaker **12**
Don't Tell Mama **5**
Dublin House **2**
Fine & Rare **8**
Flaming Saddles **3**
The Honey Well **1**
King Cole Bar **9**
Metropolitan Museum
   Roof Garden/
   Great Hall
   Balcony Bar **13**
Music Hall
   of Williamsburg **16**
Old Town Bar **12**
Ophelia Lounge **10**
Radegast Hall
   & Biergarten **17**
Rum House **6**
The Shanty **20**
Swing 46 **4**
Union Pool **19**
Westlight **15**

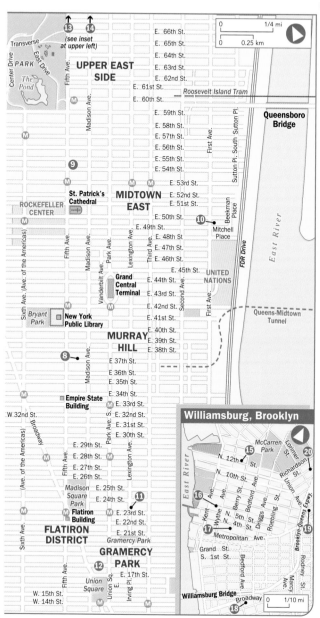

Nightlife A to Z

Bars & Cocktail Lounges

★★ Aldo Sohm TIMES SQUARE
Named for its sommelier/owner, this ultra-classy, contemporary wine bar is the perfect place for a splash after a show. *151 W. 51st (in the courtyard). www.aldosohmwinebar. com.* ☎ *212/554-1113. Subway: 1/2/3/N/Q/R/S to Times Square.*

★★★ Bar Goto LOWER EAST
SIDE   The force behind this sophisticated drinkery, Kenta Goto, formerly of the late great Pegu Club, has put a Japanese spin on its decor, cocktails, and snacks. That might mean liquors mixed with green tea powder, miso, or even a topping of marshmallow. All is served in a woodsy, square room that wouldn't be out of place in Kyoto. *245 Eldridge St. (near E. Houston). www.bargoto.com.* ☎ *212/475-4411. Subway: F to Second Ave.*

Bartender at Bemelmans Bar.

★★ Bemelmans Bar UPPER
EAST SIDE   A playful mural by illustrator Ludwig Bemelmans, author of the *Madeline* children's books, decorates this old-school white-gloved lounge in the Carlyle hotel. Perched at one of the tables set around a piano that tinkles with show standards, you might even forget to check your cell phone while sipping perfectly made classic cocktails. *35 E. 76th St. (at Madison Ave.).* ☎ *212/744-1600. Subway: 6 to 77th St.*

★★★ Broken Shaker FLATIRON
DISTRICT   This indoor/outdoor rooftop tiki bar raises its freak flag with drinks that mix in blueberry jam, taste like a creamsicle, or come with a dreidel floating atop (the "Hebrew Hammer"). Models and the finance bros who squire them seem to be the target audience. *In the Freehand Hotel, 23 E. 23rd St. www.freehandhotels.com. Subway: 6 to 23rd St.*

★★ Brooklyn Street Art Beer
Garden BUSHWICK BROOKLYN Local brewers supply the beers, and borough artists the ever-changing art, at this warm-weather-only venue, which features a sand pit, a gallery space, and a 30-foot bar shack, all set in a former empty lot. It rocks. *33 Wyckoff Ave. (at Starr St.). www.thebrooklynbeer garden.* ☎ *718/366-2337. Subway: L to Jefferson St.*

★★ Dante GREENWICH VILLAGE
In the 1920s and 1930s, Dante's Café was where struggling artists gathered for a cheap cuppa joe and conversation. The place looks the same today, although a blaring indie soundtrack and dense crowds

It's a trippy scene at the Brooklyn Street Art Beer Garden.

make conversation a challenge. But you may not mind after tasting the encyclopedic variety of *apperativos* at what was ranked number one on 2019's "Best 50 Bars of the World" list. **Tips:** Happy hour (3–6pm) slices the cost of Negronis; outdoor tables are the most serene spots here. *79–81 MacDougal St. (near Houston). http://dante-nyc.com. ☎ 212/983-5275. Subway: 1 to Houston, A/B/C/ D/E/F to West 4th St.*

★ **d.b.a.** EAST VILLAGE   Lounges dominate the city, but d.b.a. is a refreshing change of pace. It's an unpretentious neighborhood bar—a beer- or whiskey-lover's dream. The collection of single-malt scotches is phenomenal. *41 First Ave. (btw. 2nd and 3rd sts.). ☎ 212/475-5097. Subway: F to Second Ave.*

★ **Decibel** EAST VILLAGE   A gritty, underground sake bar, Decibel is a center of social life for many of the ex-pat Japanese living in NYC. In fact, most of the clientele are Japanese, the soundtrack is Japanese rock, and the bar food can be exotic (dried squid,

anyone?). *240 E 9th St. (btw. Second and Third aves.). www.sakebar decibel.com. ☎ 212/979-2733. Subway: 6 to Astor Place.*

Don't Tell Mama TIMES SQUARE Broadway's up-and-comers head here to belt out a tune or two when their shows have let out. It's a club-house, of sorts, but all are welcome and the pianist can play anything (just don't order the food, or a cocktail more complex than a gin and tonic). *343 W. 46th St. www. donttellmamanyc.com. ☎ 212/757-0788. Subway: A/C/E/1/2/3/N/Q/R to 42nd St.*

Dublin House UPPER WEST SIDE An unapologetic dive, this Irish pub was founded over 80 years ago to slake the thirst of sailors docking at the nearby boat basin. It still opens daily at 8am, and serves ice-cold Guinness. *225 W. 79th St. (near Broadway). www.thedublinhousenyc. com. Subway: 1 to 79th St.*

★★★ **Ear Inn** SOHO   The Ear Inn is set in one of the oldest build-ings on Manhattan: a gable-roofed, two-story Federal town house built by African American Revolutionary

Bellying up to the vintage King Cole Bar.

War hero James Brown in 1817. It got its current name when the "B" on the neon sign outside went on the fritz. Today, this mini-museum of a bar (there's historical ephemera everywhere) is popular with a wide range of New Yorkers, from 20-something gallery-hoppers to 50-something motorcycle enthusiasts. *326 Spring St. (near Greenwich St.). www.earinn.com.* ☎ *212/226-9020. Subway: 1 to Canal St., C/E to Spring St.*

★★ **Fine and Rare** MIDTOWN EAST "Rare" comes into play because of the limited-edition bottles served here (bourbons, scotches, and rums primarily); "fine" defines this joint's old-timey good looks (tufted leather banquettes, brass railings, mahogany bar). A sophisticated evening out, with cover-free jazz to boot (and good food, too). *9 East 37th St. (off Fifth Ave.). www.fineandrare.nyc.* ☎ *212/725-3866. Subway: B/D/F/N/R to 34th St.*

★★ **The Honey Well** HARLEM Evoking a 1970's basement rec room, this sepia-toned charmer offers homey snacks (Ritz crackers & spinach dip, anyone?) next to seriously accomplished cocktails. The soundtrack is funk from that era, and the vibe laid back. *3604 Broadway (btw. 148th and 149th sts.). www.thehoneywellnyc.com. Subway: 1 to 145th St.*

★ **Kavasutra** EAST VILLAGE No liquor is served here, just kava and kratum, legal Polynesian psychotropic liquids. They taste awful, but once downed will leave you with a mellow, floaty high. *261 E. 10th St. (btw. First Ave, and Ave. A). www.kavasutra.com. Subway: L to First Ave.*

★★ **King Cole Bar** MIDTOWN EAST The Bloody Mary was born here, in the tony St. Regis Hotel. The Maxfield Parrish mural alone is worth the price of a classic cocktail (but egads, what a price!). It's a small but memorable spot. *2 E. 55th St. (at Fifth Ave.). www.kingcolebar.com.* ☎ *212/744-4300. Subway: E to Fifth Ave./53rd St.*

★★ **Metropolitan Museum Roof Garden/Great Hall Balcony Bar** UPPER EAST SIDE Every Friday and Saturday night

The Old Town, a vintage charmer near Union Square.

from 4 to 8:30pm, the mezzanine level of the Met's lobby transforms into a lounge with live classical music. When the weather warms, take the elevator up to the **Roof Garden** for drinks with sumptuous views of the park. *Metropolitan Museum of Art, 1000 Fifth Ave. (at 82nd St.). www.metmuseum.org. ☎ 212/535-7710. Subway: 4/5/6 to 86th St.*

Old Town UNION SQUARE You know a bar is old when the burgers and fries are shuttled from the kitchen via dumbwaiter. This place was immortalized by David Letterman in the opening credits of his late-night show but has been around a lot longer than Dave. A classic dive bar. *45 E. 18th St. (btw. Broadway and Park Ave. S.). www. oldtownbar.com. ☎ 212/529-6713. Subway: 4/5/6/L/N/R/Q to 14th St./ Union Sq.*

★★★ Ophelia Lounge MIDTOWN EAST Ravishing cityscape views are the draw, but you'll want to linger thanks to jovial,

talented bartenders, and a kitchen that serves up better-than-usual bar food. At the top of a 1928 skyscraper, it can get very loud Thurs–Sat (the DJ plays at a sternum-thumping level) but is serene the rest of the week. *3 Mitchell Pl. (at 49th St. and First Ave.). www. opheliany.com. ☎ 212/980-4796. Subway: E to Lexington Ave./50th St.*

★★ PDT EAST VILLAGE The ultimate speakeasy, "Please Don't Tell" is entered through the false wall at the back of a phone booth in a hot dog shop. The menu features drinks with oddball ingredients and combos (plum brandy with salted caramel, pisco with green peas) and the mystery becomes: How do they taste so good? Get advance reservations—no standing allowed here. *113 St. Marks Pl. (btw, First Ave. and Ave. A). www.pdtnyc. com. ☎ 212/614-0386. Subway: L to First Ave.*

PDT (Please Don't Tell), a modern speakeasy.

Learn about LGBTQ history, and down a pint, at The Stonewall Inn

★★ The Rum House TIMES
SQUARE   You don't expect to find a place that's both this hip and this unpretentious in the heart of Times Square, but here it is. Set in the Edison Hotel, this classic watering hole serves up a mean cocktail and decent bar food. On most nights, a live pianist adds to the ambience, softly playing hits from the days of Gershwin and Irving Berlin. *228 W. 47th St. (btw. Broadway and Eighth Ave.).* www.edisonrumhouse.com. ☎ *646/490-6924. Subway: N/Q/R to 49th St.*

★★ Swing 46 MIDTOWN WEST
Gotham's active swing dance community supports this wonderful supper club (though you can come to dance without eating). With live music 6 nights a week (on Mondays a DJ takes over), locals Lindy Hop, jitterbug, waltz, and freestyle well into the wee hours. *349 W. 46th St. (btw. Eighth and Ninth aves.).* www. swing46.com. ☎ *212/262-9554. Subway: C or E to 50th St.*

The Gay & Lesbian Scene

★★ Flaming Saddles HELLS
KITCHEN   Yee-haw! This country-western bar is Coyote Ugly reversed, with hot, shirtless male bartenders dancing atop the bar. Along with hunky guys, this place attracts a lot of bachelorette parties, but there's one rule: no "woo-hooing" female customers! *739 Ninth Ave. (at 39th St.).* ☎ *212/713-0481. Subway: C, E to 50th St.*

★ Henrietta Hudson WEST
VILLAGE   This popular ladies' lounge has been calling out to lipstick lesbians since 1991. The theme nights pack the house. *438 Hudson St. (at Morton St.).* www. henriettahudson.com. ☎ *212/924-3347. Subway: 1 to Houston St.*

★★ Marie's Crisis WEST
VILLAGE   The "Church of Show Tunes" is in joyous session 7 nights a week at Marie's Crisis, a basement piano bar that has an atmosphere like no other. In a low-ceilinged room, covered with Christmas lights, dozens of men (and some women) gather each evening to belt out Sondheim, Porter, and Rodgers and Hammerstein. *59 Grove St. (at Seventh Ave.).* ☎ *212/243-9323. Subway: 1 to Christopher St.*

★★ The Stonewall Inn GREEN-
WICH VILLAGE   Pride began here! And while some may come for the drag shows and piano bar, most just want to down a pint in the place where history changed for the better. A plaque in the park opposite tells the story. *53 Christopher St (nr Seventh Ave.).* www.thestonewallinnnyc.com. ☎ *212/488-2705. Subway: 1 to Christopher St.* ●

Arts & Entertainment **Best Bets**

Most **Unusual Venue**
Bargemusic, *Fulton Ferry Landing, Brooklyn* (p 145)

Best **Free Concerts**
New York Philharmonic Concerts in the Park, *City Parks* (p 145)

Best **Historic Venue**
Apollo Theater, *253 W. 125th St.* (p 147)

Best **Classical Dance Troupe**
New York City Ballet, *Lincoln Center, Broadway and 64th St.* (p 147)

Best **Modern Dance Venue**
Joyce Theater, *175 Eighth Ave.* (p 146)

Best **Author Readings**
92nd Street Y, *1395 Lexington Ave.* (p 147)

Best **Off-Broadway Theater**
The Public Theater, *425 Lafayette St.* (p 152)

Best **Comedy Club**
Caveat, *21 A Clinton St.* (p. 146)

Best **Rock-'n'-Roll Bar**
Mercury Lounge, *217 E. Houston St.* (p 150)

Most **Unforgettable Visual Spectacle**
Metropolitan Opera, *Lincoln Center, Broadway and 64th St.* (p 150)

Best **Jazz Club**
Smoke, *2751 Broadway* (p 150)

Most **Cutting-Edge Major Venue**
Brooklyn Academy of Music, *30 Lafayette Ave., Brooklyn* (p 147)

Best **Church Concert Series**
Church of the Transfiguration, *1 E. 29th St.* (p 146)

Previous page: Katrina Lenk starring in the hit, gender-reversed version of Stephen Sondheim's musical Company. Above: The Public Theater.

Downtown A&E

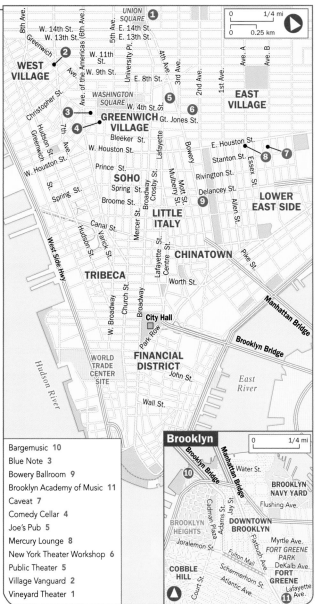

Bargemusic **10**

Blue Note **3**

Bowery Ballroom **9**

Brooklyn Academy of Music **11**

Caveat **7**

Comedy Cellar **4**

Joe's Pub **5**

Mercury Lounge **8**

New York Theater Workshop **6**

Public Theater **5**

Village Vanguard **2**

Vineyard Theater **1**

Midtown & Uptown A&E

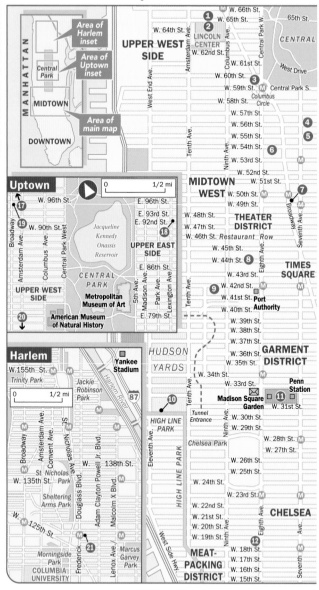

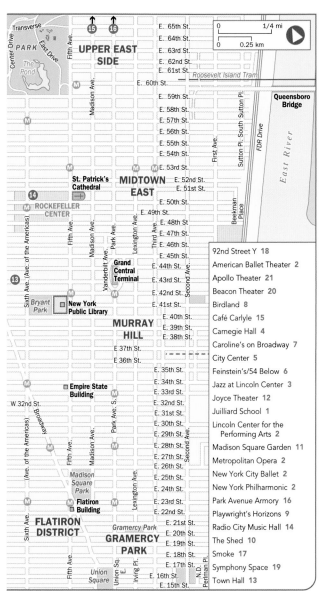

92nd Street Y **18**

American Ballet Theater **2**

Apollo Theater **21**

Beacon Theater **20**

Birdland **8**

Café Carlyle **15**

Carnegie Hall **4**

Caroline's on Broadway **7**

City Center **5**

Feinstein's/54 Below **6**

Jazz at Lincoln Center **3**

Joyce Theater **12**

Juilliard School **1**

Lincoln Center for the
Performing Arts **2**

Madison Square Garden **11**

Metropolitan Opera **2**

New York City Ballet **2**

New York Philharmonic **2**

Park Avenue Armory **16**

Playwright's Horizons **9**

Radio City Music Hall **14**

The Shed **10**

Smoke **17**

Symphony Space **19**

Town Hall **13**

The Best Arts & Entertainment

Broadway Theaters

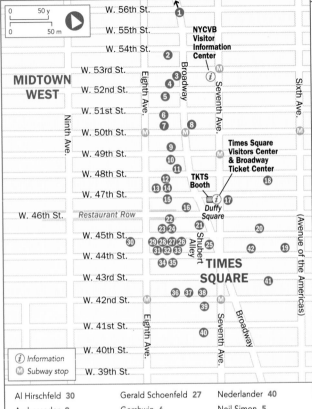

Al Hirschfeld **30**	Gerald Schoenfeld **27**	Nederlander **40**
Ambassador **9**	Gershwin **6**	Neil Simon **5**
American Airlines **36**	Helen Hayes **35**	New Amsterdam **39**
August Wilson **4**	Hudson **42**	New Victory **38**
Belasco **19**	Imperial **23**	Palace **17**
Bernard B. Jacobs **28**	John Golden **29**	Richard Rogers **22**
Booth **26**	Longacre **12**	Samuel J. Friedman **13**
Broadhurst **32**	Lunt-Fontanne **16**	St. James **34**
Broadway **3**	Lyceum **20**	Shubert **33**
Brooks Atkinson **15**	Lyric **37**	Stephen Sondheim **41**
Circle in the Square **7**	Majestic **31**	Studio 54 **2**
Cort **18**	Marquis **21**	Vivian Beaumont **1**
Ethel Barrymore **14**	Minskoff **25**	Walter Kerr **11**
Eugene O'Neill **10**	Music Box **24**	Winter Garden **8**

A&E A to Z

A chamber ensemble performs at Bargemusic.

Classical Music

★ Bargemusic BROOKLYN
Manhattan skyline views and ethereal tunes as you gently bob on the water—what could be lovelier? An evening at the intimate theater on this permanently docked steel barge, at the foot of the Brooklyn Bridge, is an ideal night out for chamber music lovers. *At Fulton Ferry Landing (just south of the Brooklyn Bridge), Brooklyn. www. bargemusic.org. ☎ 718/624-2083. Tickets $35, $30 seniors, $20 students. Subway: 2/3 to Clark St.; A/C to High St.*

★★★ Juilliard School LINCOLN
CENTER America's premier music school sponsors more than 500 concerts a year, most at no charge, performed by the most talented young people in the nation. *60 Lincoln Center Plaza (Broadway at 65th St.). www.juilliard.edu. ☎ 212/799-5000. Subway: 1 to 66th St.*

★★★ New York Philharmonic
LINCOLN CENTER Founded in 1842, this is one of the most gifted orchestras anywhere. Its free summertime **Concerts in the Park** take place at green spaces in all five boroughs, and are magical evenings (as are the performances at the Phil's home theater in Lincoln Center). *At Avery Fisher Hall, Lincoln Center, Broadway and 65th St. www. nyphil.org. ☎ 212/875-5656 for audience services, 212/875-5030 for box office information, or 212/721-6500 for tickets. Tickets $32–$149. Subway: 1 to 66th St.*

The famous Juilliard School sponsors hundreds of free concerts by its students.

Comedy Clubs

★★★ Caveat LOWER EAST SIDE
Intellectual topics—art history, biology, climate science, U.S. history—discussed by really funny, smart people, sometimes in a game-show-like format. Hard to describe, a kick to watch. *21A Clinton St. (near Houston). www.caveat.nyc.* ☎ *212/228-2100. Subway: F to Delancey.*

★★ Caroline's On Broadway
MIDTOWN WEST With a Theater District location, and a slightly more upscale vibe than the Comedy Cellar, Caroline's hosts some of the biggest names in comedy (Sarah Silverman, Dave Chappelle, Tracy Morgan). In 2021, it celebrated 40 years as a woman-owned business. *1626 Broadway (at 50th St.). www.carolines.com.* ☎ *212/757-4100. Subway: C/E/1 to 50th St.*

★ Comedy Cellar GREENWICH
VILLAGE This intimate subterranean club is a favorite among comedy cognoscenti. It gets names you'd expect (Dave Chappelle, Chris Rock) and a few you wouldn't (William Shatner). *117 Macdougal St. (btw. Minetta Lane and W. 3rd St.). www.comedycellar.com.* ☎ *212/254-3480. Subway: A/B/C/D/E/F/M/S to W. 4th St.*

Dance

★★★ American Ballet Theater
LINCOLN CENTER Renowned for its dazzling story ballets—Coppelia, Swan Lake, Sleeping Beauty—ABT features several bravura stars, including prima ballerina Misty Copeland, whose performances are always a huge draw. *Metropolitan Opera House, Lincoln Center, Broadway and 64th St. www.abt.org.* ☎ *212/477-3030. Subway: 1 to 66th St.*

★★ City Center MIDTOWN
WEST Alvin Ailey and Paul Taylor companies perform here, along with other major dance companies. You'll understand why, once you've attended a show in this splendid, Moorish-revival space (formerly a temple). In the basement are the stages of the excellent off-Broadway Manhattan Theatre Club. *131 W. 55th St. (btw. Sixth and Seventh aves.). www.citycenter.org.* ☎ *877/247-0430. Subway: F/N/Q/R/W to 57th St.; B/D/E to Seventh Ave.*

★★ Joyce Theater CHELSEA
In this renovated Art Deco–era movie theater, the audience sits slightly above the dancers, meaning that you won't be seeing just the feet or just the bodies—you'll get the whole picture. In past years, Pilobolus has performed here, as

Heavenly Sounds

New York churches may play traditional hymns during their religious services, but many also host afternoon and evening concerts in a variety of secular styles, from classical to opera, from instrumental to thrilling soloists. And the price is right: A few concerts require tickets, but most have a "requested donation" from $2 to $10. Check the websites for schedules. Some of the best include **Church of the Transfiguration** (1 E. 29th St.; www.littlechurch.org), **St. Bart's** (325 Park Ave.; www.stbarts.org), **St. Paul's Chapel and Trinity Church** (p 16), **the Cathedral of St. John the Divine** (p 61), and **St. Ignatius Loyola** (980 Park Ave.; www.stignatiusloyola.org).

New York City Ballet dancers perform at Lincoln Center.

well as MOMIX and Savion Glover. *175 Eighth Ave. (at 19th St.). www. joyce.org.* ☎ *212/691-9740. Subway: C/E to 23rd St.; 1 to 18th St.*

★★★ New York City Ballet
LINCOLN CENTER   The legendary George Balanchine founded this stellar company, which still performs his diamond-sharp choreography. *At the New York State Theater, Lincoln Center, Broadway and 64th St. www.nycballet.com.* ☎ *212/870-5570. Subway: 1 to 66th St.*

Landmark Venues
★★ 92nd Street Y UPPER EAST
SIDE   Forget what you know about the YMCA—this Jewish community center offers concerts, literary readings, and superb cultural events with the top newsmakers of the day. *1395 Lexington Ave. (at 92nd St.). www.92y.org.* ☎ *212/415-5500. Subway: 4/5/6 to 86th St.; 6 to 96th St.*

★★ Apollo Theater HAR-
LEM   A legendary institution, with annual jazz concerts and a popular Amateur Night on Wednesdays. *See p 62.*

★★★ Brooklyn Academy of Music BROOKLYN
Just 25 minutes by subway from Midtown, the five theaters that make up this renowned arts institution bring cutting-edge performances of theater, opera, dance, and music (Peter Brooks, Philip Glass, and more) from around the world. *30 Lafayette Ave. (off Flatbush Ave.), and 651 Fulton St., Brooklyn. www.bam.org.* ☎ *718/636-4100. Subway: 2/3/4/5/B/D/M/N/Q/R to Atlantic Ave./Barclays Center.*

★★★ Carnegie Hall MIDTOWN
WEST   Perhaps the world's most famous performance space, Carnegie Hall hosts everything from world-renowned orchestras to solo sitar stars in its three concert halls (big, medium, and small). Tickets for 1-hour tours (offered Oct–late June) are available at the box office. ⏲ *1 hr. (for tour). 881 Seventh Ave. (at 56th St.). www.carnegiehall.org.* ☎ *212/247-7800. Tours $19 adults, $16 students and seniors. Tours Mon–Fri 11:30am, 12:30, 2, and 3pm; Sat 11:30am and 12:30pm. Subway: A/B/C/D/1 to Columbus Circle; N/Q/R/W to 57th St./Seventh Ave.*

★★★ Lincoln Center for the Performing Arts UPPER WEST
SIDE   One of the most important cultural complexes on the planet. See individual listings for the **American Ballet Theater** (p 146), **Jazz at Lincoln Center** (p 150), **Juilliard School** (p 145), **New York Philharmonic** (p 145), **New York City Ballet** (above), and **Metropolitan Opera** (p 152) for more information. *10 Lincoln Center Plaza (Broadway from 62nd–66th sts.). www.lincolncenter.org.* ☎ *212/875-5456. Subway: 1 to 66th St.*

★★★ Park Avenue Armory
UPPER EAST SIDE   Bona fide cultural events take place in this

Radio City Music Hall.

historic and massive space, which hosts opera, dance, and theater from the world's most esteemed artists (de Keersmaeker, Satoshi Miyagi). *643 Park Ave. (at 66th St.). www.armoryonpark.org.* ☎ *212/616-3930. Subway: 6 to 68th St.*

★★★ Radio City Music Hall

MIDTOWN WEST   This stunning 6,200-seat Art Deco theater is home to the annual Christmas Spectacular and the Rockettes, plus many concerts year-round. *See p 8.*

★★★ The Shed HUDSON

YARDS   Alex Poots, the mastermind who helmed the Park Avenue Armory (see above) for many years, is artistic director of this new venue, in a whiz-bang building whose spaces can all be reconfigured to fit the performance (some change from indoor to outdoor). His debut season featured Bjork, Renee Fleming, and choreographer William Forsyth. Every piece is specially commissioned for The Shed, making its debut here. *545 W. 30th St. https://theshed.org.* ☎ *646/455-3494. Subway: 7 to 34th St./Hudson Yards.*

★ **Symphony Space** UPPER WEST SIDE   Now in its 35th year, this innovative institution offers a varied program of dance, film, readings, and music. We particularly like the "New Voices" series of concerts from young Broadway composers. *2537 Broadway (at 95th St.). www.symphonyspace.org.* ☎ *212/864-5400. Tickets $25–$40. Subway: 1/2/3 to 96th St.*

★ **Town Hall** MIDTOWN WEST A National Historic Site, Town Hall has pin-drop acoustics and has hosted performers ranging from Trisha Yearwood to Bela Fleck to a number of Broadway stars. *123 W. 43rd St. (btw. Sixth and Seventh aves.). www.thetownhall.org.* ☎ *212/840-2824. Tickets $24–$150. Subway: N/Q/R/S/W/1/2/3/7 to 42nd St./Times Sq.; B/D/F/M to 42nd St.*

Live Music

★★★ **Beacon Theater** UPPER WEST SIDE   Every seat at this Art Deco landmark has a good view, and while you won't get the mega-names, you will see talented stars

Live performances debut at The Shed, in the new Hudson Yards development.

Choosing the Right Broadway Show

You can traipse the entire Metropolitan Museum of Art, attend a Yankees game, and ascend to the top of the Empire State Building, but you can't really say you've done New York until you spend an evening at the theater. It's an essential element in a NYC vacation. Once you've accepted that you may not be able to score tickets to a mega-hit like *Hamilton*, how do you choose from among the many other shows? *Some tips:* Avoid shows that have been running for over 2 years, as they won't have the electricity of a younger show (the casts get bored). And look at whether the show garnered Tony nominations; that's a good measure for how high quality the production is (this info can be easily Googled and compared). Finally, don't forget that Off-Broadway shows can be as satisfying (and often as filled with stars). To save money on a show, see "Getting Broadway Tickets" (p 151); for where the Broadway theaters are, see our map on p 144.

Marquee above the Ambassador Theater, in the Broadway Theater District.

either on their way up or down, such as the Tedeschi Trucks Band, Cyndi Lauper, and comedian Jerry Seinfeld. *2124 Broadway (at 74th St.). www.beacontheatre.com.* ☎ *212/465-6500. Subway: 1/2/3 to 72nd St.*

★★ **Birdland** MIDTOWN WEST This legendary jazz club is one of the few (beyond Jazz at Lincoln Center) with room for really big bands. The weekly **Jim Caruso's Cast Party,** an open-mic night for Broadway performers (and would-be ones), is a hoot. *315 W. 44th St. (btw. Eighth and Ninth aves.). www. birdlandjazz.com.* ☎ *212/581-3080. Subway: A/C/E to 42nd St.*

Blue Note GREENWICH VILLAGE The Blue Note has some issues. Tables are jammed together, the bar area is even more crowded, and the second floor is given over to a tacky souvenir stand. But since it still attracts genuine talent, it can't be overlooked. *131 W. 3rd St. (at Sixth Ave.). www.bluenote.net.* ☎ *212/475-8592. Subway: A/B/C/D/ E/F/M to W. 4th St.*

★★ **Bowery Ballroom** LOWER EAST SIDE Another Art Deco wonder—this one with a big stage and good sightlines from every corner. Such alt-rockers as Kurt Vile perform here, as do stalwarts like

Emmylou Harris. *6 Delancey St. (at Bowery). www.boweryballroom.com.* ☎ *212/533-2111. Subway: F/J/M/Z to Delancey St.*

★ Café Carlyle UPPER EAST SIDE

This classic cabaret lounge is the venue of choice for a rotating lineup of musical stars; Woody Allen and his New Orleans–style jazz band perform often. *Carlyle Hotel, 35 E. 76th St. www.thecarlyle. com.* ☎ *212/744-1600. Subway: 6 to 77th St.*

★★ Feinstein's/54 Below

MIDTOWN WEST   Another cabaret venue, but with a twist: The majority of the entertainers who perform here are playing hooky from their real jobs at the big Broadway houses nearby—like Patty Lupone and Matthew Morrison (of *Glee*). The club itself is charming, with a 1930s speakeasy decor. *254 W. 54th St. (btw. Eighth Ave. and Broadway). www.54below.com.* ☎ *646/476-3551. Subway: C/E to 50th St.*

★★★ Jazz at Lincoln Center

UPPER WEST SIDE   The gold standard, meaning that the biggest stars in the genre vie to play in these three spectacular venues (two with eye-popping views of Central Park behind the musicians). Director of the program, legendary trumpeter Wynton Marsalis, helms the in-house orchestra. *In the Time Warner Center (at Broadway and 60th St.). www.jalc.org.* ☎ *212/258-9800. Subway 1/A/E/C to 59th St.*

★★ Joe's Pub EAST VILLAGE

Located in the Public Theater and named for its founder, Joseph Papp, this eclectic supper club hosts a range of performers from monologists to world music to hip hop, often by emerging stars (and some big names, too). *425 Lafayette St. (btw. Astor Place and E. 4th St.).* *www.joespub.com.* ☎ *212/539-8778. Subway: 6 to Astor Place.*

Madison Square Garden

GARMENT DISTRICT   Billy Joel has a "residency" here; he's just one of the mega-names in popular music that regularly play this cavernous 20,000-seat arena. *Seventh Ave. (from 31st–33rd sts.). www.the garden.com.* ☎ *212/465-MSG1 (465-6741). Subway: A/C/E/1/2/3 to 34th St.*

★ Mercury Lounge LOWER EAST SIDE

The ideal live-music rock-'n'-roll bar. Top talent, just the right amount of grit. *217 E. Houston St. (btw. Essex and Ludlow sts.). www.mercuryloungenyc.com.* ☎ *212/260-4700. Subway: F to Second Ave.*

★★ Smoke UPPER WEST SIDE

Going strong for almost 14 years— and even despite expanding and adding a supper club—Smoke still hasn't forgotten its initial objective of offering intimate, reliable jazz. Such mainstays as Mike LeDonne, John Farnsworth, and Eric

Smoke Jazz & Supper Club.

Getting Broadway Tickets

On average, only five or six shows per year get away with charging full price for their seats eight shows per week. For those productions, buying advance tickets well in advance from **TeleCharge** (www.telecharge.com; ☎ 212/239-6200) or **Ticketmaster** (www.ticketmaster.com; ☎ 212/307-4100) is key, though you can sometimes score tickets on StubHub.com and SeatGeek.com. With other shows you can buy in advance or day of, and get discounts of up to 50% through such websites as www.broadwaybox.com and www.playbill.com. The app **TodayTix** (for day- and month-of shows) is also a primo discount-getter. I think using these websites is preferable to waiting on line at the **TKTS booth** (www.tdf.org; ☎ 212/912-9770), since that eats up your valuable vacation time. Still, good show discounts can be had at the **Times Square booth** (47th St. and Broadway; Mon and Wed–Sat 3–8pm, Tues 2–7pm, and, for matinees only, Wed and Sat 10am–2pm and Sun 11am–2pm); the **South Street Seaport TKTS booth** (Mon–Sat 11am–6pm, Sun 11am–4pm; corner of Front and John sts.); or near **Lincoln Center** (in the atrium at 61 W. 62nd St.; Mon–Sat noon–7pm, Sun noon–5pm). Most tickets are sold at half-price, although some are discounted only 25%. A $4 TKTS service charge is added. *Tip:* Keep the ticket stubs if you plan to use TKTS more than once in a week; they'll allow you to jump the line the second time. There's also a special, usually shorter, line for plays.

Alexander, who helped launch Smoke, still make it their home with regular gigs. *2751 Broadway (btw. 105th and 106th sts.). www.smoke jazz.com. ☎ 212/864-6662. Subway: 1 to 103rd St.*

★ The Village Vanguard

GREENWICH VILLAGE Since 1935, this club has been showcasing jazz artists. Many of the greats, including Sonny Rollins and John Coltrane, have recorded live jazz albums here. *178 Seventh Ave. S. (just below 11th St.). www.village vanguard.com. ☎ 212/255-4037. Subway: 1/2/3 to 14th St.*

Off-Broadway Theaters
★★ New York Theater Workshop

EAST VILLAGE Intellectually heady and sometimes avant-garde, this company has launched some big hits, such as *Once* (Tony Award), *Hadestown* (Tony Award), *What the Constitution Means to Me* and *Rent* (Pulitzer Prize). *79 E. 4th St. (btw. Second Ave. and the Bowery). www.nytw.org. ☎ 212/460-5475. Subway: 6 to Astor Place.*

★ Playwrights Horizons

MIDTOWN WEST Dedicated to nurturing the art of the writer (lyricists and librettists as well as playwrights), Playwrights has always had

Opera-goers head for the Metropolitan Opera House on Lincoln Center Plaza.

a great eye for talent, producing the works of Stephen Sondheim, Christopher Durang, and A. R. Gurney. *416 W. 42nd St. (btw. Seventh and Eighth aves.). www.playwrights horizons.org.* ☎ *212/564-1235. Subway: 1/2/3/N/Q/R/ S to Times Sq. or A/E/C to 42nd St.*

★★★ Public Theater NOHO

Come here for groundbreaking stagings of Shakespeare's plays as well as new plays, musicals (*Hamilton* started here!), classical dramas, and solo performances. *425 Lafayette St. (btw. Astor Place and E. 4th St.). www.publictheater.org.* ☎ *212/ 539-8500. Subway: 6 to Astor Place.*

The Vineyard Theater UNION

SQUARE   The biggest risk-taker of the major Off-Broadway theaters, the Vineyard Theater presents out-and-out performance art along with less far-out plays and musicals. When they're good, they're great; even when their shows miss the mark, they're still usually intriguing. *Avenue Q* (Tony Award) debuted here before moving to Broadway. *108 E. 15th St., off Union Sq. www. vineyardtheatre.org.* ☎ *212/353-0303. Subway: 4/5 6/ N/Q/R/L to Union Sq.*

Opera

★★★ Metropolitan Opera

LINCOLN CENTER   Opera aficionados consider this one of the most electrifying companies in the world. *At the Metropolitan Opera House, Lincoln Center, Broadway and 64th St. www.metopera.org.* ☎ *212/ 362-6000. Subway: 1 to 66th St.*

New York City Opera AROUND

TOWN   Though it has risen from the ashes, NYC Opera is a shadow of its former self, offering only a handful of performances each year. *At different venues across the city. www.nycopera.com.* ●

Hotel Best Bets

Most Romantic
Crosby Street Hotel $$$ *79 Crosby St. (p 159)*

Hotel with the Best Restaurant & Bars
Freehand New York City $$$ *23 Lexington Ave. (p 160)*

Best Boutique Hotel
MADE Hotel $$$ *42 W. 29th St. (p 162)*

Best Old-School Glamour
The Beekman $$$$ *123 Nassau St. (p 158)*

Most Luxurious Hotel
The Peninsula—New York $$$$ *700 Fifth Ave. (p 163)*

Best Budget Hotel
Nesva Hotel $ *39–12 29th St. (at 39th Ave.), Long Island City, Queens (p 162)*

Best for Kids
Beacon Hotel $$$$ *230 Broadway (p 158)*

Best Value
NobleDen $$–$$$ *196 Grand St. (p 162)*

Best Hotel in the Middle of Everything
The Knickerbocker $$$ *151 W. 54th St. (p 161)*

Best Hotel Pool
The Greenwich Hotel $$$ *377 Greenwich St. (p 160)*

Best for Business Travelers
The Beekman $$ *123 Nassau St. (p 158)*

Best Views
Mr. C Seaport $$$$ *33 Peck Slip (p 162)*

Best Beds
MADE Hotel $$$$ *42 W. 29th. St. (p 162)*

Stays by Season

Hotel prices can shift drastically season-to-season, and even day-by-day in Gotham. In terms of days of the week to visit, Sunday night stays are traditionally the cheapest, with prices peaking, oddly enough on Tuesdays. Seasonally, prices plunge in the months of January (after the 4th), February, and early March. It is not at all uncommon in deep winter to score a very nice hotel room for just above $100 a night. Sadly, that very same hotel room will usually cost triple that amount the rest of the year. So if you're looking to save, brave the cold! Many of the city's top sights and experiences are indoors anyway.

Previous page: The lobby of the MADE Hotel.

Downtown Hotels

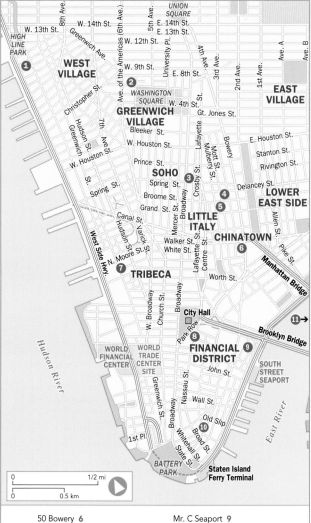

50 Bowery **6**

The Beekman **8**

Crosby Street Hotel **3**

The Greenwich Hotel **7**

The Hoxton **11**

The Jane **1**

Mr. C Seaport **9**

NobleDen **5**

The Nolitan **4**

Wall Street Inn **10**

Washington Square Hotel **2**

Midtown & Uptown Hotels

Andaz Fifth Ave **12**

Beacon Hotel **1**

The Boro Hotel **18**

Carlton Arms **7**

The Carlyle **17**

Casablanca Hotel **3**

Citizen M **2**

The Evelyn **8**

Freehand NYC **6**

The High Line Hotel **5**

Hotel Hendricks **11**

The Knickerbocker Hotel **4**

The Library **13**

MADE Hotel **10**

The Nesva **18**

The NoMad Hotel **9**

The Peninsula **16**

The Pod Hotel **15**

Sofitel New York **14**

TWA Hotel **18**

Hotels A to Z

Atrium shot of the Grand Salon at the Beekman Hotel.

★★ 50 Bowery CHINATOWN

This purpose-built skyscraper hotel is an unusually pleasant place to stay, boasting smart, larger-than-usual rooms (all with floor-to-ceiling windows); a sensational rooftop bar; and staff who give VIP service to every guest. *50 Bowery (near Canal St.). www.joiedevivrehotels.com. ☎ 212/508-8000. 229 units. $139-$239 double. AE, DC, MC, V. Subway: 1/2/3/4/5/6/N/Q/R to Canal St.*

★★ Andaz Fifth Avenue

MIDTOWN   Behind a nameless facade lies one of the city's smartest hotels. The striking interior of this historic 1916 building has become a thoughtful homage to the city, with tall, factory-style shutters and edgy artwork. Rooms have extravagantly high ceilings, rainfall shower heads, and soaking tubs. Some have spectacular views of the New York Public Library, across the street. *485 Fifth Ave. (at 41st St.). www.newyork.5th avenue.andaz.hyatt.com. ☎ 212/601-1233. 184 units. $247-$546 double, plus $30 resort fee. AE, DISC, MC, V. Subway: 4/5/6 to Grand Central and B/D/F to Bryant Park/42nd St.*

★ Beacon Hotel UPPER WEST

SIDE   This solid, family-friendly choice is a short walk from **Central Park** (p 100) and the **American Museum of Natural History** (p 50). The good-value perks include large rooms with kitchenettes. *230 Broadway (at 75th St.). www.beaconhotel. com. ☎ 800/572-4969. 260 units. $164-$314 double. AE, DC, MC, V. Subway: 1/2/3 to 72th St.*

★★★ The Beekman FINANCIAL

DISTRICT   Opened in 2016, this dazzler restores one of the city's first skyscrapers, built in 1881. Over the swank bar is a soaring nine-story atrium, with a pyramidal glass skylight; next to it is a restaurant by celeb chef Tom Colicchio (he's also in charge of room service). Rooms are carved out of former offices, so each has a different shape and size, but all have quietly elegant furnishings. *123 Nassau St. (at Beekman St.). www.thompsonhotels.com. ☎ 212/233-2300. 287 rooms. Double from $299-$458. AE, DISC, MC, V. Subway: 4/5/6/R Brooklyn Bridge/City Hall, 2/3 Park Pl., A/C Fulton St.*

★★ The Boro Hotel QUEENS

Floor-to-ceiling windows,

larger-than-usual rooms, sleek decor, and an affordable room service menu are just a few reasons to consider this outer borough winner. Oh, and the prices are primo. *32–28 27th St. (at 39th Ave.), Long Island City. www.borohotel.com.* ☎ *718/433-1375. 108 units. $109–$229 double, plus $22 resort fee. Subway: 7 to Queensboro Pl. or N/W to 39th Ave.*

★ Carlton Arms MIDTOWN EAST
Quirky, and definitely NOT for all travelers, the Carlton Arms is as much art gallery as it is hotel. Each room is decorated by a different artist (there's an Egyptian mummy–themed room, a Steampunk room, etc.) and many are mind-bending environments . . . which hopefully keeps guests' minds off the age of the mattresses, peeling paint, and the shared bathrooms (for some rooms). Still, prices and location are good. *160 E. 25th St. (at Third Ave.). www.carltonarms.com.* ☎ *212/679-0680. 44 units. $85–$147 double. AE, DC, DISC, MC, V. Subway: B/D/F/M/N/R to 34th St.*

★★★ The Carlyle UPPER EAST
SIDE   The old-school glamour in this 1930 white-glove landmark is tasteful, understated, never over the top. But baby, it's plenty luxe, all gleaming marble and custom fabrics. **Bemelmans Bar** (see p 132) is a jewel. *35 E. 76th St. (at Madison Ave.). www.rosewoodhotels.com/the-carlyle.* ☎ *212/744-1600. 188 units. Double $389–$950, suite from $950. AE, DC, DISC, MC, V. Subway: 6 to 51st St.; E/F to Lexington Ave.*

★★ Casablanca Hotel TIMES
SQUARE   An oasis in the middle of the Times Square mayhem, the Casablanca is one of the best options in the area. Rooms are good-sized for the price, and a homey lounge with fireplace where daily complimentary wine and cheese and breakfast are served adds to the value. *147 W.43rd St.*

(btw. Broadway and Sixth Ave). www. casablancahotel.com. ☎ *212/869-1212. 48 units. $224–$487 double. AE, DC, MC, V. Subway: N/R/Q/1/2/3 to Times Sq.–42nd St.*

★★ Citizen M TIMES SQUARE
On a budget? Try these unapologetically pre-fab, tiny, shiny white "pod" rooms, each with a modular shower/toilet enclosed unit, and a huge bed that pushes right up to a wall-to-wall window, with bright red pillows bearing notes encouraging pillow fights. The lobby is a hipster haunt, as is the roof bar. *218 W. 50th St. (btw. Seventh and Eighth aves.). www.citizenm.com.* ☎ *212/461-3638. 230 units. $152–$349 double. Subway: C/E to 50th St, B/D to Seventh Ave. or N/R to 49th St.*

★★★ Crosby Street Hotel
SOHO   This art-besotted hotel is a top choice for honeymooners and other romantics, for the elegance and whimsy of its decor (which makes use of fine art works throughout) and the high quality of its room service. The staff, too, couldn't be a nicer bunch. Its sister hotel, The Whitby, brings the same type of charm to midtown. *79 Crosby St. (btw. Prince and Spring sts.). http://crosbystreethotel.com.* ☎ *212/226-6400. 86 units. $555–$825 double.*

Artists give each room at the Carlton Arms its own character.

AE, DC, MC, V. Subway: N/R to Prince St.; 6 to Spring St.

★★ The Evelyn FLATIRON DISTRICT

Evelyn Nesbit, the famed Gilded Age beauty at the heart of a famous murder, is the muse here. Which means decor references that period and has a delicate elegance: pale blue velvet armchairs, diaphanous curtains, and luminous portraits of Nesbit everywhere. *Tips:* Book directly and they'll match any Internet rate, plus throw in free breakfast. Free walking tours daily for guests. *7 E. 27th St. (near Fifth Ave.). www.theevelyn.com. ☎ 212/545-8000. 562 units. $169–$341 double, plus $29 resort fee. AE, DC, MC, V. Subway: 6/R/W to 28th St.*

★★★ Freehand New York City MIDTOWN EAST

The Freehand has unusually sociable public areas: a game room, two lava-hot bars (p 132), three superb restaurants, and a second floor lobby that's so comfy and pleasant, locals hang out there as well as guests. Rooms are equally congenial, if small, some so tiny they're sold only to singles, often at a deep discount. *23 Lexington Ave. (at 23rd St.). www.freehandhotels.com. ☎ 212/715-2500. 209 units. $95–$305 double,* plus $15 resort fee. AE, DC, DISC, MC, V. Subway: 6 to 23rd St.

Sociable public areas are a plus at the Freehand Hotel.

★★★ The Greenwich Hotel TRIBECA

No detail or expense has been spared at this beautiful small luxury hotel (whose owners include Robert De Niro), where even the bricks are handcrafted. It's meant to feel like an 88-room home—if home is a rustically elegant country manor filled with art and antiques. It's everything a hip, edgy downtown hotel isn't—and that makes it plenty hip. *377 Greenwich St. (at N. Moore St.). www.thegreenwichhotel. com. ☎ 212/941-8900. 88 units. $625–$855 double. AE, DC, DISC, MC, V. Subway: 1 to Franklin St.*

★★★ The High Line Hotel CHELSEA

Very few NYC hotels deserve the high price tag they wear. This one just may. Set in a former ecclesiastical building (a beaut of a red-brick Victorian), The High Line Hotel looms like a castle over Tenth Avenue. Its interior is as grand, though delightfully quirky, with rooms that look like they could have been inhabited by a Gatsby type in the 1920s. And the hotel has outdoor courtyards and restaurants that are a delight in the warm weather months. *180 Tenth Ave. (at 20th St.). www.thehighlinehotel.com. ☎ 212/929-3888. 60 units. $209–$509 double, plus $24 resort fee. Subway: C to 23rd St.*

★★ Hotel Hendricks MIDTOWN

Animal prints throughout and Murano glass chandeliers in the bar bring a surprising sexiness to this business travelers' hotel in the Garment District. Rooms are small but very quiet, with Empire State Building views. *25 W. 38th St. (btw. Fifth and Sixth aves.). www.hotel hendricksny.com. ☎ 833/436-3745. 175 units. $114–$240 double. AE, DC, MC, V. Subway: B/D/F/7 to 42nd St./Bryant Park.*

Skyline views at the rooftop lounge at Brooklyn's Hoxton Hotel.

★★ The Hoxton BROOKLYN
Floor-to-ceiling windows catch Instagram-worthy views of the Manhattan skyline in half the rooms here. But all guests have access to the hotel's three hopping hotel/bars, including a rooftop one with those same fab vistas. *97 Wythe Ave. (at N. 10th St.), Williamsburg. www.thehoxton.com.* ☎ *718/215-7100. 150 units. $129–$349 double w/breakfast. AE, DC, MC, V. Subway: L Bedford Ave.*

★ The Jane WEST VILLAGE
Two-thirds of the units in this "micro hotel" are 50-square-foot spaces complete with bed (or bunk bed), flatscreen TV, Wi-Fi, A/C, and shared bathrooms—all yours for $125 a night. But with such fabulous public spaces—a massive lobby bar with fireplace, a rooftop lounge overlooking the Hudson River—who needs a big, pricey room to rattle around in? *113 Jane St. (at the West Side Hwy.). www.thejanenyc.com.* ☎ *212/924-6700. 210 units. Basic doubles $88–$135. AE, MC, V. Subway: A/C/E to 14th St.*

★★ The Knickerbocker TIMES SQUARE   Set in a landmarked, 1902 Beaux Arts knockout of a skyscraper, this hotel makes smart use of the building's grand bones: Guest rooms all have soaring ceilings and massive windows. Topnotch service, zen decor, and amenities such as on-site gourmet restaurants keep things calm in the midst of all the Times Square hoopla. *6 Times Square (on 42nd St., near Broadway). www.theknicker bocker.com.* ☎ *212/204-4980. 230 units. $196–$565 double. Subway: 1/2/3/7/N/R/Q/S to 42nd St./Times Sq.*

Hotel Hendricks' fashion-forward bar.

Money-Saving Tips on Lodging

New York has the most expensive lodgings in the Americas—a fact you'll comprehend when you try to book a hotel. To get the best price, consider these tips. **Look for outer borough and nearby New Jersey locations:** A number of big chains, such as Red Roof Inn and La Quinta, offer affordable offshoots in safe but less touristy Queens and Jersey City. Check out our reviews for the Nesva Hotel (p 161) and the Boro Hotel (p 157), both excellent options in Queens. **Check hotel websites** for exclusive online deals; you'll need to be members of the loyalty program to see the lowest rates, but joining is free. **Consider hotels where rooms share baths**—this one small inconvenience can save you big at hotels like downtown's **The Jane** (p 160), the **Carlton Arms** (p 157), and the **Pod Hotels** (p 163). *Don't assume air/hotel packages will be cheaper,* though; usually they don't save any money in NYC.

★ **The Library Hotel** MIDTOWN EAST Each of the 10 floors here is dedicated to a major category of the Dewey Decimal System. Rooms have a Deco elegance, done in buttery yellow and loaded with books to read. The Petite Rooms are a solid value, but yes, quite petite. The **Writer's Den,** on the 14th floor, has the dog-eared feel of a beloved book. *299 Madison Ave. (at 41st St.). www.libraryhotel.com.* ☎ *212/983-4500. 60 units. $239–$500 double. AE, DC, MC, V. Subway: 4/5/6/7/S to 42nd St.*

★★ **MADE Hotel** FLATIRON DISTRICT Extraordinary Sapira hybrid beds—half memory foam, half coils, for body contouring without heat—mean that sleeps here are unusually deep. Also soothing are the quiet, chicly rough-hewn rooms and the ministrations of an unusually kindly staff. Final perks: a nice rooftop bar and fab basement restaurant. *42 W. 29th St. (btw. Sixth Ave. and Broadway). www.madehotels.com.* ☎ *212/213-4429. 72 units. $139–$539 double. AE, DISC, MC, V. Subway: N/R to 28th St.*

★★ **Mr. C Seaport** SEAPORT DISTRICT In the shadow of the Brooklyn Bridge (fab views) is this stylish, Italian-souled hotel from the Cipriani family of restaurant fame. Not surprisingly, the on-site pasta house is topnotch. Since it's set in a historic warehouse, some of the rooms are oddly shaped, but all are classy and comfortable. *33 Peck Slip. www.mrcseaport.com.* ☎ *877/528-4249. 66 units. $170–$425 double. AE, DC, DISC, MC, V. Subway: 2, 3, 4, 5, J, Z to Fulton St.*

★ **Nesva Hotel** QUEENS Very pleasant rooms with quality beds and non-cookie-cutter contemporary decor make staying in nowheres-ville Queens more than palatable. Another huge plus is that the hotel's area is safe and just two stops from midtown Manhattan. *39–12 29th St. (at 39th Ave.), Long Island City, Queens. www.nesvahotel.com.* ☎ *917/745-1000. 36 units. $95–$162 double. Subway: N, Q to 39th Ave.*

★★ **NobleDen** CHINATOWN Mostly Europeans book this sleek new hotel, which sits on the porous border between Chinatown and

Little Italy. My guess is they're drawn by the clean Scandinavian-style design (lots of neutral colors offset by pops of red, hidden drawers that double your storage space, angular lamps, and two-room bathrooms). I like the king units best for their floor-to-ceiling windows. *196 Grand St. (btw. Mulberry and Mott sts.). www.nobleden.com.* ☎ *212/390-8988. 54 units. $141–$264 double. Subway: B, D to Grand St. or N, Q, R, 6 to Canal St.*

★ **The Nolitan** NOLITA   Located close to Chinatown, Little Italy, Soho, and Nolita, the Nolitan fits in snugly with those unique neighborhoods. This boutique charmer features cozy rooms, many with balconies, all with open views from oversize windows. The hotel even offers free bike rentals. *30 Kenmare St. (btw. Elizabeth and Mott sts.). www.nolitanhotel.com.* ☎ *212/925-2556. 55 units. $160–$525 double. AE, DC, MC, V. Subway: 6 to Spring St.*

★★★ **The NoMad** FLATIRON DISTRICT   Circular bedrooms—those are the lure for the honeymooners who go for the suites at this swank hotel. But even the cheaper digs are sensual, with fabric dressing screens dividing the rooms, beds piled high with fluffy duvets, a European *fin de siècle* vibe, and unique art on the walls. Room service comes from the superb **NoMad Restaurant** (see p 35). *1170 Broadway (at 28th St.). www.thenomad hotel.com.* ☎ *212/796-1500. 168 units. $310–$581 double, plus $27 resort fee. Subway: N, R, 6 to 28th St.*

★★★ **The Peninsula—New York** MIDTOWN   Housed in a 1905 landmark building, the Peninsula has some of the most tastefully luxurious (and priciest) rooms in town. Take the curving stairway up from the world-class spa to the 22nd-floor heated pool, with Central

Park and Fifth Avenue views. *700 Fifth Ave. (at 55th St.). www.peninsula. com.* ☎ *800/262-9467. 239 units. $490–$1,400 double. AE, DC, DISC, MC, V. Subway: E/F to Fifth Ave.*

★ **The Pod Hotel** MIDTOWN   High style and high jinks at low rates—those are what travelers who stay here get. There's a trade-off of space (and, in some cases, a private bathroom) for groovy-looking if Lilliputian rooms—hence the word "pod." But the common areas are so fun-filled, with hopping bar/restaurants and Ping-Pong tables, that most don't mind. The Pod has one sister hotel in Brooklyn and two in midtown Manhattan. *230 E. 51st St., off Third Ave. www.thepodhotel. com.* ☎ *800/742-5945 or 212/355-0300. 348 units. $85–$195 double. AE, MC, V. Subway: 6 to 50th St.*

★ **Sofitel New York** MIDTOWN WEST   Built in 2000, the 30-story Sofitel has an elegant, marbled lobby with a Deco-style restaurant and bar. Rooms are standard but spacious and soundproofed. *45 W. 44th St. (btw. Fifth and Sixth aves.). www.sofitel.com.* ☎ *212/354-8844.*

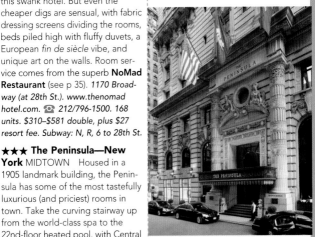

The ultra-luxe Peninsula Hotel.

The Best Hotels

The lounge of the Sofitel.

398 units. $191–$674 double, plus $17 resort fee. AE, DC, MC, V. Subway: B/D/F/M to 42nd St.

★ **TWA Hotel** JFK AIRPORT I don't usually recommend staying out at the airport (the commute sucks), but this hotel so successfully channels the 1960s, in its architecture (by Eero Saarinen back in the day) and the decor of its public spaces, that it's catnip to fans of that era. Guest rooms are crisply contemporary. *1 Idlewild Dr. (at JFK). www. twahotel.com. ☎ 212/806-9000. 512 units. $197–$249 double, day rates available. AE, DC, DISC, MC, V.*

The Wall Street Inn FINANCIAL DISTRICT This intimate, seven-story Lower Manhattan oasis is warm, comforting, and very inexpensive on weekends. One warning, though: The rooms that overlook rowdy Stone Street can get loud in warm weather because of all the outside bars. *9 S. William St. (at Broad St.). www.thewallstreetinn. com. ☎ 212/747-1500. 46 units. $116–$314 double, plus $3.50 resort fee. AE, DC, DISC, MC, V. Subway: 2/3 to Wall St.; 4/5 to Bowling Green.*

★ **Washington Square Hotel** GREENWICH VILLAGE Itsy-bitsy rooms, but well-appointed and in a hotel with a storied history. Plus you're overlooking one of the loveliest parks in the city. *103 Waverly Place (btw. Fifth and Sixth aves.). www.wshotel.com. ☎ 212/777-9515. 150 units. $158–$267 double. AE, MC, V. Subway: A/B/C/D/E/F/M to W. 4th St. (use 3rd St. exit).* ●

B&Bs & Apartment Stays

Yes, hotel prices are high in New York, and the costs climb even higher for families paying for extra people in the room. Oh, and did we mention resort fees and hotel room taxes? (Tack on 14.25% to your total bill for the latter.) Save big bucks, enjoy more room, and live among the locals by staying in a B&B? Alas, apartment rentals of less than 30 days are illegal, but many flout the law and find rooms through **Airbnb.com**, **FlipKey.com**, and **VRBO.com**. If that idea makes you nervous (and the city of New York has hit property owners with fines over the years, causing them to pull rentals at the last minute), know that you can stay legally in a room in an apartment so long as the owner is still in residence—and this can often yield BIG savings. You'll find such rooms through **Wimdu.com** and **Airbnb**.

Before You Go

There's no denying that New York City was hit hard and early by Covid 19. But as we go to press, the city is back to its bustling, exuberant self. Despite what you may have heard, NYC remains a safe place to visit, with the lowest crime rate of any large American city according to the FBI. As importantly, the welcome visitors receive is warmer than ever. During the long months of the pandemic New Yorkers missed the energy and enthusiasm tourists bring to the city—we're thrilled to have you back.

The Best Times to Go

July and August are hot and humid, but because the local population tries to escape, the city is far less crowded. There are plenty of free alfresco events, too. September through December bring crowds and the highest hotel rates; January and February are the cheapest months to visit, by far, but very chilly. Ideal time? There's nothing like New York in late spring when the weather is mild.

Festivals & Special Events

WINTER From early November through New Year's, the city puts on its Christmas decorations, highlighted by the **Rockefeller Center Christmas Tree** and displays at various department stores. On **New Year's Eve,** the most famous party of them all takes place in Times Square (www.timessquarenyc.org). During **Chinese New Year** (first week in February), Chinatown comes alive with parades and special celebrations (www.explorechinatown.com).

SPRING St. Patrick's Day Parade (http://nycstpatricksparade.org) on March 17th is a big drunken party and parade, while the **Easter Parade**— not a traditional parade, but a flamboyant fashion display along Fifth Avenue from 48th to 57th streets—is on Easter Sunday. The **Dance Parade** (http://danceparade.org) which features dancers from across the globe strutting their stuff in downtown Manhattan, is a May event.

SUMMER In July and August, **Lincoln Center** (www.lincolncenter. org) celebrates the best of the performing arts from all over the world. **SummerStage** (www.summerstage. org; ☎ 212/360-2756) is a summerlong festival of outdoor performances in Central Park, featuring world music, pop, folk, and jazz artists. At the same time and also in Central Park, well-known actors take on the Bard in the Public Theater's long-running **Shakespeare in the Park** series (http://publictheatre. org). On **July 4th** Macy's puts on a fireworks spectacle (go to www. macys.com for details). Dance till you drop at **Midsummer Night Swing** (www. lincolncenter.org), 3 weeks of outdoor dance parties held in Lincoln Center's Damrosch Park.

FALL The **Greenwich Village Halloween Parade** (www.halloween-nyc. com) on October 31 is a flamboyant parade that everyone is welcome to join. Two things everyone should see at least once are the **Radio City Music Hall Christmas Spectacular** (www.radiocitychristmas. com/newyork; ☎ 212/247-4777 or Ticketmaster at 212/307-1000) and

Previous page: New York is full of one-of-a-kind spots, like the Lower East Side's Economy Candy.

the **Macy's Thanksgiving Day Parade** (☎ 212/494-4495).

Useful Websites

- **www.nycgo.com:** A wealth of free information about the city

- **www.nymag.com:** Terrific coverage of arts and events from *New York* magazine

- **www.timeout.com/newyork:** Full listings, restaurant reviews, shopping, and nightlife

- **www.panynj.gov** and **www.mta.info:** Transit info

- **www.weather.gov:** Up-to-the-minute weather

Restaurant & Theater Reservations

We can't say it enough: Book well in advance if you're determined to eat at a particular spot or see a very popular show (like *Hamilton*)—especially if you're visiting at a peak time. If you're determined to eat at a hot restaurant, ask for early or late hours—often tables are available before 6:30pm and after 9pm. Or ask about seating at the bar, which doesn't require reservations and is often the best venue in the house anyway.

For advance theater bookings, try a discounter website like **Broadway Box.com** or the app **TodayTix**, as you may be able to get a less expensive seat that way. If that doesn't work, look at www.telecharge.com, the official seller. A last-ditch effort could mean **SeatGeek.com** for resold tickets (if you have the stomach for it, prices at the latter plunge in the hour before show time), though there are no guarantees you'll get a seat that way.

Getting **There**

By Plane

Three major airports serve New York City: **John F. Kennedy International Airport** in Queens is about 15 miles (24km; 1 hr. driving time) from midtown Manhattan; **LaGuardia Airport,** also in Queens, is about 8 miles (13km; 30 min.) from Midtown; and **Newark International Airport** in nearby New Jersey is about 16 miles (26km; 45 min.) from midtown. Always allow extra time, though, especially during rush hour, peak holiday travel times, and if you're taking a bus. Info on all three is available at **www.panynj.gov/airports**.

For ease and convenience, your best bet is to stay away from public transportation when traveling to and from the airport. **Taxis** are a quick and convenient alternative. Taxis are available at designated taxi stands outside the terminals; all take credit cards. Fares, whether fixed or metered, do not include bridge and tunnel tolls ($8–$10), a tip for the cabbie (15–20% is customary) or the new congestion and rush hour fees (which vary by time of day, but always include the $4.05 state tax surcharge). Fares do include all passengers in the cab and luggage. **From JFK:** Taxis charge a flat rate of $52 to Manhattan (plus tolls and tip). **From LaGuardia:** $24 to $30, metered, plus tolls and tip. **From Newark:** The dispatcher for New Jersey taxis gives you a slip of paper with a flat rate ranging from $50 to $75 (toll and tip extra), depending on where you're going in New York City. The yellow-cab fare from Manhattan to Newark is the meter amount plus $15 and tolls (about $70–$85, perhaps a few dollars more with tip).

Uber, Lyft and private limo companies provide convenient

24-hour door-to-door airport transfers. They usually are equal in cost to taxis. If you don't want to do Uber or Lyft on your phone when you arrive, you can get advance reservations for car services such as **Dial 7** (www.dial7.com; ☎ 800/777-7777) or **Carmel** (☎ 800/922-7635 or 212/666-6666).

AirTrains ($16–$17) are available at Newark and JFK and will certainly save you money, but skip the AirTrain JFK if you have mobility issues, mountains of luggage, or small children. You'll find it easier to rely on a taxi, car service, or shuttle service that can offer you door-to-door transfers. For information, check out **AirTrain JFK** (www.airtrainjfk.com) and **AirTrain Newark** (www.airtrainnewark.com). The latter works pretty well, but you will have to change trains at a NJ Transit station to get to Penn Station in midtown Manhattan.

Bus and shuttle services provide a comfortable and less expensive (but usually more time-consuming) option than taxis and car services. **The New York Airport Service** (www.nyairportservice.com) buses travel from JFK and LaGuardia to the Port Authority Bus Terminal (42nd St. and Eighth Ave.), Grand Central Terminal (Park Ave., between 41st and 42nd sts.), and to select midtown hotels. One-way fares run between $16 and $25 per person.

By Car

From New Jersey and points west, there are three Hudson River crossings into the city's west side: the **Holland Tunnel** (lower Manhattan), the **Lincoln Tunnel** (Midtown), and the **George Washington Bridge** (upper Manhattan). From upstate New York, the **Tappan Zee Bridge** spans the Hudson. For the east side, the **Brooklyn, Manhattan, Williamsburg,** and **Queensboro bridges,** as well as the **Queens Midtown Tunnel,** cross the East River from Brooklyn and Queens.

Once you arrive in Manhattan, park your car in a garage (expect to pay $35–$55 per day) and leave it there. You really don't need your car for traveling within the city—in fact, it can be more of a hindrance to drive it around the city, especially during rush hours.

By Train

Amtrak (www.amtrak.com; ☎ 800/USA-RAIL; book early—as much as 6 months in advance—and travel on weekends for best rates) runs frequent service to New York City's **Penn Station,** on Seventh and Eighth Avenue between 31st and 33rd streets, as do **New Jersey Transit** and **Long Island Railroad. Metro-North Railroad** runs out of **Grand Central Terminal** (p 7). You can easily pick up a taxi, Uber, subway, or bus to your hotel from either station.

Getting **Around**

By Subway

The **subway** system is the fastest way to travel around New York, especially during rush hours. The subway runs 24 hours a day, 7 days a week. The rush hour are roughly from 7:30 to 9:30am and from 5 to 6:30pm on weekdays. The fare is

$2.75 (half-price for seniors and those with disabilities); children under 44 inches tall (111cm) ride free. Fares are paid either with credit/debit card scanners inset in most subway turnstiles (smart phones and watches with the right credit card tech also work) or with a

MetroCard, a magnetically encoded card that debits the fare when swiped through the turnstile (or the fare box on any city bus). MetroCards also allow you free transfers between the bus and subway within a 2-hour period. There are Pay-Per-Ride and Unlimited-Ride MetroCards; both can be purchased at any subway station.

By Bus

Less expensive than taxis, with better views than subways—buses would be the perfect alternative if they didn't sometimes get stuck in traffic. They're best for shorter distances or east-to-west journeys (in areas where the subways don't go crosstown). Like the subway fare, bus fare is $2.75, payable with a MetroCard or exact change. At some bus stops, you pay on the sidewalk; look for kiosks. Bus drivers don't make change, and fare boxes don't accept dollar bills or pennies. If you pay with a Metro-Card, you can transfer to another bus or to the subway for free within 2 hours. If you pay cash, request a free transfer slip that allows you to change to an intersecting bus route only (legal transfer points are listed on the transfer paper) within 1 hour of issue. Transfer slips cannot be used to enter the subway.

By Taxi, Uber, Lyft & Via

Yellow taxi cabs are licensed by the Taxi and Limousine Commission (TLC). Base fare on entering the cab is $2.50, plus $2.50 congestion charge (if you're in Manhattan below 96th Street) and an 80¢ state tax. The cost is 50¢ for every ⅕ mile or 50¢ per 1 minute in stopped or very slow-moving traffic (or for waiting time); all take credit cards. There's no extra charge for each passenger or for luggage, but you must pay bridge or tunnel tolls. You'll also pay a 50¢ night surcharge after 8pm and before 6am, and a $1 peak-hour surcharge Monday to Friday 4 to 8pm. A 15 to 20% tip is customary. You can hail a taxi on any street. Taxis can carry a maximum of four passengers, a rule that is strongly enforced.

As in other American cities, Uber, Lyft, and Via have become popular alternatives to taxis, and generally charge equivalent rates (Via is much cheaper, at $5 per person for rides of any distance). To use these services, download the apps to your smart phone.

By Bike

The CitiBike bike-sharing program (www.citibikenyc.com) is a wonderful way to get around, especially now that bike lanes have been built on many streets. Anyone over age 16 can purchase a single ride ($3.50) or a daily pass ($15), which gives you access to any CitiBike at 300-plus stations throughout the city for unlimited 30-minute trips (there are overtime fees if you don't dock a bike within 30 min.). After downloading the free app and entering your payment info, you'll scan the QR code on a bike to unlock it. Google Maps show which streets have protected bike lanes.

Fast **Facts**

ATMS (CASHPOINTS)   You'll find automated teller machines (ATMs) every few blocks, all of which charge a fee to withdraw if you're not a customer of that bank (usually $3, not including any fees your home bank may charge).

BABYSITTING Many hotels have babysitting services or will provide you with lists of reliable sitters. If this doesn't pan out, contact the **Babysitters' Guild** (www.babysitters guild.com). Its sitters are licensed, insured, and bonded, and can even take your child on outings.

BANKING HOURS Banks tend to be open Monday through Friday 9am–6pm, plus Saturday mornings.

BUSINESS HOURS Most stores stay open until 7pm or later, with drugstores and groceries usually going strong until 9pm, and delis and corner produce markets lasting into the wee hours. Most stores (except in the Financial District) are open on Sunday, although they may not open until 11am or noon.

CONSULATES New York has a consulate for virtually every country. The consulate of **Australia** is at 150 E. 42nd St., 34th floor (☎ 212/351-6500). The consulate of **New Zealand** is at 295 Madison Ave. (www. nzembassy.com; ☎ 212/832-4038). The consulate of **Canada** is at 466 Lexington Ave. (www.canadianembassy.org; ☎ 212/596-1628). The consulate of **Ireland** is at 345 Park Ave., 17th floor (www.irelandemb. org; ☎ 212/319-2555). The consulate of the **United Kingdom** is at 885 Second Ave. (www.gov.uk; ☎ 212/745-0200).

DOCTORS & DENTISTS Ask your hotel concierge to recommend a local doctor or dentist—his or her own. There are also many walk-in medical centers, like **City MD** (www.citymd.com), which offers 26 clinics in Manhattan plus others in the outer boroughs. Because of a shortage of hospitals in New York City, I don't recommend emergency room visits except in, well,

dire emergencies.

ELECTRICITY Like Canada, the U.S. uses 110 to 120 volts AC (60 cycles), compared to 220 to 240 volts AC (50 cycles) in most of Europe, Australia, and New Zealand. If your small appliances use 220 to 240 volts, you'll need a 110-volt transformer and a plug adapter with two flat parallel pins to operate them here. Converters that change 220–240 volts to 110–120 volts are difficult to find in the U.S., so bring one with you.

EMERGENCIES Dial ☎ **911** for fire, police, and ambulance.

GAY & LESBIAN TRAVELERS All over Manhattan, but especially in such neighborhoods as the **West Village, Hell's Kitchen,** and **Chelsea,** shops, services, and restaurants cater to a gay and lesbian clientele. It's unlikely you'll experience any forms of discrimination in New York City.

HOLIDAYS Banks, government offices, post offices, and many stores, restaurants, and museums are closed on the following legal national holidays: January 1 (New Year's Day), the third Monday in January (Martin Luther King, Jr., Day), the third Monday in February (Presidents' Day), the last Monday in May (Memorial Day), July 4 (Independence Day), the first Monday in September (Labor Day), the second Monday in October (Columbus Day), November 11 (Veterans' Day), the fourth Thursday in November (Thanksgiving Day), and December 25 (Christmas). The Tuesday following the first Monday in November is Election Day, a federal government holiday in presidential-election years (held every 4 years, and next in 2020).

INSURANCE Not all trips need to be insured, but for big-ticket expenses, we suggest looking at such marketplace sites as **Square Mouth.com** and **TravelInsurance. com**.

MAIL & POSTAGE The main post office is at 421 Eighth Ave. (at 33rd St.); other branches can be found by logging onto **www.usps.gov**. At press time, domestic postage rates were 35¢ for a postcard and 55¢ for a letter.

PHARMACIES **Duane Reade** (www. duanereade.com) has 24-hour pharmacies in **Midtown** at 530 Fifth Ave. at 46th St. (☎ 212/687-8641) and 1627 Broadway at 50th St. (☎ 212/586-0374); on the **Upper East Side** at 1111 Third Ave. at 66th St. (☎ 212/838-0195); and other locations. **CVS** (www.cvs.com) also has 24-hour pharmacies around the city.

SAFETY New York is one of the safest large cities in the U.S. But that doesn't mean you should take a stroll through Central Park in the wee hours of the morning, leave unsecured valuables in your car, or flash wads of cash in Times Square. No, no, and no. Avoid being the victim of petty crime by using common sense: Store your wallet in a safe place; wear your purse so it's not snatchable; and lock valuables in the hotel safe.

SENIOR TRAVELERS New York subway and bus fares are half-price ($1.35) for people 65 and older. Many museums and sights (and some theaters and concert halls) offer discounted admission to seniors, so don't be shy about asking and always bring an ID.

SMOKING Smoking is prohibited on public transportation, in hotel and office-building lobbies, in taxis, in bars and restaurants, and in all shops except cigar stores.

SPECTATOR SPORTS You've got your choice of baseball teams: the **Yankees** (www.yankees.com; ☎ 718/293-6000) or the **Mets** (www.mets.com; ☎ 718/507-TIXX). For basketball, there's the **Knicks** (www.nyknicks.com; ☎ 877/NYK-DUNK), the **New York Liberty** (www.liberty.wnba.com; ☎ 212/564-9622), and the **Brooklyn Nets** (www.nba.com/nets; ☎ 718/933-3000). The **New York Giants** (www.giants.com; ☎ 201/935-8222) and **Jets** (www. newyorkjets.com; ☎ 800/469-JETS) cover your football options. The **U.S. Open** (www.usopen.org) takes place every August and is considered one of the premier events in tennis.

TAXES **Sales tax** is 8.875% on meals, most goods, and some services. **Hotel tax** is 14.75% plus $3.50 per room per night (including sales tax). **Parking garage tax** is 18.375% (residents get a reduced rate).

TELEPHONE For directory assistance, dial ☎ 411; for long-distance information, dial 1, then the appropriate area code and 555-1212. There are four area codes in the city: two in Manhattan, the original **212** and the newer **646,** and two in the outer boroughs, the original **718** and the newer **347.** The **917** area code is assigned to cellphones, pagers, and the like. Calls between these area codes are local, but you'll have to dial the area code plus seven digits, even within the same area code.

TICKETS Tickets for concerts at all larger theaters can be purchased through **Ticketmaster** (www.ticket master.com; ☎ 212/307-7171). For advance tickets at smaller venues, contact **Ticketweb** (www.ticketweb. com; ☎ 866/468-7619). You can buy theater tickets in advance from **TeleCharge** (www.telecharge.com; ☎ 212/239-6200) or **Ticketmaster** (www.ticketmaster.com; ☎ 212/307-4100). For sporting events, theater, and concerts, the resellers **Stubhub.com** and **SeatGeek.com** can come in handy, especially for sold-out events.

TIPPING   In hotels, tip **bellhops** at least $1 per bag ($2–$3 if you have a lot of luggage) and tip the **chamber staff** $1 to $2 per day (more if you've left a disaster area for him or her to clean up, or if you're traveling with messy kids and/or pets). Tip the **doorman** or **concierge** only if he or she has provided you with some specific service (such as calling a cab). In restaurants, bars, and nightclubs, tip **service staff** 15 to 20% of the check, tip **bartenders** 10 to 15%, and tip **checkroom attendants** $1 per garment. Tipping is not expected in cafeterias and fast-food restaurants. Tip **cab drivers** 15 to 20% of the fare and tip **skycaps** at airports at least $1 per bag ($2–$3 if you have a lot of luggage).

TOILETS   Grand Central Terminal (42nd St. btw. Park and Lexington aves.), and the High Line entrance at 16th St. and Tenth Ave. have clean restrooms. Otherwise, your best bet is **Starbucks** or another city java chain—you can't walk more than a few blocks without seeing one. The big **chain bookstores** are good bets, too.

TOURIST OFFICES   **NYC & Company** is the city's official marketing and tourism organization (www.nycgo.com).

TOURS   Scholar-led private or group walking tours with award-winning tour operator **Context Travel** (www.contexttravel.com) offer in-depth looks at the city's art, architecture, and urban history. Less expensive, but arguably as compelling, are the walking tours given by **Free Tours by Foot** (www.freetoursbyfoot.com; you tip about $20 at the end). **Urban Oyster** (www.urbanoyster.com) is tops for food and/or drink tours. **Big Apple Greeter** (www.bigapple-greeter.org) provides free neighborhood walking tours given by locals (they're terrific and very personal). I'm not a fan of hop-on, hop-off double-decker bus tours (they tend to be time-wasters with poorly trained guides), but those offered by **Big Bus** (www.bigbus tours.com) are the best of the bunch.

TRAVELERS WITH DISABILITIES   **Public buses** are an inexpensive and easy way to get around New York. All buses' back doors are equipped with wheelchair lifts. Buses also "kneel," lowering their front steps for people who have difficulty boarding. Passengers with disabilities pay half-price fares ($1.35). The **subway** isn't yet fully wheelchair accessible, but a list of nearly 100 accessible subway stations is on the MTA website (http://web.mta.info/accessibility/stations.htm). All Broadway and most off-Broadway theaters have areas set aside for people in wheelchairs; call in advance to ask. You'll also find loaner wheelchairs and services for people with disabilities at such major sites as the Metropolitan Museum and the 9/11 Memorial Museum.

A Brief **History of New York**

1524 Giovanni da Verrazano sails into New York Harbor.

1609 Henry Hudson sails up the Hudson River.

1621 The Dutch West India Company begins trading from New York City.

1626 The Dutch pay 60 guilders ($24) to the Lenape Tribe for the island of New Amsterdam.

1664 The Dutch surrender New Amsterdam to the British, and the island is renamed after the brother of King Charles II, the Duke of York.

1765 The Sons of Liberty burn the British governor in effigy.

1776 Independence from England is declared.

1789 The first Congress is held at Federal Hall on Wall Street, and George Washington is inaugurated.

1792 The first stock exchange is established on Wall Street.

1820 New York City is the nation's largest city, with a population of 124,000.

1863 Draft riots rage throughout New York; 125 people die, including 11 African Americans who are lynched by mobs of Irish immigrants.

1883 The Brooklyn Bridge opens.

1886 The Statue of Liberty is completed.

1892 Ellis Island opens and begins processing more than a million immigrants a year.

1904 The first subway departs from City Hall.

1920 Babe Ruth joins the New York Yankees.

1929 The stock market crashes.

1931 The Empire State Building opens and is the tallest building in the world.

1947 The Brooklyn Dodgers sign Jackie Robinson, the first African American to play in the Major Leagues.

1969 The Gay Rights movement begins with the Stonewall Rebellion in Greenwich Village.

1990 David Dinkins elected as the city's first African-American mayor.

2001 Terrorists use hijacked planes to crash into the Twin Towers of the World Trade Center, which brings both towers down and kills more than 3,000 people.

2009 The New York Yankees win the World Series in their first year in the new Yankee Stadium, giving them 27 World Series championships.

2012 Hurricane Sandy, the worst storm ever to hit New York, inflicts billions of dollars' worth of damage.

2019 Hudson Yards, the largest private real estate development in U.S. history, opens half its campus.

2020 New York City becomes the first major city in the US to be hit by Covid-19. Nearly 34,000 New Yorkers die of the disease.

New York Architecture

New York is famous for its great buildings, but the truth is that the most interesting thing about its architecture is its diversity. From elegant Greek Revival row houses to soaring glass skyscrapers, the city contains examples of just about every style. Constructed over 300 years, these buildings represent the changing tastes of the city's residents from Colonial times to the present.

Georgian (1700–76)

This style reflects Renaissance ideas made popular in England, and later in the U.S., through the publication of books on 16th-century Italian architects. Georgian houses are characterized by a formal arrangement of parts employing a symmetrical composition enriched with classical details, such as columns and pediments.

St. Paul's Chapel (p 16), the only pre-Revolutionary building in Manhattan, is an almost perfect example of the Georgian style, with a pediment, colossal columns, Palladian window, quoins, and balustrade above the roofline.

Federal (1780–1820)

The first American architectural style, Federal was an adaptation of a contemporaneous English style called Adam (after Scottish architects Robert and James Adam), which included ornate, colorful interior decoration. Federal combined Georgian architecture with the delicacy of the French rococo and the classical architecture of Greece and Rome. The overall effect is one of restraint and dignity.

In the **West Village**, near and along Bedford St. between Christopher and Morton sts., are more original Federal-style houses than anywhere else in Manhattan. House nos. 4 through 10 (built in 1834) on Grove St., just off Bedford, present one of the most authentic groups of late-Federal-style houses in America.

Greek Revival (1820–60)

The Greek Revolution in the 1820s, in which Greece won its independence from the Turks, recalled to American intellectuals the democracy of ancient Greece—and its elegant architecture. With many believing America to be the spiritual successor of Greece, the use of classical Greek forms came to dominate residential, commercial, and government architecture.

Perhaps the city's finest Greek Revival building is **Federal Hall National Memorial** (built 1842; p 58), 26 Wall St., at Nassau St. The structure has a Greek temple front, with Doric columns and a simple pediment, resting on a high base

Lintel   Sash Window   Cornice

Side Light   Pilaster   Transom

A typical Federal exterior.

called a plinth, with a steep flight of steps.

Gothic Revival (1830–60)

The term "Gothic Revival" refers to a literary and aesthetic movement of the 1830s and 1940s in England and the U.S. that harkened back to medievalism. Some structures had only one or two Gothic features, while others, usually churches, were copies of English Gothic structures.

Trinity Church (p 16), at Broadway and Wall St. (Richard Upjohn, 1846), is one of the most celebrated Gothic Revival structures in the U.S. Here you see all the features of a Gothic church: a steeple, battlements, pointed arches, Gothic tracery, stained-glass windows, flying buttresses (an external bracing system for supporting a roof or vault), and medieval sculptures.

Italianate (1840–80)

The architecture of Italy inspired this building style, which could be as picturesque as the Gothic or as restrained as the classical. In New York, the style was used for urban row houses and commercial buildings. The development of cast iron at this time permitted mass production of decorative features that few could have afforded in carved stone. This led to the creation of cast-iron districts in nearly every American city.

New York's **SoHo Cast Iron Historic District** has 26 blocks jammed with cast-iron facades, many in the Italianate manner. The single richest section is **Greene Street** between Houston and Canal sts.

Early Skyscraper (1880–1920)

The invention of the skyscraper evolved directly from the use of cast iron in the 1840s. Experimentation with cast and wrought iron in the construction of interior skeletons eventually allowed buildings

to rise higher. These buildings were spacious, cost-effective, efficient, and quickly erected—in short, the perfect architectural solution for America's growing downtowns. But solving the technical problems of the skyscraper did not resolve how the buildings should look. Most solutions relied on historical precedents, including decoration reminiscent of the Gothic, Romanesque (characterized by rounded arches), or Beaux Arts styles.

Examples include the **American Surety Company,** at 100 Broadway (Bruce Price, 1895); the triangular **Flatiron Building** (p 34), at Fifth Ave. and 23rd St. (Daniel H. Burnham & Co., 1902), with strong Renaissance Revival detail; and the **Woolworth Building** (Cass Gilbert, 1913; p 18), on Broadway at Park Place.

Second Renaissance Revival (1890–1920)

Compared to the Italianate, or First Renaissance Revival (1840–90), this style showed a studied formalism, with greater faithfulness to Italian Renaissance precedents in its window and doorway treatments. It also differed in that it was used for larger-scale buildings, such as banks, swank town houses, government buildings, and private clubs.

New York's Upper East Side has two fine examples of this building type: the **Racquet and Tennis Club,** 370 Park Ave. (McKim, Mead & White, 1918), based on the style of an elegant Florentine palazzo; and the **Metropolitan Club,** 1 E. 60th St. (McKim, Mead & White, 1894).

Beaux Arts (1890–1920)

This style takes its name from the Ecole des Beaux-Arts in Paris, where a number of prominent American architects trained, beginning around the mid–19th century.

These architects adopted the academic design principles of the Ecole, which emphasized the study of Greek and Roman structures, composition, and symmetry. Because of the idealized classical origins, the Beaux Arts in America was seen as the ideal style for expressing civic pride. Grandiose compositions, an exuberance of detail, and a variety of stone finishes typify most Beaux Arts structures.

The **New York Public Library** (p 39), at Fifth Ave. and 42nd St. (Carrère & Hastings, 1911), is perhaps the best example. Others of note are **Grand Central Terminal** (p 7), at 42nd St. and Park Ave. (Reed & Stem and Warren & Whetmore, 1913), and the **Alexander Hamilton U.S. Custom House** (Cass Gilbert, 1907), on Bowling Green between State and Whitehall sts.

International Style (1920–45)

In 1932, the Museum of Modern Art hosted its first architecture exhibit, titled simply *Modern Architecture*. Displays included images of International Style buildings from around the world. The structures all share a stark simplicity and vigorous functionalism, a definite break from historically based, decorative styles. The International Style was popularized in the U.S. through the teachings and designs of **Ludwig Mies van der Rohe** (1886–1969), a German émigré based in Chicago. Interpretations of the "Miesian" International Style were built in most U.S. cities as late as 1980.

Two famous examples of this style in New York are the **Seagram Building,** at 375 Park Ave. (Ludwig Mies van der Rohe, 1958), and the **Lever House,** at 390 Park Ave., between 53rd and 54th sts. (Skidmore, Owings & Merrill, 1952).

Art Deco (1925–40)

Art Deco is a decorative style that took its name from a Paris exposition in 1925. The jazzy style embodied the idea of modernity, and it influenced all areas of design, from jewelry and household goods to cars, trains, and ocean liners. Art Deco buildings are characterized by a linear, hard edge, or angular composition, often with a vertical emphasis and highlighted with stylized decoration.

Despite the effects of the Depression, several major Art Deco structures were built in New York in the 1930s, often providing crucial jobs. **Rockefeller Center** (Raymond Hood, 1940; p 8) includes 30 Rockefeller Plaza, a tour de force of Art Deco style, with a soaring vertical

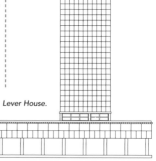

Lever House.

shaft and aluminum details. The **Chrysler Building**'s needle-like spire (William van Alen, 1930; p 35), with zigzag patterns in glass and metal, is a distinctive feature on the city's skyline. The **Empire State Building** (Shreve, Lamb & Harmon, 1931; p 7) contains a black- and silver-toned lobby among its many Art Deco features.

Art Moderne (1930–45)

Art Moderne strove for modernity and an artistic

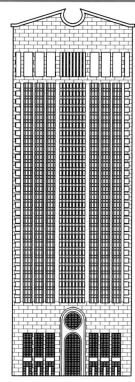

The Chrysler Building.

expression for the sleekness of the Machine Age. Unbroken horizontal lines and smooth curves visually distinguish it from Art Deco and give it a streamlined effect. It was popular with movie theaters and was often applied to cars, trains, and boats to suggest the idea of speed.

Radio City Music Hall (p 8), on Sixth Ave. at 50th St. (Edward Durrell Stone and Donald Deskey, 1932), has a sweeping Art Moderne marquee.

Postmodern (1975–90)

Postmodernism burst on the scene in the 1970s with the reintroduction of historical precedents in architecture. With many feeling that the office towers of the previous style were too cold, postmodernists began to incorporate classical details and recognizable forms into

The Sony Building.

their designs—often applied in outrageous proportions.

The **Sony Building,** at 550 Madison Ave. (Philip Johnson/John Burgee, 1984), brings the distinctive shape of a Chippendale cabinet to the New York skyline.

Contemporary (1990–Today)

In just the last two decades, such "Starchitectects" as Frank Gehry, Jean Nouvel, and others have added sinuous, fractured, and asymmetrical buildings to the cityscape, in forms that couldn't have been achieved without the help of computer modeling. You'll see our picks for some of the best of these newbies on p 36.

Index

See also Accommodations and Restaurant indexes, below.

A

Abby Aldrich Rockefeller
Sculpture Garden
(MoMA), 54
ABC Carpet & Home, 96
Abyssinian Baptist Church, 63
Accessibility, 172
Accommodations. *See*
Accommodations
index; Hotels
Adam Clayton Powell, Jr.
Blvd and 125th St., 61–62
Admission. *See* Tickets
African Burial Ground
National Monument, 59
Air travel, 167–168
Aldo Sohm, 134
Alexander Hamilton U.S.
Custom House, 176
The Algonquin, 29
Alice in Wonderland
Statue, 26
Alison and Roberto Mig-
none Halls of Gems and
Minerals (AMNH), 51
All Birds, 97
American Ballet Theater, 146
American Museum of Natu-
ral History (AMNH), 3,
12–13, 26, 50–51
American Surety
Company, 175
American Wing (The Met),
44–45
Anna Wintour Costume Col-
lection (The Met), 45
Annie's Blue Ribbon Gen-
eral Store, 75
Antique districts, 90
Apartment rentals, 164
Apollo Theater, 62, 147
The Apple Store, 92
Architecture, 32–37, 174–177
Area codes, 171
Arms & Armor (The Met), 44
The Arsenal (Central
Park), 103
Art Deco architecture,
176–177
Art galleries in Chelsea, 64–67
Art Moderne
architecture, 177
Artists & Fleas, 79
Artist's studios, 23
ArtMuse Selects app, 23

Arts & entertainment, 4,
139–152
Asian Art (The Met), 44
Astor Row, 63
Astor Wines & Spirits, 94
ATMs, 169–170

B

B&Bs (bed-and-
breakfasts), 164
B&H Photo-Video-Pro
Audio, 92
Baby's All Right, 130
Babysitting services, 170
Banking hours, 170
Bar Goto, 134
Bargemusic, 145
Barnes & Noble Union
Square, 90
Bars, 130, 134–138
Battery Park, 57
The Bayard-Condict
Building, 34
Beacon Theater, 148–149
Beauty/apothecary
shopping, 90
Beaux Arts architecture,
175–176
Bedford Avenue, 79
Belvedere Castle, 12
Bemelmans Bar, 134
Bergdorf Goodman, 91
Bethesda Terrace, 102
Bike-sharing, 169
Birdland, 149
Bloomingdale's, 91–92
Blue Note, 149
Blumstein's Department
Store, 62
Book Culture, 90
Books Are Magic, 91
Books of Wonder, 97–98
Bookstores, 90–91
Bowery Ballroom, 149–150
Broadway shows.
See Theater
Broadway Theater District, 9
Broken Shaker, 134
Bronx Zoo, 25
Brooklyn Academy of Music,
75, 147
Brooklyn Art Library, 77
Brooklyn artisans &
outlets, 92
Brooklyn Botanic Garden, 73
Brooklyn Brewery, 79
Brooklyn Bridge, 4, 33
Brooklyn Museum, 73
Brooklyn Street Art Beer
Garden, 134
Bus travel, 169
Bushwick Inlet Park, 79
Business hours, 170

C

C. O. Bigelow, 90
Café Carlyle, 150
CAMP, 98
Camper, 97
Canal Street, 82–83
Carnegie Hall, 147
Caroline's On Broadway, 146
Carousel in Central Park, 26,
102–103
The Cathedral of St. John
the Divine, 61, 146
Cathedral of the Transfigu-
ration of our Lord, 78
Caveat, 146
Central Park, 3, 12, 26,
100–103
Central Park Zoo, 26, 103
The Chapel (Green-Wood
Cemetery), 109
Chapel Crescent (Green-
Wood Cemetery), 109
Chelsea, 64–67
Chelsea Grasslands (High
Line), 106
Chelsea Thicket (High
Line), 106
Cherry Lane Theatre, 71
Children's books & clothing
stores, 97–98
Children's Museum of Man-
hattan, 25–26
Chinatown, 4, 80–84
Chinese New Year, 166
Christmas Spectacular, 26
Chrysler Building, 7, 35, 177
Church concerts, 146
Church of the
Transfiguration, 146
City Center, 146
City Hall Park, 18
City Reliquary, 77
Classical music, 145
The Cloisters, 45
Clothing stores, 93–94
Cocktail lounges, 134–138
Collection 1880s–1940s
(MoMA), 53
Collection 1940–1970
(MoMA), 53
Collection 1970s–Today
(MoMA), 53
Colonial Fence, 58
Columbus Park, 81
Comedy Cellar, 146
Comedy clubs, 146
Coney Island, 27
Conservatory Garden, 101
Consulates, 170
Contemporary architecture,
36, 177
Cooper Hewitt, 47
Cushman Row, 65

D

The Dakota, 13
Dance, professional, 146–147
Dance Parade, 166
Dante, 134–135
David Zwirner Gallery, 65
D.b.a., 135
Decibel, 135
Dentists, 170
Department stores, 91–92
Desserts, 122
The Diamond District, 96
Diller–Von Furstenberg Sundeck & Water Feature (High Line), 106
Dining, 113–128. *See also* Restaurants index
　best of, 114
　desserts, 122
　food halls, 119
　outdoors, 4
　pizza, 126
　reservations, 167
　Restaurant Week, 114
Doctors, 170
Don't Tell Mama, 135
Doyers Street, 81–82
Driving to New York City, 168
Dublin House, 135

E

Ear Inn, 135–136
Early Skyscraper architecture, 175
Easter Parade, 166
Eataly, 94
Economy Candy, 94
The Edge, 112
Edgar Allan Poe Cottage, 29
Edward Mooney House, 82
Egyptian Art (The Met), 44
Electricity, 170
Electronics stores, 92
Ellis Island Immigration Museum, 4, 16
Emergencies, 170
Empire State Building, 7, 112, 177
Entertainment. *See* Arts & entertainment; Nightlife
European Paintings: 19th & Early 20th Centuries (The Met), 45
European Paintings: Old Masters (The Met), 45
European Sculpture & Decorative Arts (The Met), 43–44
Everlane, 93

F

Family Art Lab & Creativity Lab (MoMA), 54
Fannie the Dog (Green-Wood Cemetery), 110
F.A.O. Schwartz, 98
Fashion Institute of Technology (FIT), 40
Fashion shopping, 93–94
Favorite moments, 1–4
FDR Four Freedoms Park, 39
Federal architecture, 174
Federal Hall National Memorial, 58–59, 174
Federal Reserve Bank of New York, 40
Feinstein's/54 Below, 150
Festivals, 39, 166
Fifth Avenue, 3, 9
Financial District, 56–59
Fine and Dandy, 93
Fine and Rare, 136
Fireworks, 166
Fishs Eddy, 96
Flaming Saddles, 138
The Flatiron Building, 34, 175
Flight Club, 97
Foley Square, 18
Food halls, 119
Food shopping, 94–95
Forbidden Planet, 95
40 Bond Street, 36
48 Commerce St., 71
14th Street Passage (High Line), 105–106
Fraunces Tavern Museum, 58
Free & dirt-cheap tour, 38–40
Frick Madison, 48

G

Gagosian Gallery, 66
Gansevoort Stair Entry (High Line), 105
General Theological Seminary, 65
Georgian architecture, 174
Gift stores, 95–96
Gladstone Gallery, 66
Gothic Revival architecture, 175
Governors Island, 110
Grand Army Plaza, 74
Grand Central Terminal, 7–8, 35, 176
Grand Street, 83
Grant's Tomb, 37
The Great Hall (The Met), 43
The Great Lawn (Central Park), 102
Greek & Roman Galleries (The Met), 43

Greek Revival architecture, 174
Greeley Gravesite (Green-Wood Cemetery), 110
Greene Street, 175
Greenstones, 98
Greenwich Village, 4, 68–71, 90, 166
Green-Wood Cemetery, 108–110
Grove Court, 71
Gudrun Sjödén, 93
Guggenheim Museum, 36–37, 48

H

Hamilton Grange, 63
Harbor cruises, 23
Harlem, 60–63
Harlem Meer, 101
Harry Potter NY, 98
Harry's Shoes, 97
Hayden Planetarium (AMNH), 51
Henrietta Hudson, 138
The High Line, 3–4, 66–67, 104–107
High Line Hotel, 65
History
　of the High Line, 106
　of New York City, 173
Holiday activities, 26
Holiday Train Show, 26
Holidays, list of, 170
Home design stores, 96
The Honey Well, 136
The Hotel Chelsea, 30
Hotels, 153–164. *See also* Accommodations index
　B&Bs & apartment rentals, 164
　best of, 154
　saving money, 154, 162
　taxes, 171
Housewares shopping, 96
Hudson Yards, 67

I

IAC Building, 36, 65
Ina, 93
Industry City, 92
Insurance, 170–171
International Style architecture, 176
Intrepid Sea, Air & Space Museum, 27
Italianate architecture, 175

J

Jazz at Lincoln Center, 150
Jewelry stores, 96–97
The Jewish Museum, 47

Joe's Pub, 150
John Derian Company, 95
Joyce Theater, 146–147
Juilliard School, 145
July 4th fireworks, 166

K

Kalustyan's, 95
Kavasutra, 136
Kid-friendly tour, 24–27
Kiehl's, 90
Kimlau War Memorial, 81
King Cole Bar, 136
Koch Dinosaur Wing
    (AMNH), 51
Kossar's Bialys, 83–84

L

The Lake (Central Park), 12,
    21–22, 102
Landmark venues, 147–148
Landscape Avenue (Green-
    Wood Cemetery), 110
Le Fanion, 95
Lee Avenue, 77
Lever House, 36, 176
LGBTQ travelers
    bar scene, 138
    fast facts, 170
Library Way, 30
Lin Sister Herb Shop, 81
Lincoln Center for the Per-
    forming Arts, 13, 147, 166
Lincoln Center Plaza, 22
Literary Gotham tour, 28–31
Little Island, 105
Little Italy, 80–84
Live music, 148–151
Louis Armstrong House
    Museum, 49
Lovelace Tavern Site, 58
Lower East Side, 80–84

M

Macy's, 92
Macy's Thanksgiving Day
    Parade, 26, 167
Madison Square Garden, 150
Mail, 171
Main Gate (Green-Wood
    Cemetery), 109
The Mall (Central Park), 102
Manhattan Art and Antiques
    Center, 90
Marie's Crisis, 138
Martha P. Johnson State
    Park, 79
McCarren Park, 78–79
Mercury Lounge, 150
Metropolitan Club, 175
Metropolitan Museum of Art
    Store, 95

Metropolitan Museum of Art
    (The Met), 3, 11, 42–45
Metropolitan Museum of Art
    Roof Garden/Great Hall
    Balcony Bar, 136–137
Metropolitan Opera, 152
Midsummer Night
    Swing, 166
Mies van der Rohe,
    Ludwig, 176
Milstein Hall of Ocean Life
    (AMNH), 51
Minetta Street, 71
Minetta Tavern, 71
Mmuseumm, 40
Modern Art Wing (The
    Met), 43
MoMA Store, 96
The Montauk Club, 75
The Morgan Library &
    Museum, 30
Mott Street, 82
Mount Morris Park Historic
    District, 61
Mt. Olivet Baptist Church, 61
Mulberry Street, 83
Museum at Eldridge, 83
The Museum at FIT, 40
Museum of Art and
    Design, 48
Museum of Chinese in
    America (MOCA), 83
Museum of Jewish Heri-
    tage—A Living Memorial
    to the Holocaust, 49
Museum of Modern Art
    (MoMA), 3, 9, 52–54
Museum of Sex, 23
Museum of the Moving
    Image, 4, 48–49
Museums, best of, 41–54
Music
    church concerts, 146
    classical, 145
    live, 148–151
    opera, 152
Music Hall of
    Williamsburg, 130

N

National Museum of the
    American Indian, 57
Neighborhood walks
    Chelsea, High Line,
        Hudson Yards, 64–67
    Chinatown, Little Italy,
        Lower East Side,
        80–84
    Financial District, 56–59
    Greenwich Village,
        68–71
    historic Harlem, 60–63

Prospect Park & Park
    Slope, 72–75
Williamsburg, Brooklyn,
    76–79
Neue Galerie New York, 21
New Museum, 84
New Victory Theater, 27
New Year's Eve, 166
New York City
    architecture, 174–177
    arrival information,
        167–168
    fast facts, 169–172
    favorite moments, 1–4
    history of, 173
    traveling within, 168–169
    websites for informa-
        tion, 167
    when to visit, 66
New York City Ballet, 147
New York City Opera, 152
New York Distilling
    Company, 77
New York Philharmonic, 145
New York Public Library, 8,
    39, 176
New York Stock
    Exchange, 59
New York Theater
    Workshop, 151
New Yorker former offices,
    29–30
New-York Historical
    Society, 48
Nightlife, 4, 129–138
9/11 Memorial and Museum,
    17, 59
92nd Street Y, 147
Nordstrom's, 92
North American Mammals
    (AMNH), 51
Nouvelle's glass patchwork
    tower (100 Eleventh
    Ave.), 36
NYC & Company, 40

O

The Obelisk (Central Park),
    12, 102
Observation decks, 111–112
Off-Broadway theaters,
    151–152
Old Town, 137
One World Observatory,
    17, 112
1-day tour, 6–9
101 Spring Street, 33
130 MacDougal St., 70–71
Opera, 152
Ophelia Lounge, 137
Orchard Street, 83
Outdoor activities, 99–112

P

The Pace Gallery, 66
Parades, 166
Park Avenue Armory, 147–148
Parking garage tax, 171
Patchin Place, 30
Paula Cooper Gallery, 66
PDT, 137
Pershing Square Beams (High Line), 107
Pharmacies, 171
Philip A. and Lisa Maria Falcone Flyover (High Line), 107
Pippin Vintage Jewelry, 96–97
Pizza, 126
Playgrounds, 101
Playwrights Horizons, 151–152
The Plaza, 9, 22, 29
Postage, 171
Postmodern architecture, 177
Prospect Park, 74–75
Prospect Park Zoo, 75
P.S. 1, 54
Public Theater, 152
Public transportation, 168–169

R

Racquet and Tennis Club, 175
Radegast Hall & Biergarten, 130
Radio City Music Hall, 8–9, 148, 177
Radio City Music Hall Christmas Spectacular, 166
The Ramble (Central Park), 102
Reservations, 167
The Reservoir (Central Park), 101–102
Restaurant Week, 114
Ridesharing, 169
The Rink in Rockefeller Center, 22
Riverside Church, 37
Rizzoli, 91
Rockefeller Center, 8, 22, 36, 112, 166, 176
Romantic New York tour, 20–23
Roosevelt Island Tram, 39
Rose Center for Earth & Space, 13
Rose Center for Earth & Space (AMNH), 51
Ross Hall of Meteorites (AMNH), 51
The Row, 70
Rubin Museum of Art, 48
The Rum House, 138

Russ & Daughters, 84

S

Safety, 171
Sailboat Pond, 26
Saks Fifth Avenue, 92
Sales tax, 86, 171
Saving money
    free & dirt-cheap tour, 38–40
    on hotels, 154, 162
    on theater tickets, 151
Schomburg Center for Research in Black Culture, 63
Seagram Building, 176
Seating steps & Lawn (High Line), 106–107
Second Renaissance Revival architecture, 175
Senior travel, 171
17 Grove St., 71
Shakespeare Garden, 12
Shakespeare in the Park, 166
The Shanty, 130
The Shed, 148
Sheep Meadow, 22
Shoe stores, 97
Shopping, 3, 85–98
    antique districts, 90
    beauty/apothecary, 90
    best of, 86
    bookstores, 90–91
    Brooklyn artisans & outlets, 92
    children's books, toys & clothing, 97–98
    department stores, 91–92
    electronics, 92
    fashion, 93–94
    food & wine, 94–95
    gifts, 95–96
    home design & housewares, 96
    jewelry & precious stones, 96–97
    sales tax, 86
    shoes, 97
Silver Center, 69
Skyscraper Museum, 33
Smoke, 150–151
Smoking, 171
SoHo Cast Iron Historic District, 175
Solomon R. Guggenheim Museum, 36–37, 48
Sony Building, 177
Spectator sports, 171
The Spur (High Line), 107
St. Bart's, 146
St. Ignatius Loyola, 146

St. Luke in the Fields, 71
St. Patrick's Cathedral, 8
St. Patrick's Day Parade, 166
St. Paul's Chapel, 16–17, 146, 174
Staten Island Ferry, 40
The Statue of Liberty, 15–16
Stettheimer Doll House, 25
Stone Street Historic District, 33, 58
The Stonewall Inn, 138
The Strand, 31, 91
Strawberry Fields, 13
Strivers' Row, 63
Subway travel, 168–169
SummerStage, 166
Summit at 1 Vanderbilt, 112
Sunset cruises, 3
Swing 46, 138
Sylvan Water (Green-Wood Cemetery), 110
Symphony Space, 148

T

Taxes, 86, 171
Taxis, 169
Telephone area codes, 171
Television show tapings, 40
Temporary exhibitions at MoMA, 53
The Tenement Museum, 84
Tenth Avenue Square & Viewing Platform (High Line), 106
Theater, 3
    Broadway Theater District, 9
    choosing shows, 149
    off-Broadway, 151–152
    tickets, 151, 167
Theodore Roosevelt Memorial Hall (AMNH), 51
30th Street Cutout & Viewing Platform (High Line), 107
3-day tour, 14–18
Tickets, 171–172
    The American Museum of Natural History (AMNH), 51
    Broadway shows, 151, 167
    Chelsea galleries, 67
    The High Line, 105
    Little Island, 105
    The Metropolitan Museum of Art (The Met), 44
    The Museum of Modern Art (MoMA), 53
    P.S. 1, 54
    television show tapings, 40

Accommodations Index

Tiffany & Co., 22, 97
Tipping, 172
Toilets, 172
The Tomb of the Soda
    Fountain King (Green-
    Wood Cemetery), 109–110
Top of the Rock, 112
Tourist offices, 172
Tours, 172. *See also* Neigh-
    borhood walks
        architecture, 32–37
        free & dirt-cheap, 38–40
        kid-friendly, 24–27
        literary Gotham, 28–31
        1-day, 6–9
        romantic New York,
            20–23
        3-day, 14–18
        2-day, 10–13
Town Hall, 148
Toy stores, 97–98
Toy Tokyo, 98
Train travel, 168
Transportation, 168–169
Travel insurance, 170–171
Triangle Shirtwaist factory
    (29 Washington Place), 69
Trinity Church, 16, 59,
    146, 175
29 Washington Place, 69
2-day tour, 10–13

U

Ulla Johnson, 93
Union Pool, 130
Union Square
    Greenmarket, 95
UNIQLO, 93–94
The United Nations, 35–36

V

Valley Water (Green-Wood
    Cemetery), 109
Victorian Gardens Amuse-
    ment Park, 26–27, 103
The Village Vanguard, 151
The Vineyard Theater, 152

W

Walking tours. *See* Neigh-
    borhood walks
Wall Street, 58
The Washington Mews, 69
Washington Square, 31
Washington Square Arch, 70
Washington Square Park,
    69–70
Websites for information, 167
West Bleecker Street Shop-
    ping District, 71

West Side Rail Yards
    extension (High Line), 107
West Village, 174
Westlight, 130
Whisk, 96
The Whispering Gallery,
    22–23
The Whitney Museum of
    American Art, 49
Wildflower Field (High
    Line), 107
Williamsburg, Brooklyn,
    76–79, 130
Wine shopping, 94–95
Wollman Rink/Victorian
    Gardens, 26–27, 103
Woolworth Building, 175
World Trade Center
    Transportation Hub,
    18, 36

Y

Yankee Stadium, 25

Z

Zabar's, 95

Accommodations

Andaz Fifth Avenue, 158
Beacon Hotel, 158
The Beekman, 158
The Boro Hotel, 158–159
Carlton Arms, 159
The Carlyle, 159
Casablanca Hotel, 159
Citizen M, 159
Crosby Street Hotel, 159
The Evelyn, 160
50 Bowery, 158
Freehand New York City, 160
The Greenwich Hotel, 160
The High Line Hotel, 160
Hotel Hendricks, 160
The Hoxton, 161
The Jane, 161
The Knickerbocker, 161
The Library Hotel, 162
MADE Hotel, 162
Mr. C Seaport, 162
Nesva Hotel, 162
NobleDen, 162–163
The Nolitan, 163
The NoMad, 163
The Peninsula—New
    York, 163
The Pod Hotel, 163
Sofitel New York, 163
TWA Hotel, 164
The Wall Street Inn, 164
Washington Square
    Hotel, 164

Restaurants

Adda Indian Canteen, 118
American Museum of Natural
    History (AMNH), 51
Amy Ruth's, 118
Balthazar, 118
Barney Greengrass, 118
Berimbau, 118
Blue Hill, 119
Boulud Sud, 13
Caffe Reggio, 70
Chelsea Market, 119
Chikalicious, 122
City Kitchen, 119
Claro, 75
Coppelia, 120
Cosme, 120
Cote, 120
Crown Shy, 59
Danji, 120
The Dead Rabbit Grocery
    and Grog, 18
Dekalb Market, 119
Dominick's, 120
Dominique Ansel, 122
Eataly, 16, 119
Eleven Madison Park, 121
Emmy Squared, 126
Ernesto's, 121
Farida, 121
Frenchette, 122
The Fulton, 122
Gage & Tollner, 122
Grand Central Oyster Bar, 8
Gray's Papaya, 123
Great NY Noodletown, 123
Gyu-Kaku, 123
The High Line food court, 106
Ippudo, 123
Iris, 123
Jacob's Pickles, 124
John's Pizza, 126
Juliana's, 126
Katz's Delicatessen, 124
Keens, 124
Keste, 126
Kiki's, 124
Lady M Cake Boutique, 122
Le Bernardin, 125
Le Pavillon, 125
Lilia, 79
Llama San, 125
The Loeb Boathouse, 102
Los Tacos No. 1, 125
McSorley's, 31
Mercado Little Spain, 67, 119
Metropolitan Museum of Art
    (The Met), 11, 44
The Modern, 54
Mokyo, 126
Morgenstern's, 122
Museum of Modern Art
    (MoMA), 54

Nami Nori, 126
Nom Wah Tea Parlor, 82
The NoMad, 35
Nyonya, 127
One If By Land, Two If By
Sea, 23
Pete's Tavern, 30
Prince Street Pizza, 126
Red Rooster Harlem, 62

Rice to Riches, 122
The River Café, 23
Serendipity 3, 26
Shake Shack, 13
Shalom Japan, 77
Smorgasburg, 119
Speedy Romeo, 126
Sushi Yasuda, 127
Thai Diner, 127

Time Out Market, 119
Tom's Restaurant, 73
Tong, 127
Totonno's, 126
Venieros, 122
Veselka, 128
Via Carota, 128
Xian Famous Foods, 128
Yoon Haeundae Galbi, 128

Photo **Credits**